# Executive
# Skills

# Executive Skills

## A Management by Objectives Approach

**George Odiorne**
*University of Massachusetts*

**Heinz Weihrich**
*Arizona State University*

**Jack Mendleson**
*Arizona State University*

wcb
Wm. C. Brown Company Publishers
*Dubuque, Iowa*

# Contents

# Preface

One of the most enduring managerial approaches is Management by Objectives (MBO). It is practiced by managers and nonmanagers, by profit and nonprofit organizations, in the United States and abroad. (A detailed definition of MBO may be found on page ix.) Organizations aim at results and MBO is a way to clarify the aims toward which activities are directed. In general, then, the clearer the objectives, the better are the chances of achieving them. To accomplish this clarification is the purpose of this book.

There are seven sections in this book. The first one discusses the evolution of the concept and the practice of MBO. Section 2 deals with the broad view of MBO. Strategic planning and the hierarchy of objectives becomes an integral part of the MBO process. Section 3 discusses the very important aspects of setting objectives. Furthermore, the planning for action, especially necessary for critical and complex objectives, is also included in this part. Section 4 focuses on practical suggestions for the implementation of MBO. Section 5 deals with the control of organizational performance and appraisal of individuals. Selected subsystems such as selection of managers, human resource development, and compensation are discussed in section 6. Finally, section 7 contains the experiences with MBO by specific organizations. Moreover, recommendations are made for the application of MBO to nonprofit organizations.

The individual sections are integrated in a model in the first part of the book. This model serves as the framework and shows the interrelationships of the concepts and sections.

We intend the book for three primary uses. First, this book is a supplement to virtually any textbook on general management taught in junior colleges, colleges, and universities. The theoretical base is supported by real-world applications of the concepts. Second, the book is intended for participants in Executive Development Programs conducted by educational institutions or within a company. We have conducted many such programs in the United States and abroad and noted the need for readings on MBO which contain conceptual depth and practical applications. It is unrealistic—and impractical—to expect executives participating in Executive Programs to search the library for pertinent articles. Furthermore, to be effective, articles are more meaningful in context. This book shows how the concepts fit together into a system.

The third user of the book is the executive or the new manager who would like to learn about MBO or to deepen his or her understanding of it. It may help to read this book in conjunction with books such as

*Management by Objectives and MBO II* by George S. Odiorne;
*Improving Business Results* by John W. Humble; or
*Managing by Objectives* by Anthony P. Raia.

The authors would like to thank the publishers and authors who have granted permission to use their articles. Special appreciations go to Professors Harold Koontz, Frederic R. Wickert, and Anthony P. Raia who stimulated our interest and refined our thinking about MBO, and to several major writers and consultants, such as John W. Humble and Peter F. Drucker, for their work in integrating various aspects of MBO.

George S. Odiorne
Heinz Weihrich
Jack L. Mendleson

# An Overview of the Book

Management by Objectives (MBO), which focuses on results, is one of the most successful approaches to management. As a consequence of the popularity of MBO, many articles deal with this topic. Unfortunately, most of them focus only on specific aspects of this managerial process rather than on MBO as a *system* of management. The MBO student and practitioner could be overwhelmed by the many writings on the various aspects of the MBO system. In our consulting work and in management development seminars, we have found a great need for bringing together important articles and grouping them into a framework. This book is the result.

## A New MBO Model

The MBO concept has changed during the evolutionary stages, ranging from being used as an appraisal tool to a way of managing (Section 1). We view MBO as a comprehensive managerial system that integrates many key managerial functions and activities. There is evidence that when MBO is treated as a limited subsystem of the managerial process, such as focusing on appraisal only, difficulties arise. Therefore, we consider MBO as a way of managing, rather than an addition to the manager's job.

Various authors focus on different aspects of MBO; consequently, definitions may vary accordingly. We employ a frequently quoted and very descriptive definition.

> The system of management by objectives can be described as a process whereby the superior and subordinate managers of an organization jointly identify its common goals, define each individual's major areas of responsibility in terms of the results expected of him, and use these measures as guides for operating the unit and assessing the contribution of each of its members.[1]

Because MBO is a complex system, a framework has to be established. The MBO model (Figure 1) not only identifies the important aspects and relationships, but it will also be the structural outline of the book. For each part of the model, therefore, readings have been selected that address in detail that subject matter.

## Figure 1
A New Management by Objectives Model.

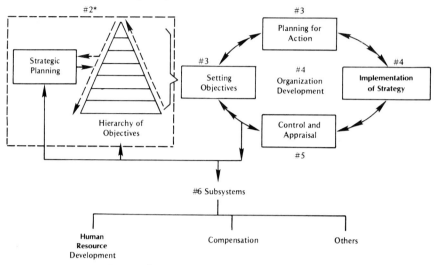

*The numbers (#2 through #6) pertain to the sections in which these concepts are discussed. Section 1 concerns the evolution of MBO and section 7 discusses organizational experience with MBO.

## Strategic Planning and the Hierarchy of Objectives (Section 2)

MBO programs traditionally focus on one-year cycles. However, short-term objectives may be incongruent with the long-range plans. Consequently, an integration of long- and short-term aims is necessary. In addition, customers and clients are outside the organization and the focus of managers must go beyond the organizational boundaries. Similarly, competition—often a restraining factor—also operates external to the firm and must be considered in strategic planning. In short, the environment has to be scanned to identify opportunities for and threats to the firm. In turn, they have to be matched with the internal strengths and weaknesses of the firm so that resources can be deployed effectively and efficiently.

In determining the strategy, the aims of the organization must be evaluated and, if necessary, redefined. The ends toward which the activities of the organization are directed form a hierarchy (Figure 2). This hierarchy may be viewed as follows:

1. The socioeconomic purpose is the fundamental reason why the organization exists.
2. The mission is a basic end of the organization and gives direction for planning.

**Figure 2**
Hierarchy of Objectives.

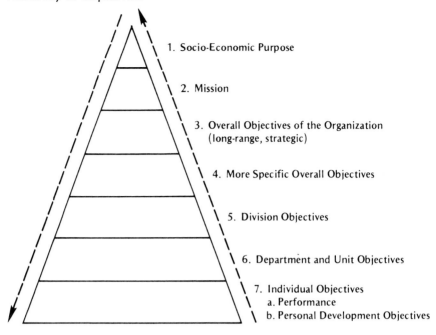

1. Socio-Economic Purpose

2. Mission

3. Overall Objectives of the Organization (long-range, strategic)

4. More Specific Overall Objectives

5. Division Objectives

6. Department and Unit Objectives

7. Individual Objectives
   a. Performance
   b. Personal Development Objectives

3. The overall objectives of the organization consider its long-range health. They are also an essential part of strategic planning, which involves aspects vital to the firm.
4. Specific objectives, which are important for the success of the company, are set in all areas. An example may be "to introduce three new products in markets X and Y by December 31, 1982 at a cost not to exceed one million dollars."
5. Division objectives are derived from the organizational objectives as they relate to a specific division in a large company.
6. Department and unit objectives are set so that they contribute to divisional objectives.
7. Finally, individual objectives are set for positions throughout the organization.

This hierarchy breaks down the broader organizational aims into specific objectives, As indicated in Figure 2, the process of setting objectives is a two-way process: top down *and* bottom up. This means, for example, that the subordinate sets the objectives and discusses them with the superior.

The next parts of the model—setting objectives, planning for action, implementation of strategy, control and appraisal—are the more traditional aspects of the MBO process.

## Setting Objectives and Planning for Action (Section 3)

Setting of verifiable objectives is not easy, but is essential. At the end of the planned period it should be possible to verify whether or not objectives have been achieved. An effective MBO program includes different kinds of objectives for individuals, such as extraordinary objectives, creative as well as improvement objectives, personal development, and, to a lesser extent, routine objectives.

The verifiable objectives—set in a collaborative manner between the superior and subordinate—become the basis for control and evaluation of performance.

Objectives are the ends toward which activities should be directed. The action plan is concerned with *what* functions, tasks, and activities have to be carried out, and *how* to best do this. In addition, it has to be determined *when* things have to be done and *who* is going to do it. Action planning, which should be done with discretion, is especially useful for complex programs, as will be further explained in the acticle dealing with this topic.

## Implementation of MBO and Organization Development (Section 4)

Objectives and action plans have to be implemented. For an MBO program to be successful, top management commitment and involvement are essential. Moreover, the organization must be analyzed to decide on the implementation strategy. It should be determined where in the organization MBO is to be introduced. A few failures at the beginning will surely kill MBO. Although many of the benefits of MBO only become evident after considerable time and effort, the wise administrator certainly wants to produce some short-term improvements.

Experience has shown that the organizational climate must be congruent with the MBO philosophy. This is where new knowledge from the behavioral sciences can be applied effectively to initiate change—and managing with MBO is a major change for most companies. Organizational development is important in all phases of MBO. However, it is absolutely crucial in the implementation stage. Critical organizational constraints should be identified and a change strategy must be developed. Success in MBO does not come by accident; it is planned.

MBO is for many managers a new way of managing. Thus, MBO helps them to make a transition from "crisis management," or "putting out fires," to professional managing with a clear direction, well-developed plans, and a commitment to their own development.

## Control and Appraisal (Section 5)

Control involves (1) setting performance standards, (2) measuring performance, and (3) taking corrective actions, if necessary. The verifiable objectives set in the planning process become the standards against which performance is measured. If deviations occur, superior and subordinate together engage in problem solving. Their motive is not to find fault, but rather to determine the cause of deviation.

The MBO philosophy emphasizes self-control. If there is agreement between the superior and subordinates on verifiable objectives, then subordinates can evaluate their own performance. Consequently, the superior is relieved of the role as a judge telling subordinates how well or how poorly they performed. Also, during the appraisal process past performance is analyzed; but, at the same time, new objectives are set for the future. In short, MBO helps managers learn from the past and commit themselves to future action.

## Selected MBO Subsystems (Section 6)

There are several subsystems that can be integrated into MBO. A case in point is *human resource development*. During the objective-setting and action-planning processes, manpower needs are usually identified. Consequently, a manpower plan is developed to achieve the objectives. The inventory of present manpower and the forecast of future needs often reveals a gap that may be filled by training people from within the organization or by hiring them from the outside.

Another aspect of goal setting is that as individuals set personal *development* goals for themselves, manager development becomes essentially self-development with the superior acting more in the role of a counselor. Therefore, the responsibility for growth is on the individual with an opportunity for better integration of personal and company objectives.

*Compensation* is another subsystem of MBO. The evaluation of performance against objectives can be a sound basis for fair compensation. Another subsystem of MBO may be *selection* by objectives, whereby people for new positions, promotions, or transfers are selected. The goal is to obtain a good fit between the person and the job. Besides the obvious benefits for the organization, personal satisfaction is one of the important outcomes of effective selection by objectives.

## Organizational Experiences with MBO (Section 7)

Management by Objectives is results-oriented, a practical approach based on solid theoretical concepts. This may be the reason why many companies have embraced MBO. These enterprises range from manufacturing companies to banks, and even to nonprofit organizations. It is in its application that MBO has to prove itself as an effective way of managing, and section 7 discusses a great variety of organizational experiences with MBO.

## Conclusion

This book is for the practitioner and those who want to become professional managers. The MBO model was introduced not to deal with abstractions but rather to provide the framework for the collection of readings.

The numbers shown in the model indicate the sections in which the topic is discussed. Moreover, each section is introduced by the part of the model that is the focal point of the discussions. Because many authors contributed, there is, of course, some overlap and even some differences of opinion. In selecting articles, we have attempted to present the best current thinking. We believe the result—even allowing for some diversity and disagreements among authors—is a collection of articles which fit well into the system of Management by Objectives we envision.

1. George S. Odiorne, *Management by Objectives* (New York: Pitman Publishing Company, 1965), pp. 55-56.

# Executive
# Skills

# 1

# The Evolution of MBO

**Objectives**
1. To understand the philosophy of MBO that emphasizes self-control.
2. To appreciate the long and complex history of MBO and the major contributions to MBO by many scholars, consultants, and practitioners.
3. To recognize that MBO is a way of managing, not an addition to the managerial job.
4. To project the future direction of MBO.

## The Evolution of MBO

There are few approaches to management that have enjoyed as much popularity as Management by Objectives (MBO). The great amount of literature certainly shows no lack of interest in MBO. What is often overlooked is that MBO has changed over the years and probably will have to continue changing if it is to remain a viable managerial approach.

Peter Drucker is usually credited with popularizing MBO in his book, *The Practice of Management.* Indeed, excerpts from his chapter are the first reading. He envisioned MBO as a way of managing and even called it a "philosophy of management." At the same time—or even before Drucker's writing—General Electric used key aspects of MBO in its reorganization plan. In its early application, MBO was primarily used as an appraisal tool to overcome the shortcomings of traditional appraisal instruments that emphasized personality traits of subordinates. MBO was a departure from this orientation; it focused on performance, measured against objectives.

Later in its development, the motivational potentials of MBO were also recognized. Especially writers who were also often consultants saw MBO as a way of integrating the demands of the organization with the needs of individuals who become active participants in the MBO process. The underlying assumption is that people at all levels of the organization are capable of contributing.

During the next phase in the development of MBO the short-term orientation has been expanded to integrate long-range and strategic planning in the MBO process. This approach requires top management involvement in MBO which gives additional credence to the commitment of top executives to MBO. It also welds together short-term objectives with the long-term aims of the enterprise.

The evolution and application of the MBO concept starting with an emphasis on appraisal, continuing as a means of integrating individual and organizational objectives, and finally considering MBO as a long-range planning instrument is a healthy development. But, to be truly effective, MBO has to be even more, it has to become a way of managing that integrates most key managerial activities into a comprehensive system, as shown in the introduction.

The first reading contains excerpts from *The Practice of Management,* in which Drucker suggests that everyone in the organization, from the highest to the lowest level, needs clearly identified objectives. The emphasis is on the contribution a manager makes to the organization as a team member. The set of objectives should include not only tangible business objectives but also goals for managers and for organization development. MBO is not management by "drives," rather it is managing through self-control. This means that managers set the objectives for themselves and then select means for achieving them. The activities necessary to obtain results have to be, of course, ethical, professional, within the law, and congruent with company policy. But MBO is essentially an approach that provides freedom, accountability, and motivation to contribute to the aims of the enterprise. At the same time, MBO facilitates the achievement of personal goals and self-fulfillment.

The second reading, "MBO: A Backward Glance" by George S. Odiorne, traces the history of MBO. Even before the term *MBO* was used, there was great concern about purpose and goals because they give direction to individual and organized efforts. Later the goal orientation with the organizational setting was enhanced by Drucker's perceptive writings. More recently, systems concepts have been applied in developing a systems approach to MBO. Although MBO has many devotees, it also has its critics. Indeed MBO has its shortcomings, but often it is the implementation that is at fault, not the MBO concept itself.

# 1

# Management by Objectives and Self-control

## What Should the Objectives of a Manager Be?

Each manager, from the "big boss" down to the production foreman or the chief clerk, needs clearly spelled-out objectives. These objectives should lay out what performance the man's* own managerial unit is supposed to produce. They should lay out what contribution he and his unit are expected to make to help other units obtain their objectives. Finally, they should spell out what contribution the manager can expect from other units toward the attainment of his own objectives. Right from the start, in other words, emphasis should be on teamwork and team results.

These objectives should always derive from the goals of the business enterprise. In one company, I have found it practicable and effective to provide even a foreman with a detailed statement of not only his own objectives but those of the company and of the manufacturing department. Even though the company is so large as to make the distance between the individual foreman's production and the company's total output all but astronomical, the result has been a significant increase in production. Indeed, this must follow if we mean it when we say that the foreman is "part of management." For it is the definition of a manager that in what he does he takes responsibility for the whole—that, in cutting stone, he "builds the cathedral."

The objectives of every manager should spell out his contribution to the attainment of company goals in *all areas* of the business. Obviously, not every manager has a direct contribution to make in every area. The contribution which marketing makes to productivity, for example, may be very small. But if a manager and his unit are not expected to contribute toward any one of the areas that significantly affect prosperity and

From pp. 126-132 and 135-136 from *The Practice of Management* by Peter F. Drucker. Copyright 1954 by Peter F. Drucker. Reprinted by permission of Harper & Row, Publishers, Inc.
*Note from the editors. We would prefer the term "persons" here. We note that Professor Drucker wrote this well over 20 years ago when women managers were less prevalent.

survival of the business, this fact should be clearly brought out. For managers must understand that business results depend on a balance of efforts and results in a number of areas. This is necessary both to give full scope to the craftsmanship of each function and specialty, and to prevent the empire-building and clannish jealousies of the various functions and specialties. It is necessary also to avoid overemphasis on any one key area.

To obtain balanced efforts the objectives of all managers on all levels and in all areas should also be keyed to both short-range and long-range considerations. And, of course, all objectives should always contain both the tangible business objectives and the intangible objectives for manager organization and development, worker performance and attitude and public responsibility. Anything else is shortsighted and impractical.

## Management by "Drives"

Proper management requires balanced stress on objectives, especially by top management. It rules out the common and pernicious business malpractice: management by "crisis" and "drives."

There may be companies in which management people do not say: "The only way we ever get anything done around here is by making a drive on it." Yet, "management by drive" is the rule rather than the exception. That things always collapse into the *status quo ante* three weeks after the drive is over, everybody knows and apparently expects. The only result of an "economy drive" is likely to be that messengers and typists get fired, and that $15,000 executives are forced to do $50-a-week work typing their own letters. And yet many managements have not drawn the obvious conclusion that drives are, after all, not the way to get things done.

But over and above its ineffectiveness, management by drive misdirects. It puts all emphasis on one phase of the job to the inevitable detriment of everything else.

> "For four weeks we cut inventories," a case-hardened veteran of management by crisis once summed it up. "Then we have four weeks of costcutting, followed by four weeks of human relations. We just have time to push customer service and courtesy for a month. And then the inventory is back where it was when we started. We don't even try to do our job. All management talks about, thinks about, preaches about, is last week's inventory figure or this week's customer complaints. How we do the rest of the job they don't even want to know."

In an organization which manages by drives people either neglect their job to get on with the current drive, or silently organize for collective sabotage of the drive to get their work done. In either event they become deaf to the cry of "wolf." And when the real crisis comes, when all hands should drop everything and pitch in, they treat it as just another case of management-created hysteria.

Management by drive, like management by "bellows and meat ax," is a sure sign of confusion. It is an admission of incompetence. It is a sign that management does not know how to plan. But, above all, it is a sign that the company does not know what to expect of its managers—that, not knowing how to direct them, it misdirects them.

## How Should Managers' Objectives Be Set and by Whom?

By definition, a manager is responsible for the contribution that his component makes to the larger unit above him and eventually to the enterprise. His performance aims upward rather than downward. This means that the goals of each manager's job must be defined by the contribution he has to make to the success of the larger unit of which he is a part. The objectives of the district sales manager's job should be defined by the contribution he and his district sales force have to make to the sales department, the objectives of the project engineer's job by the contribution he, his engineers and draftsmen make to the engineering department. The objectives of the general manager of a decentralized division should be defined by the contribution his division has to make to the objectives of the parent company.

This requires each manager to develop and set the objectives of his unit himself. Higher management must, of course, reserve the power to approve or disapprove these objectives. But their development is part of a manager's responsibility; indeed it is his first responsibility. It means, too, that every manager should responsibly participate in the development of the objectives of the higher unit of which his is a part. To "give him a sense of participation" (to use a pet phrase of the "human relations" jargon) is not enough. Being a manager demands the assumption of a genuine responsibility. Precisely because his aims should reflect the objective needs of the business, rather than merely what the individual manager wants, he must commit himself to them with a positive act of assent. He must know and understand the ultimate business goals, what is expected of him and why, what he will be measured against and how. There must be a "meeting of minds" within the entire management of each unit. This can be achieved only when each of the contributing managers is expected to think through what the unit objectives are, is led, in other words, to participate actively and responsibly in the work of defining them. And only if his lower managers participate in this way can the higher manager know what to expect of them and can make exacting demands.

This is so important that some of the most effective managers I know go one step further. They have each of their subordinates write a "manager's letter" twice a year. In this letter to his superior, each manager first defines the objectives of his superior's job and of his own job as he sees them. He then sets down the performance standards which he believes are being applied to him. Next, he lists the things he must do himself to attain these goals—and the things within his own unit he considers the major obstacles. He lists the things his superior and the company do that help him and the things that hamper him. Finally, he outlines what he proposes to do during the next year to reach his goals. If his superior accepts this statement, the "manager's letter" becomes the charter under which the manager operates.

This device, like no other I have seen, brings out how easily the unconsidered and casual remarks of even the best "boss" can confuse and misdirect. One large company has used the "manager's letter" for ten years. Yet almost every letter still lists as objectives and standards things which completely baffle the superior to whom the letter is addressed. And whenever he asks: "What is this?" he gets the answer: "Don't you remember what you said last spring going down with me in the elevator?"

The "manager's letter" also brings out whatever inconsistencies there are in the demands made on a man by his superior and by the company. Does the superior demand both speed and high quality when he can get only one or the other? And what compromise is needed in the interest of the company? Does he demand initiative and judgment of his men but also that they check back with him before they do anything? Does he ask for their ideas and suggestions but never uses them or discusses them? Does the company expect a small engineering force to be available immediately whenever something goes wrong in the plant, and yet bend all its efforts to the completion of new designs? Does it expect a manager to maintain high standards of performance but forbid him to remove poor performers? Does it create the conditions under which people say: "I can get the work done as long as I can keep the boss from knowing what I am doing?"

These are common situations. They undermine spirit and performance. The "manager's letter" may not prevent them. But at least it brings them out in the open, shows where compromises have to be made, objectives have to be thought through, prior ties have to be established, behavior has to be changed.

As this device illustrates: managing managers requires special efforts not only to establish common direction, but to eliminate misdirection. Mutual understanding can never be attained by "communication down," can never be created by talking. It can result only from "communications up." It requires both the superior's willingness to listen and a tool especially designed to make lower managers heard.

## Self-Control Through Measurements

The greatest advantage of management by objectives is perhaps that it makes it possible for a manager to control his own performance. Self-control means stronger motivation: a desire to do the best rather than just enough to get by. It means higher performance goals and broader vision. Even if management by objectives were not necessary to give the enterprise the unity of direction and effort of a management team, it would be necessary to make possible management by self-control.

So far in this book I have not talked of "control" at all; I have talked of "measurements." This was intentional. For "control" is an ambiguous word. It means the ability to direct oneself and one's work. It can also mean domination of one person by another. Objectives are the basis of "control" in the first sense; but they must never become the basis of "control" in the second, for this would defeat their purpose. Indeed, one of the major contributions of management by objectives is that it enables us to substitute management by self-control for management by domination.

That management by self-control is highly desirable will hardly be disputed in America or in American business today. Its acceptance underlies all the talk of "pushing decisions down to the lowest possible level," or of "paying people for results." But to make management by self-control a reality requires more than acceptance of the concept as right and desirable. It requires new tools and far-reaching changes in traditional thinking and practices.

To be able to control his own performance a manager needs to know more than what his goals are. He must be able to measure his performance and results against the goal. It should indeed be an invariable practice to supply managers with clear and common measurements in all key areas of a business. These measurements need not be rigidly quantitative; nor need they be exact. But they have to be clear, simple and rational. They have to be relevant and direct attention and efforts where they should go. They have to be reliable—at least to the point where their margin of error is acknowledged and understood. And they have to be, so to speak, self-announcing, understandable without complicated interpretation or philosophical discussion.

Each manager should have the information he needs to measure his own performance and should receive it soon enough to make any changes necessary for the desired results. And this information should go to the manager himself, and not to his superior. It should be the means of self-control, not a tool of control from above.

This needs particular stress today, when our ability to obtain such information is growing rapidly as a result of technological progress in information gathering, analysis and synthesis. Up till now information on important facts was either not obtainable at all, or could be assembled only so late as to be of little but historical interest. This former inability to produce measuring information was not an unmixed curse. For while it made effective self-control difficult, it also made difficult effective control of a manager from above; in the absence of information with which to control him, the manager had to be allowed to work as he saw fit.

Our new ability to produce measuring information will make possible effective self-control; and if so used, it will lead to a tremendous advance in the effectiveness and performance of management. But if this new ability is abused to impose control on managers from above, the new technology will inflict incalculable harm by demoralizing management, and by seriously lowering the effectiveness of managers.

That information can be effectively used for self-control is shown by the example of General Electric:

> General Electric has a special control service—the traveling auditors. The auditors study every one of the managerial units of the company thoroughly at least once a year. But their report goes to the manager of the unit studied. There can be little doubt that the feeling of confidence and trust in the company that even casual contact with General Electric managers reveals, is directly traceable to this practice of using information for self-control rather than for control from above.

But the General Electric practice is by no means common or generally understood. Typical management thinking is much closer to the practice exemplified by a large chemical company.

> In this company a control section audits every one of the managerial units of the company. The results of the audits do not go, however, to the managers audited. They go only to the president who then calls in the managers to confront them with the audit of their operations. What this has done to morale is shown in the nickname the company's managers have given the control section: "the president's Gestapo." Indeed, more and more managers are now running their units not to obtain the best performance but to obtain the best showing on the control-section audits.

This should not be misunderstood as advocacy of low performance standards or absence of control. On the contrary, management by objectives and self-control is primarily a means to obtain standards higher than are to be found in most companies today. And every manager should be held strictly accountable for the results of his performance.

But what he does to reach these results he—and only he—should control. It should be clearly understood what behavior and methods the company bars as unethical, unprofessional or unsound. But within these limits every manager must be free to decide what he has to do. And only if he has all the information regarding his operations can he fully be held accountable for results.

## A Philosophy of Management

What the business enterprise needs is a principle of management that will give full scope to individual strength and responsibility, and at the same time give common direction of vision and effort, establish team work and harmonize the goals of the individual with the common weal.

The only principle that can do this is management by objectives and self-control. It makes the common weal the aim of every manager. It substitutes for control from outside the stricter, more exacting and more effective control from the inside. It motivates the manager to action not because somebody tells him to do simething or talks him into doing it, but because the objective needs of his task demand it. He acts not because somebody wants him to but because he himself decides that he has to—he acts, in other words, as a free man.

The word "philosophy" is tossed around with happy abandon these days in management circles. I have even seen a dissertation, signed by a vice-president, on the "philosophy of handling purchase requisitions" (as far as I could figure out "philosophy" here meant that purchase requisitions had to be in triplicate). But management by objectives and self-control may be legitimately be called a "philosophy" of management. It rests on a concept of the job of management. It rests on an analysis of the specific needs of the management group and the obstacles it faces. It rests on a concept of human action, human behavior and human motivation. Finally, it applies to every manager, whatever his level and function, and to any business enterprise whether large or small. It insures performance by converting objective needs into personal goals. And this is genuine freedom, freedom under the law.

# 2

# MBO: A Backward Glance

In the world of the academic and the industrial manager, few people are neutral about management by objectives (MBO). In the United States and abroad, popular and scholarly management periodicals are replete with articles by both university-based researchers and operating managers about this managerial technique. An abundance of doctoral dissertations, trade books by consultants and professors, and case studies for use in academic classrooms deals with various facets of MBO as a modern management technique. New applications and adaptations, sometimes matched by critical and satirical comments, keep coming forth.

Recently, a Canadian scholar prepared a list of books and articles in the area of MBO, consisting of some fifty-five pages with over 700 books, articles, monographs, dissertations, and theses listed.[1] In addition to these, it would be possible to identify more than 300 readings, foreign journal articles, and audio and video cassette training packages on MBO. Hundreds of company-prepared manuals and documents are designed for internal company training and guidance in applying MBO. At least one regular monthly journal and several newsletters on MBO are currently in existence. Keeping track of new developments in the growth and modification of MBO is, therefore, a prodigious task.

Writers, consultants, practitioners, and researchers who deal with MBO can be classified into three major categories.

1. The *constructors* are those managers, writers, and researchers who have shaped the form and direction of MBO.
2. The *devotees* are those who advocate it, cite its successes in their own organization, improve upon it, and espouse it for others' use.
3. The *haters* are those who find in MBO a seriously defective management system and are strong in their condemnation. While this group is surprisingly small in numbers, it has existed and made loud, objectionable sounds since MBO's inception.

George S. Odiorne, "MBO: A Backward Glance," *Business Horizons*, October 1978, pp. 14-24. Copyright 1978 by the Foundation for the School of Business at Indiana University. Reprinted by permission.

## The Constructors

### Origins

One of the more popular pastimes among academics is uncovering the origins of MBO. A plethora of originators has been proposed. Old Testament quotations and examples, including Abraham's covenant with God and Moses' search for the Promised Land, have been cited. The Koran is quoted: "If you don't know where you are going, any road will get you there." Several ancient Greeks, including Aristotle, noted the importance of a definite purpose to ultimate success. Disraeli proposed that "success is a product of unremitting attention to purpose." C. West Churchman, trained as a philosopher and recognized as a leading figure in the systems approach, has also noted that the earliest constructions of that approach are found in the writings of Plato, Aristotle, St. Thomas Aquinas, Nietzsche, Descartes, Hobbes, Leibniz, Bentham, Kant, and Marx, among others.[2]

The definition of goals as a preliminary step to action seems to have permeated most management theory. It would be easy to construct an underlying management theory of goals and results-centered management from the histories of organizers of great corporations, such as Andrew Carnegie or Pierre Du Pont.

When young Pierre Du Pont, at the turn of the century, joined his family business, he came under the tutelage of Arthur Moxham, who taught him the virtues of cost accounting. But even more, "he came away profoundly impressed with analytical management."[3] Moxham's balance sheets told, at a glance, which parts of the company made money and which did not, thus making it possible to have a rational basis for investment decisions. This attention to accounting and its development through statistical analysis was in its formative stage at the turn of the century, and offered a set of lessons that DuPont was to carry successfully to other places and times. Upon moving to the presidency of General Motors in 1920, one of Pierre Du Pont's first acts was to reorganize GM into divisions and to initiate the development of impersonal statistical and financial controls. When Du Pont resigned as president of General Motors in 1923, he left in place a management system with clear targets in such areas as inventory, ROI, sales, and output.

Starting in 1925, General Motors adopted a concept created by Donaldson Brown that related "a definite long-term return on investment objective to average or standard volume expectations over a number of years."[4] Goals were set for volume, costs, prices, and rates of return on capital. Standard cost hours, amounts paid for each purchased part, and the hours of labor required for each function were determined. These breakdowns were, at least in part, accounting techniques, for they included statistical data, ratios, rates, and amounts for every business purpose. As Alfred P. Sloan has written, "The guiding principle was to make our standards difficult to achieve, but possible to attain, which I believe is the most effective way of capitalizing on the initiative, resourcefulness, and capabilities of operating personnel."[5]

This concept, Sloan point out, makes profit residual for most managers and makes it possible to estimate very closely what profit would be at various volumes. Tied to the executive bonus plan, based upon rewarding performance as it related to standards, the development of this concept would suggest that Sloan, with his associates Donaldson Brown and Albert Bradley, perfected the major elements of modern MBO. Indeed, Peter Drucker, who many years later conducted a study of GM's management system, reported to John Tarrant, his biographer, that he first heard the term "management by objectives" used by Alfred P. Sloan.

In the marketing field, it was neither Du Pont nor Sloan who evidenced the first rudimentary examples of MBO, but John Henry Patterson of National Cash Register. Patterson had acquired the sagging National Manufacturing Company and changed its name. After overhauling the design of the cash register so that it could be manufactured economically, he turned his attention to launching a selling and sales training program of unmatched effectiveness. As one business historian has noted, "He established a quota system and guaranteed territory, altering a competitive concept which, in the past, had pitted one salesman against another in the same circumscribed area."[6] This quota system ran contrary to all selling concepts prior to Patterson's time and led NCR to market domination in the field with 94 percent of the market.

It was this system under which Thomas Watson, Sr., learned his trade as a marketer; he was later to transfer it to his own firm, the International Business Machines Corporation, in 1914. By 1924, Watson had made it clear that his style of management was unique and astonishingly successful. The creation of the One Hundred Percent Clubs, open to those who had achieved their quota, was supplemented with an evangelical enthusiasm for success. Part of the new IBM spirit was that no man was to think of himself as a boss; "the farther we keep away from the boss proposition, the more successful we are going to be," Watson said in 1925.[7] On the other hand, one could be a leader on a one-to-one basis, with one man giving guidance to another, not telling him what to do but helping him to do it. Thus the supportive aspect of management—setting tough goals and showing great enthusiasm, then helping the subordinate to get there—so highly regarded in modern MBO, was commonplace in IBM under Watson.

In 1927, he told members of the Hundred Percent Club, "It is a shame for any man, if he is in good health, to put in twelve months in a territory in our business and not come through with 100 percent of quota."[8] Watson demonstrated with unremitting energy that he would set high goals and exhorted everyone toward attainment of those goals. If top management support, as is so often said, is an essential ingredient of MBO, then Watson was living proof of its effectiveness. By 1930, goals-centered management was spreading.

Quite independently, at Standard Oil of New Jersey, President Walter Teagle faced up to growing administrative problems in that giant worldwide firm. He issued a memorandum in 1933 that effected a basic MBO program, even though that label was not attached to it. In effect, that memorandum brought to an end the era of the "entrepreneurial genius" method of management. It provided for a complete delegation of operating authority to independent operating units, making each unit responsible for its operations in a given territory. A coordinating committee at the corporate level defined goals and policies, approved operating and capital budgets, and approved operating indicators proposed by the units. At annual meetings, previously secret information was widely shared, along with a strong program of training for younger managers.[9] By 1940, this model of decentralized operating authority was recognized as a necessary form of organization in most major corporations. Reduced control over means of operation was being coupled with growing attention to outputs and results.[10]

### Peter Drucker, Theoretician

In the late 1930s, Peter Drucker, an Austrian by birth and an immigrant to this country, was invited to consult with the management of General Motors. As an economist and an outsider, he brought to his study of the corporate giant the observational skills of a Tocqueville or a Darwin. Without questionnaires or statistical techniques, Drucker walked about, conducting informal interviews, making notes, and drawing conclusions from common sense and systematic observations. He later wrote perceptively of his observations in *The Concept of the Corporation* (1946).

Drucker's discovery of the significance of decentralization and divisional forms of corporate organization seemed to be his major focus. His distinction between "federal" and "functional" decentralization was widely copied. The fact that he only saw goals and objectives as a natural product of that key concept is often missed. In his lectures at New York University in later years, he impressed upon his students the importance of decentralization as a route to greater industrial democracy, the personalization of large bureaucratic corporations, and the pushing down, or delegation, of decisions.

The major drawback of MBO as a means of making divisionalization work is its tendency to draw up only financial goals. Yet it becomes apparent that no other viable concept of management will work with divisional organization. General Foods, with some seventeen divisions, General Electric with seventy divisions, or ITT with 300 divisions could not be run by the most capable individual except by control of outputs and resources. The variety and sheer volume of activity in the large corporation makes the idea of close control unthinkable.

It is not surprising, therefore, that General Mills in 1954 changed from a functional to a divisional form prior to adopting MBO as its management style. The Drucker refinement of organizational planning defined also by Louis A. Allen's NICB study supplanted the previous "principles of organizations" approach.[11]

Public concern over the size of corporations was widespread during the 1930s. In his charge to the Temporary National Economic Committee (TNEC) in 1937, President Roosevelt requested that Congress address the question of whether or not the concentration of great power in private hands was in the public interest. It is reasonable to speculate that without decentralization/divisionalization, more severe antitrust legislation or other laws to break up large corporations might have been enacted. Certainly, without divisionalization and the management processes to make it viable, no conglomerates could exist.

Drucker was undoubtedly forced into paying attention to MBO as a natural product of decentralization by the response of his audience in lectures and books. The fact that Drucker is a political scientist at heart, and a management scientist by request only, is often overlooked. For him, MBO was a simple technique brought about and made necessary and logical by the need for political reform inside the modern corporation. His structures for management behavior did not grow out of any efficiency-engineer motivation. Underlying his thinking was the strong belief that the preservation of the capitalist system required some basic structural changes in the corporate system, and preferably from within. He was probably closer to his fellow Austrians Frederick Hayek and Ludwig Von Mises than he was to Douglas McGregor, Abraham Maslow, or Rensis Likert.

In *The Concept of the Corporation*, Drucker described his concept of General Motors' plan of decentralization, which Sloan had firmly put in place and skillfully operated. Drucker characterized this decentralization as a kind of "federalism." He noted that the relationship between central management and the respective divisions was achieved "through the power of the central management to set the goals for each division," and through setting limits on authority, checking progress, offering help, and relieving divisions of all work not related to their goal attainment.[12]

In his 1954 book, *The Practice of Management*, Drucker first used the expression "management by objectives and self-control" that struck such a popular chord. In part, the expression "MBO" caught on as a concept to be copied and applied by other large firms because of

Drucker's extensive speaking schedule before management groups. In the years following the publication of *The Practice of Management*, Drucker moved the concept to the center of his thinking, rather than keeping it as a sideline to the major theme of decentralization.

**The Systems Approach**

If a theoretical basis for MBO is absolutely necessary, then it perhaps might be found in the evolution of management science, operations research, and the "systems approach." Originating in the operations research movement during World War II, the systems approach emerged when physical scientists were drafted into duty to help solve complex strategic problems for the British Navy. By applying mathematical programming and modeling, they brought new, rigorous methods of analysis to dealing with both military and social problems. This approach is commonly expressed in an almost universally accepted definition by C. West Churchman: "A system is a set of parts coordinated to accomplish a set of goals."[13] The techniques of the systems approach were mathematical and more sophisticated than most managers are accustomed to employing, but the stages are simply stated:

Identification of

1. Total system objectives.
2. The system's environment and fixed constraints.
3. The resources of the system.
4. The activities of each component of the system.
5. A method of managing to attain the goals.

The most common elements in the systems approach are inputs, activities (processes), and outputs. The first step is to define the objectives in terms of hoped-for outputs. The choice of objectives is, of course, the first step in all variations of the systems approach, and without objectives, operations research is pointless. In the years since 1946, this field has become variously known as management science, operations research, and, in colleges and university curricula, as quantitative methods. In decision making, the definition of objectives (sometimes called the "objectives function") dominates the theoretical work that follows. Operations research is thus the scientific approach to managing by objectives.

MBO has directed attention to the systems approach, and the training of thousands of managers and technical specialists in management science has perhaps had a more important effect upon decision making than is ordinarily appreciated by traditional management and MBO's devotees. The increasing use of the systems approach in the many management decisions that affect marketing, plant location, inventory control, cash management, and investment decisions has, in fact, altered substantially the ways in which more complex management decisions are made.

## Recent Developments

In more modern times, such management theoreticians as Herbert Simon, Russell Ackoff, and Martin Starr have made contributions to a goals-centered cybernetic system to solve managerial problems.

My book, *Management by Objectives*, published in 1965, is subtitled *A System of Managerial Leadership*, which implied not just operations research but rather an extension of previous theories that made MBO a kind of think-piece formulation or a behavioral device for producing participative management. Walter Mahler, a New York-based consultant, has developed a package of consulting services that draws heavily on the systems approach to describe and apply MBO to his clients.[14]

It has not been the systems approach to MBO that has drawn the most attention, however, but rather MBO's behavioral and human resource development aspects. The majority of the literature directly dealing with MBO has, in fact, centered on the management problems of managing managers, managing professionals, setting standards of performance for managerial appraisal, doing a better job of salary administration and merit increases in pay, and handling the related psychological problems of motivation, achievement, and incentives.

## Standards-of-Performance Movement

Before MBO as a philosophy could gain acceptance in the halls of corporate headquarters or in the administrative office, some deeply held attachments had to be supplanted. For one thing, performance appraisal was strongly tied to personality assessment and trait-rating systems. The early human relations movement had made amateur psychologists of many managers. Appraisal systems were often comprised of lists of such personality traits as initiative, drive, integrity, and loyalty. Managers were required to rate subordinates against these traits, and their amateur clinical judgments became a part of the subordinates' permanent personnel file.

By the 1950s, a series of widespread attacks upon personality-based management had been made by both business and academic groups. William H. Whyte wrote a widely read book, *The Organization Man*, which proposed that such personality assessment methods were an invasion of privacy and were false scientism. Meanwhile, in industrial psychology an increasing body of evidence showed that the concept of the occupational personality was not to be found, no matter how hard people searched.

The American Management Association, which became the leader in adult education of executives, came down hard in favor of more objective standards of managerial performance based upon agreed goals and targets. Hundreds of thousands of managers from leading firms attended seminars, conferences, and courses where they were admonished to avoid personality-based assessments and were urged to define, in their place, standards of managerial performance.[15]

While the standards-of-performance movement of the 1950s can be credited with our turning away from personality-based assessment systems, it often faltered and fell by the wayside because of two obstacles. Group appraisal required an inordinate amount of time, as well as reams of paper. Furthermore, evaluations were almost wholly oriented to activities and duties rather than to outputs.

The standards-of-performance movement changed our way of thinking about managerial performance, but it was unsystematic. It did however, pave the way for the MBO movement that was to emerge in the late 1950s and to blossom fully in the 1960s.

## MBO's Original Adopters

Following the publication of *The Practice of Management,* and a book and several articles by another consultant, Edward Schleh, a number of companies began to consider how to apply the basic concept to their own businesses.[16] These were not companies already following the basic MBO idea without calling it MBO, such as General Motors, but rather companies turning away from decentralization or seeking an improved managerial appraisal plan.

Among the earliest of these was General Mills, in 1955; a year earlier, it had divisionalized under its president, Charles Bell. Durward Balch, vice-president of personnel, conducted an extensive study of the MBO idea. Professor Earl Brooks of Cornell, an early pioneer in designing and installing MBO programs, became a major consultant in implementation at General Mills. Not only did the creation of twelve new divisions in 1954 call for the selection, development, and appraisal of new division general managers. This change also required that new group vice-presidents, with profit responsibility, have some clear-cut ideas of what they expected and how executive bonuses would be administered.[17]

During this period, Howard Johnson, later director of the Sloan Program, dean, and then president of MIT, was employed at General Mills as Balch's assistant. His influence was undoubtedly great, and perhaps it was he who was one of the earliest to note the important behavioral aspects of MBO in addition to its functional, profitable aspects. When he left General Mills to join MIT, it was he who told Douglas McGregor of General Mills' unique appraisal system. This was the basis for McGregor's classic article, "An Uneasy Look at Performance Appraisal," which appeared in the *Harvard Business Review* in 1959. McGregor was unabashedly a humanist, strongly advocated participative management, and supported MBO as a participative management vehicle.

At this time General Mills was instrumental in organizing an executive development course, owned jointly by four Minneapolis companies: General Mills, Honeywell, Dayton's, and the Northwest Bancorporation. Through this course, in the ensuing years, all top managers in the four companies were trained in management with a strong results-centered style. From this emerged a generation of managers whose basic management style was clearly labelled MBO. This four-company course (now the multicompany course) started with the chairmen and chief executives of the four companies, and went through the officers' ranks. It became the first example of formal implementation of what others had crept into in a more tentative fashion following decentralization.[18]

By 1960, if you didn't have an MBO system, it was assumed that you could acquire it by training your managers, starting at the top and working down through the organization. In 1959, the University of Michigan initiated the first monthly seminar to train managers in MBO. This led the way for a rash of other university and associated programs of seminars, conferences, and courses on MBO.

## The Devotees

It was during the 1960s that the flood tide of MBO plans got under way. Surprisingly, there were few, if any, books on the subject. The first book with the title *Management by Objectives* was written by me in 1962 and was published in 1965, after considerable testing in the Michigan seminar. Following that time, however, the literature grew rapidly.

One of the more important researchers in the field was Edwin A. Locke of the University of Maryland. His research was crucial to the acceptance of MBO on a widespread basis inside corporations that were professionally staffed with sophisticated human resources personnel. His first rigorous research probed such basic questions as "Does MBO change behavior?" and found that having goals improves performance results; it motivates people to work, and when people set goals and achieve them, they enjoy their work more. Locke produced an astonishing twenty-one articles, mainly in psychological journals, that probed and defined the effects of MBO. It was Locke who demonstrated in his research that MBO really works. Without his research, there might not have followed a host of other scholarly research studies that, in effect, shaped the conditions under which MBO must live to succeed in practice.[19]

This spate of rigorous study, in turn, generated further studies refining Locke's ideas. Henry Tosi and Stephen Carroll determined the kinds of people with whom goal setting would work, and more generally defined predictable responses from MBO programs when varying implementation techniques were tried.[20] The journals in which this literature appeared spanned the field of psychology, management, education, and public and hospital administration. Locke, Gary Latham, Anthony Raia, Tosi, William Reddin, Heinz Weihrich, William Reif, and Bruce Kirchoff produced a great volume of research about the psychological aspects of MBO. In addition, at least ten doctoral dissertations in MBO—its extent of use, conditions for success, and special applications—were produced during this period.

In management literature, my thirty-five books, articles, and publications led the field, with John Humble, Dale McConkey, George Morrissey, Charles Hughes, and Glenn Varney among the major writers. A division of labor existed that was most productive. The management journal writers were advocates and refiners, and wrote about MBO based upon field experience and "by construction." Major developments in the field took place, and the management writers, often fresh from successes or failures with client companies, described new areas of application and new techniques in design and implementation. The application of MBO to such chronic management problems as selection, discipline, collective bargaining, compensation, marketing, and purchasing were described in case study form and prescriptive articles. At every step, the academic researcher probed and tested, drawing up lines of reservation and constraint, questioning assumptions, pricking bubbles, and refining techniques. The management professors and consultants initiated, designed, constructed, theorized, and speculated; the behavioral researchers followed closely, deflating overly ambitious claims and clarifying the requirements of MBO in theory. Without doubt, MBO as a management technique is one of the best tested, most thoroughly researched methods in recent times.

## The Haters

While the ranks of those who detest the entire system of MBO are actually small, their vehemence has been real and their motives understandable. In one category are those who must be defined as journalistic needlers. The editor who casts about and assigns writers to "find a very popular idea and stick a pin in it" belongs in this category. An issue of *Purchasing* a few years back had a drawing of a tombstone on its front cover, with "MBO—R.I.P." etched into the stone. The story inside began with a series of provocative leads suggesting that MBO had indeed expired and proposed that the following article would comprise its obituary. The content of the article, based upon interviews with leading corporate purchasing directors, seemed to have a hedging character, for most of the stories stated conditions that could cause MBO to falter and then proceeded to describe how purchasing departments had overcome these defects. MBO was not really dead, it seemed, but it was certainly capable of failure.

Professor Ed Wrapp of the University of Chicago attracted considerable attention in the business press with an article in the magazine, *Steel*, with the provocative title "Management by Objectives—or Wheel and Deal?" He proposed that top management doesn't really set objectives but actually wheels and deals without much attention to goals, strategies, or performance measures.[21]

Dr. Harry Levinson's article, "Management by Whose Objectives?" in the *Harvard Business Review* was a more fundamental attack upon the idea of MBO, however. Levinson, a former staff psychologist at the Menninger Clinic and long interested in the mental health of managers, expressed deep concern over the suppressive and top-down effects of MBO programs. These effects were to produce barriers for people seeking their ego ideal at work, a matter of considerable importance in Levinson's mind. While the article did not bar MBO in all of its forms, it did propose serious limitations on its top-down character.[22]

Many other critical articles about MBO cannot be included in the "hater" category, for they were written in a research vein. Such articles were more apt to describe the kinds of MBO practices that would cause its ultimate failure. Tosi, Carroll, Raia, John Ivancevich, Kirchoff, and Locke certainly were not blind in their acceptance of the idea of MBO, but defined the kinds of conditions that were necessary to its effectiveness.

The National Education Association (NEA), strongly opposed to MBO's use in appraising teaching performance, expressed strong distaste for the whole idea. Teachers' unions, it suggested, should come down strongly against MBO-based rating systems by which the school board and superintendent might crack down on teachers and bust their unions. The article did concede, however, that such schemes as MBO might be satisfactory for administrators and principals rating one another. but for the classroom teacher (the "learning locale") it should be avoided like the plague.[23]

One suspects that this attitude grew more out of a basic mistrust of any kind of administrative overture relating to teachers than to the unique character of MBO, however. Indeed, teacher evaluation has been the exact use for which some school systems have employed MBO, and perhaps the position of the unions, considering their actual experience, is justified. One school superintendent in the West announced the introduction of MBO in a city-wide policy as follows: "We have adopted a new and modern management system known as MBO this fall. Every teacher will be required to submit their MBOs in September. If they are failing to achieve these MBOs by January, in detail, they will be warned. If they are still failing to achieve their MBOs at the year's end, their employment will be terminated for cause." It is not surprising that in a single memo he had created a most ample complement of fearful MBO haters.

Similar applications in firms and government agencies have likewise produced coteries of mistrustful and angry MBO haters. The use of MBO has grown rapidly in federal, state, and local government and has generated several types of opposition.

The antiplanners are a common type of manager in both business and government. Churchman has identified several types of antiplanners.[24] One is the adherent to "practical approaches" growing out of experience coupled with sound intuition, solid leadership, and a brilliant mind. A second kind of antiplanner is the skeptic, who believes that life and the world are so complicated that nobody could possibly understand it well enough to control it or even predict it. Therefore, he is considerably reluctant to try, and is hostile to those who insist that he should do so. His objectives, he believes, are grounded in "It all depends" and "We do things informally." Wrapp falls into this category, and he has ample company.

A more serious kind of antiplanner is the determinist, who believes that human choices are not in the hands of responsible people but instead are controlled by immutable social or physical forces that will produce outcomes without human intervention. Evidence and analysis are pointless, for "What will be, will be."

Governmental administrators who favor political maneuvering and incremental budgeting are often violently opposed to program planning and MBO. They believe that the determinism of changing political tastes and trends will determine goals. These goals will, in turn, determine budgets, which will inevitably rise. Religious determinists reject the idea of defining human plans, for the Almighty has already chosen what will be.

In another category of antiplanners are those concerned almost wholly with the integrity of the self and with individual differences. The major purposes of life, they propose, are to know oneself, to be oneself, and to like oneself; any formal system that would diminish these is banned. This perhaps best expresses the rationale behind Levinson's opposition. While it might also be characteristic of other behavioral scientists, it would not include the "third force" group of psychologists such as McGregor, Maslow, or Frederick Herzberg, for they place work and its fruits high in the scheme of things by which individuals find their self-expression and identity.

A final category of anti-MBO groups is that of the existentialist. Members adhere to a philosophical system that detests systems. Camus expressed it: "If you lack character, you need a system." The world and human personality are rooted in existence and determined by luck, guilt, situations, and death; all else is futile. Existence precedes essence, and man makes himself by his own choice. Yet a close study reveals that purposes even comprise an important part of the existentialist's scheme of things.

It is apparent, from its history, that MBO is much more than a set of procedural rules for managing a business. As a philosophy it is consistent with the temper of our times. It responds to the restlessness which people feel toward the bureaucracy—the sense of powerlessness and alienation from the remote leadership of the large organization. It is at once functional in terms of what top management demands and developmental in terms of the people at work. It calls for human commitment rather than simply assuming that orders from the top will be self-executing. It compels forward planning and living life in an anticipatory mode rather than responding to events. It isn't based upon the prediction of the future but rather upon the creation of that future.

As a technique MBO has an air of logic about it that is compelling to logical people. It is easily proven to be job related rather than related to caste, class, or personality. MBO makes achievement easier to distinguish when it occurs and helps solve some chronic areas of concern in management, such as rewarding performance, appraising performance, training to increase performance levels, and coaching people to do better.

Finally, it comprises a style of management which permits individual differences, is mainly democratic in operation, and allows previously left-behind populations such as women and minorities to demonstrate their competence in readily tested terms. MBO's future impact on personnel training and governmental budgeting and its potential behavioral applications in supervisory management look promising.

1. Richard Mansell, *A Management by Objectives Bibliography,* mimeographed (Waterloo, Ontario: University of Waterloo, 1977).
2. C. West Churchman, *The Systems Approach* (New York: Dell, 1977): 239-240.
3. Alfred D. Chandler and Stephen Salsbury, *Pierre S. Du Pont and the Making of the Modern Corporation* (New York: Harper & Row, 1971): 499.
4. Alfred P. Sloan, *My Years with General Motors* (New York: Doubleday, 1963): 144.
5. Sloan: 147.
6. William Rodgers, *Think, a Biography of Watson and IBM* (New York: New York: New American Library, 1970): 37.
7. Rodgers: 89.
8. Rodgers: 90.
9. H. M. Larson, E. H. Knowlton, and C. S. Popple, *History of Standard Oil: New Horizons 1927-1950* (New York: Harper & Row, 1971): 22.
10. See Alfred D. Chandler, *Strategy and Structure* (Cambridge, Mass.: MIT Press, 1962).
11. Louis A. Allen, *Management and Organization* (New York: McGraw-Hill, 1958).
12. Peter F. Drucker, *The Concept of the Corporation* (New York: John Day, 1946): 41-79.
13. Churchman: Chapter 3.
14. Walter R. Mahler, "A Systems Approach to Managing by Objectives," *Systems and Procedures Journal,* April 1972: 12-19.
15. See Virgil Rowlands, *Standards of Managerial Performance* (New York: Harper, 1959).

16. See Edward Schleh, *Successful Executive Action* (Englewood Cliffs, N.J.: Prentice-Hall, 1955). This was probably the first book-length exposition of MBO. Schleh also wrote on MBO in *Personnel*, May 1953.
17. See "How Am I Doing?," pamphlet issued by General Mills, Inc., Minneapolis, in 1955.
18. Walter Wikstrom, *Managing with and by Objectives*, Studies in Personnel Policy, No. 212 (New York: National Industrial Conference Board, 1968).
19. Most of Locke's twenty-one articles were published between 1965 and 1970 when MBO was becoming widespread. They appeared in numerous publications, including the *Journal of Applied Psychology*.
20. Tosi's first research report was published in *Personnel Management* in 1965; Tosi's and Carroll's work subsequently appeared in the *Academy of Management Journal, MSU Business Topics, Management Review*, and the *California Management Review*.
21. H. E. Wrapp, "Management by Objectives—or Wheel and Deal?," *Steel*, May 29, 1967: 46-47.
22. Harry Levinson, "Management by Whose Objectives?," *Harvard Business Review*, July-August 1970: 125-134.
23. See "Should Teachers Say No to MBO?," *Briefing News* (Washington, D.C.: National Education Association, 1976).
24. See Churchman; Chapter 13.

Section **2** # Strategic Planning and the Hierarchy of Objectives

**Objectives**
1. To recognize the limitations of a short-range orientation to MBO.
2. To appreciate the importance of integrating objectives, strategies, and tactics in a system.
3. To understand that objectives form a complex hierarchy.

**Figure 3**

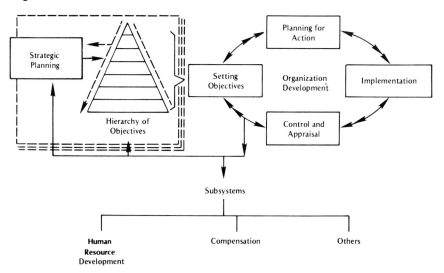

## Strategic Planning and the Hierarchy of Objectives

In the previous section it was shown that MBO has changed over the years. The early application was in appraisal, then it was seen as a means of integrating organizational and individual objectives, and more recently some enterprises have integrated MBO with strategic planning, one of the main concerns of this section.

Traditionally, MBO focused on the short-term—usually one year—planning cycle. But this often resulted in suboptimization problems because short-term objectives can be pursued at the detriment of long-term aims. For example, a production manager may neglect maintenance of machines to reduce costs. Yet, in the long-run, this may become expensive requiring early replacement of the machines or costly repairs. To prevent problems of short-sightedness and to better integrate short- and long-term efforts, the concept of MBO should be expanded to include strategic and long-range planning.

A strategy usually involves the deployment of company resources to achieve the major objectives of the firm. In other words, the strengths and weaknesses of the firm are matched with the opportunities and threats in the external environment. The emphasis is on utilizing strengths and exploiting opportunities. For example, a high technology firm may use integrated circuit knowledge to take advantage of opportunities in the market by manufacturing pocket calculators or electronic watches. The important point is that MBO becomes an integral part of strategic planning, with a long-term orientation.

A part of strategy formulation is the development of a hierarchy of aims. This means that the broad purpose of the organization and its mission statement are integrated with long-range and strategic objectives, more specific overall objectives, division, department and unit objectives, and finally objectives of each individual in the enterprise. In such a hierarchy, the lower level objectives contribute to the goals of the next higher organizational unit.

The first reading in this section, "Objectives, Strategies, and Tactics in a System," discusses the approach used at Texas Instruments. Although it is not called MBO, it has many of the elements of the comprehensive MBO model used in this book. Dove, the author of the article, conceives the goals to form a hierarchy. Thus the corporate objectives are translated into business objectives, strategies (long-term, general courses of actions), and tactics (short-term actions). By focusing on both the strategic mode and the operational mode—the day-to-day and month-to-month operation—the chances of working toward short-term goals at the expense of long-range aims are greatly reduced.

In the second reading, "The Hierarchy of Objectives," Granger develops an elaborate hierarchy ranging from the needs, values, and drives of policy-forming individuals to short-term programs at the low level. Furthermore, the author discusses the specific steps in the process of developing these aims starting with broad company objectives.

These two articles essentially describe the left part of our comprehensive MBO model. They provide the foundation for the more detailed steps that follow: specifically, the hierarchy of aims and the strategic plan are the basis for setting objectives, developing action plans, implementing them, and controlling the organizational performance, as well as appraising individual results.

# 1
# Objectives, Strategies, and Tactics in a System

One of the biggest aids in making decisions on the allocation of resources is to have a clearly defined set of goals. Over and over we at Texas Instruments find ourselves making resource commitments which impact a number of decentralized units in rather complex and involved ways. To meet these problems, we need to have clearly stated goals at all levels of the organization so that many diverse units will be working together toward common objectives. Goals are important because:

1. They form a specific expression of purpose. Our Objectives, Strategies, Tactics System (OST System) attempts to remove any uncertainty about the company's policy or about the intended purpose of any effort.
2. If properly designed, they permit measurement of progress. Without some form of progress measurement, it becomes very difficult to know if adequate resources are being applied or whether these resources are being effectively managed.
3. They aid in dealing with the interrelations between units, especially in cases where the natural goals of the separate units may not be consistent with some higher purpose. For example, a coordinated set of goals permits resources to be applied to achieve an innovation in one group in order to serve a market opportunity for another group. Or one group might need to forego a market opportunity to permit another group to capitalize on a more promising one.

The goals expressed in the OST System form a structure or hierarchy. They begin with a Corporate Objective and extend downward first to Business Objectives, then to Strategies, and then to Tactics. The Business Objectives express broadly defined goals in each business area. The Strategies define the long-term, general courses of action to be followed, with checkpoints along the way to measure progress toward these goals. The Tactics describe the short-term actions in support of the Strategies and define specific responsibility and the commitment of resources.

Reprinted by permission of the publisher, from *The Conference Board Record*, Vol. 7, No. 8, August 1970, pp. 52-55.

**The Organization Factor**

There are four groups in the operating organization of Texas Instruments. However, these groups are not based on such typical organizing categories as product lines or types of customers served. Instead, each of the four groups reflects a different perspective as to how TI products and services can relate to a customer's processes and systems: a Materials Group deals with products that would be raw materials for a customer's production process; a Components Group deals with products that would be sub-assemblies in the customer's process or replaceable parts in his equipment; an Equipment Group produces machines that would perform processing operations in the customer's system; and a Services Group provides systems support for a customer's operations. Given this organization structure, the various groups within TI are all natural customers for each other. Moreover, the development of any new product or service to be marketed by TI is quite likely to require the coordinated, cooperative effort of most, if not all, of the four groups. Thus, this organization structure may be an important factor in the functioning of the OST System of management.

The four operating groups are broken down further into divisions and then again into 77 Product Customer Centers (PCCs), which operate like complete small business organizations with their own short-term profit responsibility. Texas Instruments credits the PCCs with contributing much toward developing a spirit of customer responsiveness and innovation in management and also toward developing entrepreneurial managers.

R.G.S.

What we want to accomplish in this hierarchy is to create an environment which encourages the generation of ideas at all levels and in which resources can be deployed or re-deployed quickly in support of ideas which can have major impact on strategies or objectives. The OST structure gives us a Strategic Mode of operation for directing and controlling efforts toward long-range objectives. Of course, it interacts strongly with the Operational Mode for planning and controlling day-to-day and month-to-month operations.

We are asking our managers to become accustomed to living with both modes, i.e., with multiple goals. There is really no escape from it. Our Product Customer Center (PCC) managers can expect, as a way of life, to be dealing with simultaneous interrelated goals. The OST System is designed to help them sort these out so that the appropriate trade-offs will take place betwen short- and long-term interests and so that responsibilities to employees, community and share owners will be met simultaneously.

What are some of the common pitfalls that we are trying to avoid?

1. Classical organizations are frequently not properly aligned to exploit long-range opportunities. There may be very good, practical reasons

for organizing in a particular way to meet today's problems, but you would prefer to be organized differently if you could afford to be concerned with the long-range opportunities. In a sense, the OST structure allows you to have it both ways.

2. It is often true that long-range goals are merely expressed and given lip service while the money and people resources tend to gravitate towards short-term problems.

3. When goals are lacking or not clearly expressed, conflicts may occur at middle management levels and result in compromise solutions which are not in the best interests of the corporation but which are invisible to top management.

## Stating Goals and Plans

*The Corporate Objective.* At the top of the OST structure stands a Corporate Objective. It states the economic purpose, the reasons for existence of the corporation. It also states in broad terms our product, market, and technical goals. It defines our responsibilities to our employees, our share owners, our community and society as a whole, and it establishes the financial goals by which we measure our contribution to the economic development of society.

*Business Objectives.* The Corporate Objective is supported by a set of 12 Business Objectives. Each is expressed through a Business Charter which establishes the boundaries of the business, provides an appraisal of the potential opportunities which we perceive in this business, and includes a study of the technical and market trends together with the overall competitive structure of industry serving this business. Performance measures are established which include specific goals for financial factors such as sales, profit, return on internal assets, and market penetration five and ten years ahead. In addition, we attempt to project the market and the product mix; to establish technical goals; to identify obstacles or boundaries limiting the business; to evaluate the competition, threats, and contingencies we might have to meet; and generally to evaluate what we must make happen in order to achieve our Business Objective successfully.

The Business Objective is almost entirely goal-oriented. We devote considerable emphasis to establishing premises and defining environments, but there is almost none given to how the goals will be achieved; the "how" part is described in Strategies and Tactics.

One of the criteria of a good Business Objective is that it be challenging enough, even shocking enough, to force a radical re-thinking of strategies and tactics. Whenever we have enough well-defined strategies to give us a high confidence level in exceeding the goals stated in the objective, then that Business Objective is probably not ambitious enough and the probability of truly innovative strategic thinking is likely to be low.

*Strategy Statements.* The next level in the goal structure is the Strategy Statement. The Strategy describes in detail the environment of a particular business opportunity which will be pursued in support of the Business Objective. Normally there will be a number of Strategies supporting each Objective; all together we have more than 50 Strategies operating. For example, if we had an Objective to attain certain goals in the automobile market, we might have one Strategy involving automobile electronics, one involving materials applications, and perhaps another on safety systems.

The Strategy Statement specifies the innovations necessary; the probable obstacles to be encountered; alternative actions or contingencies; and the major commitments that will have to be made if the Strategy is to succeed. Each Strategy looks ahead a number of years, normally from five to ten, and intermediate checkpoints are defined along the way, providing milestones against which to judge progress—something not included at the Business Objective level. Finally, the contribution of the Strategy to the overall Objective is defined in quantitative measures, and a critique is formulated which assigns a success probability to the Strategy.

*Tactical Action Plans.* Next in the goal hierarchy is the Tactical Action Plan, or TAP. It details the steps necessary to reach the next major checkpoint defined in the Strategy. The TAP normally is short term, covering 6 to 18 months of effort. The TAP designates a responsible individual, establishes a start and finish schedule of activities, and defines the required resources.

Each TAP is broken down further into individual work packages, which are run by means of standard program management techniques. Detailed planning at this level provides the basis for planning and control of resources throughout the OST structure.

For management review, the status of each TAP is reported monthly in a simplified format which enables us to tell at a glance how the TAP stands on a number of critical factors. Yellow and red bars indicate that higher management action is needed to solve a problem. Detailed monthly reports on financial and manpower resources are also distributed to TAP, Strategy and Objective managers.

## OST Overlays Organization

What we have with OST is a system that gives us a method of planning, review and control which cuts across the organization structure of groups, divisions and PCCs. It provides a mechanism for assembling capabilities and challenging efforts to achieve results that could not be achieved by any one organizational element. In effect, we superimpose our hierarchy of goals on top of the traditional organization structure.

One way to visualize this overlay is by using a matrix with the traditional organizational units across the top of the matrix and the OST structure at the left margin. Typically the matrix organization concept has been used to illustrate the overlapping of a project organization with a functional organization. But here the matrix is showing something entirely different. It is showing the relationship between the Strategic Mode and Operating Mode within the same organization. There is still a single organization, but there are different, clearly defined responsibilities for long-term growth and current profitability.

One of the roles of a Strategy manager is to coordinate TAPs across the company in accordance with the Strategy plan. Many times the Strategy manager is also the manager of a PCC—especially if there is one PCC able to take a dominant role in the Strategy. Only rarely is being an Objective, Strategy, or Tactic manager a full-time assignment; there is almost always a simultaneous Operating role to be filled. Whenever this is the case, we simply have a manager wearing two hats. He has clearly defined goals for both growth and profitability. This dual role helps us to tie long-range strategic plans to our short-term operational planning and control activities.

## OST Focuses Innovation

There are two types of investments a manager can make: Operating investments and Strategic investments. An Operating investment is one necessary for current operations—one designed to maximize this year's results. On the other hand, a Strategic investment is not related to current operations; it is keyed to long-term growth.

With these definitions in mind, let us say that there is a young manager somewhere within one of the PCCs who is performing a line function within his Center, and that a large measure of his day-to-day responsibility is the profitability of that Center. Suppose that he thought he could see the possibility of a new business entry for TI or of a way to cause a major impact on one of the existing Strategies. He is excited about his idea and would like to spend more time digging into the possibilities of its success. The problem is that every minute he gives to this idea is a minute that he has not given to his PCC.

In many organizations, short-term pressures for operating profits might completely block his efforts. This would be a frustrating and a *demotivating* experience. He might soon learn to avoid wasting time on such innovative thinking. But in terms of future business growth, these are precisely the kind of ideas that the organization needs to stay alive.

This is the activity that we are attempting to institutionalize through the OST system.

Through the OST overlay, we have a goal structure for Strategic activities as well as Operating activities. Not only can we measure profit and loss performance operationally, we can also allocate resources through the OST structure and measure our performance toward these goals. Now our young manager's new idea has a home. It can be given resources for further development and, if progress warrants, heavier support later. His idea would become a part of the OST structure. It would be recognized and, as appropriate, supported by deliberate choice. It would not have to be bootlegged or dropped completely through the crack.

## Accountability for Results

If, as is usually the case, a man is both a Tactics manager and a PCC manager at the same time, he is responsible for both current Operating Mode results and for long-range Strategic Mode results. How does he reconcile those two roles and how will he avoid the temptation to delay and cut back strategic efforts every time an operating crisis comes along?

First, on his P & L statement, Strategic expense is below the Operating profit line and does not penalize his performance as an Operating manager. Second, the planned Strategic expenses are clearly identified and cannot be diverted into solving Operating problems without severely penalizing his performance as a Strategy manager. Third, he is not only expected to spend the Strategic funds, but he is also required to report regularly on his achievement of milestones. He has been given the authority—within specified limits—to obligate expense, capital, and people resources; to make adjustments as necessary to meet the Strategic goals; and to resolve conflict as it occurs.

Results and progress on Strategic Mode activities are reviewed first by the Tactic manager and then in succession by the Strategy level, the Business Objective level and by the Corporate Development function. Accountability for Operating profit, on the other hand, is through the PCC to the division and group levels.

The responsibility for Strategic and Operating activities in the same area tend to converge closer and closer to single individuals as one looks higher in the organization. As a result, group and division managers are all wearing both hats and have primary responsibility for both Operating profit and Strategic expense in their areas. This, in turn, means that they are accountable for the bottom line on the P & L statement—the Organization profit.

## OST as a Long-Range Plan

Our Objectives and Strategies contain all the essential elements of a long-range plan. In fact, the OST documentation is our long-range plan. In the Operational Mode, we budget and control to an Annual Plan, which is just a snapshot of one year of the long-range plan. In our planning cycle they are all tied together:

• Throughout the year we are concentrating on our Objectives and Strategies, revising the basic premises and checkpoints. This gives us the environment and guidelines we need for the more detailed annual planning to follow.

• In the fall and winter, with the economic and market outlooks in mind, we set our annual goals and the split of funds between Strategic and Operating Modes. Tactics are revised and new ones generated. We generally have more defined Tactics than we can afford to undertake at one time. We must, therefore, go through a program selection or decision package process, with the selected programs folded into the approved plans for the coming year.

• To give us a living and dynamic long-range plan, we attempt to space our Objective reviews throughout the year so that management can devote time for an in-depth study of each Objective and yet never be more than 12 months away from the most recent review of any Objective.

• In fact, Objectives can be revised and the long-range plan updated at any time when business or economic developments might make it desirable.

In effect, then, this is a rolling long-range plan.


## Problems and Benefits

The OST approach has worked for us. Nonetheless, it may not work for everyone. Furthermore, even after six years of experience with it, we still do encounter problems and difficulties.

For example, even with our resource reporting and follow-up systems, we still run "under plan" on our Strategic investments in many areas. Another problem is the quality of our long-range quantitative data. And we also have the objections that one would expect from TAP managers about detailed project planning being an over-regimented approach.

Another problem comes, ironically, as a result of success with the OST concept. When we generate more TAPS or good ideas than we can possibly undertake in a given year, it means that many well-developed proposals fall below the funding line. This is a major disappointment to the individuals who put their full energies into these proposals, and we work hard to motivate these key contributors in other areas where their skills can be even more productive. To help this situation, many of the programs in our innovative backlog are only temporarily shelved; they are funded whenever resources become available.

We look on the OST system at TI as a system for managing change. But it is many more things besides. It can be described as an approach to corporate self-renewal. It provides a method for translating goals into action plans. It is a way to plan and control our investments for the future. It provides a method of decentralized resource allocation within a framework of centrally established objectives. It ties together our activities on a worldwide basis. It allows us to attack major opportunities with the resources of a large company while operating with the inherent advantages of being many related small companies.

Finally, and perhaps most important of all, it is a vehicle by which we are developing our entrepreneur managers of the future. We are getting better definition and greater visibility of the Strategic and Operating Modes from our managers, and their dual responsibility is becoming well understood. As a result, there is a close tie between our short- and long-range plans. Perhaps most important of all is the commitment of the managers to both because they are preparing and executing their own plans.

# 2
# The Hierarchy of Objectives

- Why is a conceptual framework of objectives important in decision making?
  - What are the most important characteristics of good objectives?
  - How should objectives be chosen and established?
  - How can objectives be used profitably by management?

We are all faintly amused by the aptness of the old quotation, "Having lost sight of our objective, we redoubled our efforts." Everyone admits to having been caught in this situation at one time or another. But is it possible that most large organizations are in this predicament a good part of the time?

Evidence indicates that this may indeed be true. The main trouble seems to be a lack of clear understanding of questions such as the above. In discussing these questions I shall use the term *objective* in the relatively broad, nonspecific sense which it commonly has in everyday business language. In this sense an objective is "an aim or end of action"; it is also used as an aim or guide to intermediate decisions and actions. For example, a sales manager might say, "Our objective is to have our salesmen make as many calls as possible"—but he might be very conscious of the fact that a more fundamental objective is to develop high sales volume.

## Role and Importance

Everyone will admit that objectives are important. But is it really necessary to analyze them? Can they be taken for granted? On a larger scale we have evidence like this:

- In a $50-billion-a-year organization, Secretary Robert S. McNamara and professional military people are in serious dispute because of a new way of looking at objectives.

Charles H. Granger, "The Hierarchy of Objectives," *Harvard Business Review,* May-une 1964, Copyright © 1964 by the President and Fellows of Harvard College; all rights reserved.

- The Roman Catholic Church has called some 2,500 of its highest officials from their pressing daily business to help rethink that organization's objectives.
- The American Telephone and Telegraph Company was perhaps saved from government ownership in the 1930s by having thought out its objectives.
- Sears, Roebuck and Co. has expanded from being a catalog merchant into a fabulous range of services as a result of a continuing redefinition of its objectives.
- Theodore Levitt proposes that some leading industries may be in danger of going the way of the railroads because of inappropriate objectives.[1]

Less dramatic examples, because they are so much more numerous, probably have even greater importance. Think of the waste from the countless decisions made every day which could have been made better if the desired objectives had been more apparent to the decision-maker. In many organizations, if you ask a number of managers to write down their principal objectives, you may get strongly conflicting answers. The results? Research and development money is sometimes spent on projects which are later abandoned because they are inconsistent with broader corporate objectives. Committees spend countless hours thrashing over problems unrelated to the over-all purposes of their organizations. Vacillation on acquisition policies is often attributable to inadequately defined objectives. And so on.

Organization planning, marketing planning, R & D planning, financial planning, to say nothing of total corporate planning, properly begin with the question, "What are our over-all objectives?" Moreover, proponents of Douglas McGregor's "Theory Y" stress the importance of integrating the objectives of the individual with the objectives of the organization. But how can this be done if the organization's objectives are not really known? It seems that there is a major opportunity for increased effectiveness if our objectives can be made clearer by even a small amount.

### Subtle Conflicts
*Clarity* is not the only question. *Balance* is important, too. Thus:
- Many a company is in trouble because customer-service objectives are not properly related to profit objectives.
- One utility will tell you (privately) that it ran into a serious earnings problem because its managers overstressed customer-service objectives to the slighting of profit objectives, a condition that took some years to correct.
- Some companies recruit too many top-rate college graduates to be consistent with the rather modest objectives of the over-all organization.

When after a few years it becomes apparent to these high-potential individuals that the organization does not really intend to pursue very challenging objectives, the result is wasteful high turnover.

Lyndall F. Urwick sums up such problems in a refreshing and often-overlooked way:

> Unless we have a purpose there is no reason why individuals should try to cooperate together at all or why anyone should try to organize them. This, however, is very easily forgotten. Once an organization is set up, a human group is in being, all the individual and personal motives which have induced persons to join the group, which keep them in the game and playing the game, assume great importance in their minds. Most of us suspect that the main purpose of the undertaking which employs us is to provide us personally with a job. . . . People derive social satisfactions from working together. And they build up, often unconsciously, very elaborate codes of behavior, and loyalties, and affections and antipathies, which may have little or nothing to do with the formal organization of the undertaking, the official relationships which their superiors recognize. . . . Every organization and every part of every organization must be an expression of the purpose of the undertaking concerned or it is meaningless and therefore redundant.[2]

### Is a Theory Necessary?

Management literature is teeming with titles such as "How to Set Objectives," "How We Set Our Objectives," and even with articles on the appropriateness of one objective as opposed to another — profits versus survival, volume versus customer-service, and the like. Less attention has been given to the structure of objectives, pseudo-objectives, and constraints. Some sort of conceptual framework embracing the whole range of objectives seems necessary if we are ultimately going to use objectives more effectively. In some orderly way we must relate the "grand design" type of objective with the much more limited objectives lower down in the organization. And we have to examine how one type of objective can be derived from another. Again quoting Urwick:

> We cannot do without theory. It will always defeat practice in the end for a quite simple reason. Practice is static. It does and does well what it knows. It has, however, no principle for dealing with what it doesn't know. . . . Practice is not well adapted for rapid adjustment to a changing environment. Theory is light-footed. It can adapt itself to changed circumstances, think out fresh combinations and possibilities, peer into the future.[3]

## Tests of Validity

How can the validity of an objective be tested? What should an objective accomplish? Here are some important criteria to be applied to an objective:

1. *Is it, generally speaking, a guide to action?* Does it facilitate decision making by helping management select the most desirable alternative courses of action?
2. *Is it explicit enough to suggest certain types of action?* In this sense, "to make profits" does not represent a particularly meaningful guide to action, but "to carry on a profitable business in electrical goods" does.
3. *Is it suggestive of tools to measure and control effectiveness?* "To be a leader in the insurance business" and "to be an innovator in child-care services" are suggestive of measuring tools in a helpful way; but statements of desires merely to participate in the insurance field or child-care field are not.
4. *Is it ambitious enough to be challenging?* The action called for should in most cases be something in addition to resting on one's oars. Unless the enterprise sets objectives which involving reaching, there is a hint that the end of the road may be at hand. It might be perfectly appropriate for some enterprises which have accomplished their objectives to quietly disband. However, for an undertaking to have continuity, it needs the vitality of challenging objectives.
5. *Does it suggest cognizance of external and internal constraints?* Most enterprises operate within a framework of external constraints (e.g., legal and competitive restrictions) and internal constraints (e.g., limitations in financial resources). For instance, if objectives are to be a guide to action, it appears that American Motors, because of its particular set of constraints, should have somewhat different objectives than General Motors.
6. *Can it be related to both the broader and the more specific objectives at higher and lower levels in the organization?* For example, are the divisions objectives relatable to the corporate objectives, and in turn do they also relate to the objectives of the research department in that division?

If such tests as these are valid indications of the meaningfulness of objectives, then several further propositions become apparent. First, objectives, as aims or ends of action, are intimately involved in a complex of other important considerations or guides to action, such as definitions of the business, internal and external constraints, measurements of success, budgets, and long-range plans. Secondly, there is a ranking or hierarchy of objectives, proceeding in concept from the very broad to the specific. Logically, the specific or more limited objectives should not be in conflict with the broad objectives. The second proposition in particular deserves further consideration.

## Complete Framework

Much of the confusion which apparently exists about objectives can be alleviated by viewing objectives as a whole framework or complex of "aims or ends of action" and other guiding considerations. In this framework it is not helpful to think there is one overriding consideration, such as "profit," since we must also concede in the next breath that another objective is to "stay within the law." Profit may indeed be the factor to be maximized *in a particular case*, but it cannot be viewed as the sole objective. The concept of a hierarchy is illustrated in Figure 4.

### Leading Characteristics

Granted the existence of this hierarchy, what is significant about it? What are its important characteristics and implications?

1. *The full range of objectives and guiding considerations is distressingly broad.* No one individual in a large organization could consciously make each decision in light of the total framework of objectives and guiding considerations. Hence, in practice many managers are guided in their decision making by what they themselves view as their own key objectives. This creates quite a problem. Recognition that there is such a problem does not mean that we should shrug our shoulders and ignore the whole subject. It suggests the need for a greater effort to organize and compartmentalize objectives into classes that are useful for each decision-maker in the organization.

2. *The rate of change with time decreases as we go up the scale.* Short-term programs and budgetary objectives may change in less than a year. But long-range plans may exist for several years without major revision, and the "grand design'" of an enterprise may last throughout the leadership tenure of its chief executive.

3. *For most enterprises even the broad objectives are subject to change in 20 years.* The argument is sometimes advanced that the very broad objectives of an enterprise are tied in with human values which are essentially immutable or subject to change only in terms of millennia. A good case could be made for this in terms of some organizations such as the Church. In other fields, however, the "grand design" even of many large organizations has changed within a leadership generation. The airframe industry, Sears, Roebuck and Co., the Tuberculosis Association, and the U.S. Air Force are examples. In smaller organizations it is not unusual to see the needs and values of the leader change—for instance, from financial security to esteem or creative contribution to society—with a discernible change in objectives of the organization. Management consulting firms are keenly aware of the fact that, when a new chief executive comes into power, there is considerable potential for consulting services in helping the organization to rethink and redetail its objectives

in line with the new values, creeds, and grand design of the incoming chief executive.

4. *Debates on how specific an objective should be are not especially helpful.* One sometimes encounters the argument that an objective "to earn a fair return for the stockholder" is a pious but meaningless mouthing; 20% pretax return on invested capital (or some such specific target) is advanced as a more appropriate alternative. The scale of objectives in EXHIBIT I suggests that both of these are necessary (along with others). On the one hand, if we intend to use objectives as a tool for measuring progress, we are certainly much better able to do so if we have a certain percentage figure like 20% appropriate to the year. On the other hand, 20% (or any other fixed percent) may be ridiculous for a recession year when nobody in the industry can even approach the figure; it then becomes meaningless. Thus, to derive a valid measurement we must fall back on our broader objective of fair return to the stockholders.

5. *Debates on the merit of one type of objective as opposed to another are only meaningful in light of the particular circumstances.* For example:

> One frequently hears arguments as to whether profitability, public service, or perhaps customer-service or survival of the enterprise should be the ascendant objective. Arguments of this kind can quickly degenerate into a chicken-or-egg type of controversy.
>
> Figure 4 suggests that the relative merit of a particular type of objective can only be evaluated in light of the particular circumstances being faced—the internal and external constraints, the values of the individuals who control the destiny of the enterprise, and so on. It might be entirely appropriate for a large undertaking, threatened with nationalization or government-directed splitting up which it deems against its best interests, to emphasize public service objectives more than profit objectives. H. Igor Ansoff points out that the near-term profits of many rather large firms are relatively secure anyway.[4]

6. *The obviousness of the need for stated objectives appears to decrease as we approach the upper end of the hierarchy.* Consider the experience of the Defense Department:

> Until the McNamara era, much Congressional debate centered around budgetary allocations in the traditional service categories (Army, Navy, Air Force, and so on), each broken down by personnel, operation and maintenance, procurement, R & D, and military construction. These traditional budget categories represent objectives of a sort and are still being used. But Secretary McNamara and his colleagues revolutionized the concept of objectives in government by taking this line of reasoning: It is not a fundamental objective simply to have so many men in the Marine Corps or to build such and such an Army base. The real objective is maximum national security. Within what might be called a grand design

**Figure 4**
Hierarchy of Objectives in Terms of Level of Need or Activity.

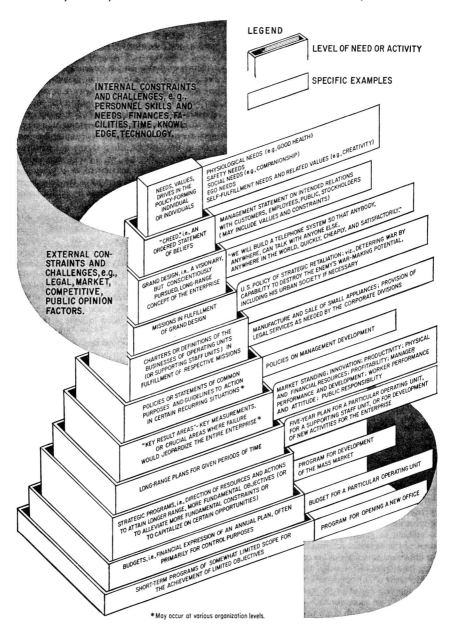

of national security, a number of "missions" were established, including strategic retaliation, continental air and missile defense, and general-purpose warfare capability. Now, for example, the Fleet Ballistic Missile System can be evaluated in terms of its contribution and cost/effectiveness relationships to the mission of the strategic retaliatory forces.

Although the advantages of evaluating the Defense Department program in light of its objectives seem obvious after the fact, and although such a system was long advocated by the Hoover Commission and other bodies, the Defense Department is the only major government department to have done this on a large scale.

This apparent casual approach to objectives is not a phenomenon of government organizations. How many talented leaders from business and other endeavors sit on boards of various churches, educational institutions, charities and the like, struggling with budgets in cases where the less obvious but more fundamental objectives have not been thought out? It is not an easy job. For example, one large church organization, after much preparatory staff work, required six early-morning-to-late-evening sessions of two days each (including the time of a large group of nationally prominent individuals) to redefine its objectives (the equivalent of grand design, missions, and charters in Figure 4) and related matters.

While formalized statements of grand design and missions apparently exist only in a small percentage of business organizations, formalized charters and policy statements are relatively common; long-range plans are becoming much more so, and almost every business has a budget.

7. *The need for broad objectives of the grand design and mission type is not restricted to the very large company.* For example:

> One moderate-size New England company is founded on a variety of specialized technologies in mechanical sealing devices. The head of this company views its *grand design* as "stopping the leaks around the world." Bizarre as this first sounds, it is a perfectly workable concept for a grand design for a highly successful undertaking—which it already is on a moderate scale. From it are spawned *missions* relating to certain markets and applications. There is a network of *charters* relating to various operating divisions both in this country and abroad. This organization seems to have a unified sense of purpose and destiny which it would otherwise lack. The whole management team seems to know where it is going, and the individual managers are excited and enthusiastic about their common purpose.

The unfortunate cases are the organizations which lack such an overall sense of purpose and are not doing anything to correct it; or perhaps their grand design is substantially accomplished or no longer appropriate to the current environment. These are the business enterprises in declining or static industries, the philanthropies for which the needs are now only marginal, and so on. The objectives of these organizations seem to be "to keep on doing what we have been doing," but the people in them are troubled and perplexed because they see that their results are not particularly satisfactory by a number of standards. A business enterprise in this situation may view its over-all objective as "10% net profit on stockholder investment"—but it does not have a ghost of a chance of achieving it on a consistent basis. People in the organization become engrossed in their personal objectives of holding onto their jobs. If only the board of directors in such cases would insist on having a written statement of the grand design!

8. *Objectives should not only guide action but also stimulate it.* Frederick R. Kappel, chairman of the board at AT&T, observes:

> "Unless the business sets demanding and exciting goals, it runs a heavy risk of losing vitality. This is an area where people in top management positions have heavy responsibilities. . . . If these goals fail to stimulate, there is something missing at the top. . . . In the sense that I am using the word, a goal is something presently out of reach; it is something to strive for, to move toward, or to become. It is an aim or purpose so stated that it excites the imagination and gives people something they want to work for, something they don't yet know how to do, something they can be proud of when they achieve it."[5]

### Steps in Derivation

When we choose and establish directives, we cannot logically proceed in one step from a grand design to a budget, although companies undoubtedly often attempt this. We are in effect confronted with a situation of goals within goals within goals.

We must start with the given statement of the broader objective (see Figure 5). Next comes the process of setting up yardsticks, criteria, "key result areas," or some other form to measure the success of the stated objective. Obviously the more tangible such yardsticks are, the more usable they will be. But if they are going to be specific and realistic (for example, so many dollars in world trade), then it is necessary to consider both the internal resources of the enterprise ("How much physically can we export?") and the environmental conditions ("What share of which world markets can we obtain?"). Hence both an analysis of internal resources and an environmental analysis are called for in setting up realistic and adequately challenging criteria.

The next step requires that management define the range of possible activities which it might use to accomplish the larger objective. For example, the question for a furniture company might be: What balance of emphasis is best between office and home furnishings? The alternatives must be weighed in terms of their effectiveness in accomplishing the objective, on the one hand, and of the consumption of available resources, on the other hand.

**Figure 5**
Process of Deriving Specific Objectives from Broader Objectives.

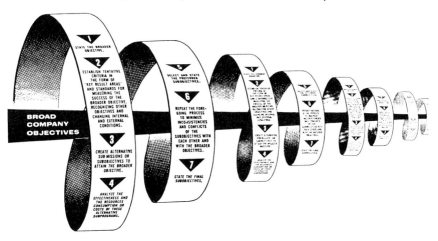

As the preferred new subobjectives and subprograms begin to emerge, one can expect numerous conflicts and inconsistencies. In the case of the exporter, for example, protection of domestic sales may not always be consistent with expansion of foreign trade. Hence some sort of reiteration or recycling is called for to minimize the inconsistencies before the final subobjectives can be decided on.

So much for the general process. What are the problems of making it work? What requirements must be observed?

### Role of Creativity
Establishing even a subobjective within the framework of a broader objective is a creative act. It involves the conceptual creation of a number of possible subobjectives, testing them against the realities of (1) consistency with internal resources, (2) consistency with environmental conditions, and (3) effectiveness/cost relationships in accomplishing the broader objective. Here we see the familiar concepts of creativity: exposure (to the broader objectives, internal and environmental constraints, and challenges), gestation, idea emergence, testing against reality, recycling.

Borrowing from the studies of creativity, we can see that the individual who is creative on the practical level, *provided he has had appropriate exposure to the company situation,* can be very helpful in establishing objectives. On the other hand, we have to beware of situations in which objectives are set without adequate *exposure* to environmental conditions (not all would-be staff planners are conscious of this); likewise we must beware of situations where objectives are set without adequate *analysis* of both internal and environmental conditions (not all line managers are conscious of this).

The creation of a workable grand-design type of objective thus emerges as an especially creative act. There are no broader objectives to be guided by. The creator of the grand design has as tools only his needs, values, and drives, and the company's environmental and internal constraints and challenges.

### Motives and Appeals

In setting meanful objectives, much help can come from creative people—those with high idea-emergence, good at censoring their own ideas against reality, persistent at recycling their ideas for improvement, having adequate exposure to internal and external factors, and possessing adequate drives. Moreover, Douglas McGregor's "Theory Y" approach to management suggests that the higher-order personal drives (such as those based on ego needs and self-fulfillment needs) of these people should be coupled with the objectives of the undertaking for the most effective accomplishment of the mission. This may be especially true in the higher echelons of a large organization. To oversimplify the thought, pay raises and threats of discharge may work with blue-collar workers, but the higher motives may be more effective with the financially more secure managers.

Frederick R. Kappel cites the visionary goal of AT&T—"the big dream stated without equivocation, the dream of good, cheap, fast, worldwide telephone service for everyone." He observes that such a goal is "not a wishful fancy. It is not a speculation. It is a perfectly clear statement that you are going to do something." He then points out three conditions which in his opinion favor setting the right goal at the right time:

1. An instinctive feeling for quality throughout the organization.
2. Freedom to make some mistakes.
3. A recognition of the pressure of external factors.

He further points out that "part of the talent or genius of the goal-setter is the ability to distinguish between the possible and the impossible—but to be willing to get very close to the latter."[6]

Eric Hoffer takes a stronger view, at least in regard to the goals of large undertakings or "mass movements." He suggests that the goals for a vital undertaking should be impossible of achievement (for example, achieving God's Kingdom on earth), and points out that the best climate for setting these visionary goals is among the groups who are down but not quite out.[7] For example, the Black Muslim movement apparently cannot reach the most abject Negroes, who seem to have little interest in anything beyond a day-to-day existence, nor does it apparently appeal much to Negroes who are currently "successful" in American society.

Does this apply to companies in the busines world? Are there any indications that the downtrodden business organization, like pre-Hitler Germany, is most susceptible to a brilliant renaissance, and all that it lacks is a deliverer, a leader who electrifies its members with visionary goals? One could say that George Romney did something of this sort with American Motors. But such examples seem rare. Why aren't there more of them? There is certainly no lack of prospective candidates!

Perhaps there is a lack of George Romneys, or perhaps they find themselves called into other fields. But any organization, in however severe straits, can probably boast a few young hotbloods who can establish visionary objectives, but who lack the other qualities of drive and leadership to carry them out.

## Need for Renewal

There is probably merit in reestablishing objectives every so often just for the sake of reestablishing them. One might think that if objectives were once set, and if internal and external conditions did not change too much, the objectives would be valid for a good long time. But the same old objectives repeated over and over produce no impact, no challenge.

Perhaps this is a failing of many religious organizations. Canonical types of objectives, produced many years ago by undoubtedly brilliant churchmen, simply do not inspire the organization member of today unless he himself has gone through the process of thinking out the objectives and reached similar conclusions.

Some "Theory Y" practitioners have gone to an extreme; they favor changing the objectives at a given level and position every time a new individual comes into the job. In other words, the new appointee, along with his own superior and others with the need to know, sits down and writes a new job description including new objectives for the work. "Theory Y" practitioners claim to have encouraging results with this approach.

## Locating Responsibility

Should the superior set the objectives for the individual groups that are subordinate to him? It is apparent that he must at least approve them if he is to discharge his own duties. Beyond this, he probably has broader exposure to internal and environmental conditions than his subordinates. But he may or may not be the creative type who can visualize a whole range of subobjectives, one for each of his various groups, the best of which are chosen after analyzing effectiveness and costs. Some of his subordinates may be better at this creation of alternatives than he is. Certainly they should have had greater exposure in depth (if not in breadth) to internal and environmental constraints, challenges, and opportunities. Accordingly, it would seem that to combine the best of these talents, the objectives for the subgroups should be worked out jointly by the leader of the subgroup and his superior.

How much help can staff give the line in this process? Certainly staff can conduct the internal analyses of resources and the environmental analyses of external conditions, always using the line for appropriate inputs in these analyses. Most line managers are accustomed to using their staffs in a similar capacity. Staff men can also propose and analyze a number of alternative subobjectives, and can sometimes make particularly brilliant contributions in proposing possible alternatives which might otherwise have been overlooked. This can be a major contribution of creative staff workers. Consultants, who are a form of temporary staff, do this frequently.

But the old principle holds true: the people with the ultimate responsibility have to make the ultimate decisions. Furthermore, they have to be brought into the decision-making process at sufficiently fundamental levels so they can have a full understanding of the context in which the final decision choices are being made. No responsible line man could be expected to accept ready-made objectives proposed by a staff person or researcher unless he, the line man, had personally weighed and debated the relation to internal and external conditions and the range of possible alternatives.

### Working-Upwards Approach

Now suppose, as is often the case, that a company has not in recent years formally developed a written statement of objectives, and that (as should more often be the case) a member of the board of directors convinces his fellow members that they should have a written statement of objectives. *Where* should the job begin?

One might reason that logic calls for starting at the top of the hierarchy displayed in Figure 4, starting with needs, values, and drives of the key individuals, and proceeding on down to creeds, grand designs, missions, and the like. For instance, Secretary McNamara and his associates, in the recent installation of program budgeting in the Defense Department, appear to have gone from a grand design to missions, to program elements (analogous to charters).

However, in our consulting practice with both business and nonbusiness enterprises, my associates and I have found that as a practical measure the top of the scale is *not* the best place to start. We have found that profit objectives in terms of growth in earnings per common share are typically the most readily graspable starting point in business. They lead very understandably to environmental analysis (first in terms of profit results of comparable companies in industry, then to analysis of market requirements, technical trends, and competitive trends in the business environment) and analysis of internal resources.

People seem to have little difficulty in understanding the need and value of analyzing profit goals. Once this understanding has been obtained, it is not too painful to work up and down the hierarchy to fill it out; going *up* to other key result areas, charters, policies, missions, and even grand designs, and *down* to long-range plans, strategic programs, budgets, and short-term programs. Suddenly there is a new clarity to the growth directions for the enterprise, the type of management development needed, and the like.

As already indicated, there is a continual process of reiteration. In this reiteration one objective is adjusted in light of another, and in light of new developments in resources and in environmental conditions. Hence it does not really matter that some managers do not readily see the need for defining the higher-level objectives, and that attempts to attack the broader questions of creeds and grand designs make them squirm. When they start with some very tangible aspect such as profits, then work into the other types of objectives as the need to do so becomes demonstrated, they can achieve as good an understanding as anyone can.

## Practical Uses

What are the practical uses of objectives? What tangible results come from giving thought and time to the clarification of objectives? An analysis was recently made by the American Management Association of companies that had developed formal company creeds.[8] In all too many cases this analysis indicated that the benefits were along the lines of "having opened up our thinking" or "a beneficial exercise for those who took part," but the practical results were rather hard to measure. This is unfortunate, for there are practical benefits indeed to be obtained.

### Better Planning

Probably the most significant use of objectives is in planning. Not many organizations can conscientiously answer the question, "What should we be doing, and how much?" But carefully worked out objectives can narrow the target area, if not altogether pinpoint it. For example:

> The new programming system in the Department of Defense is based on the nine types of missions or broad objectives of that organization (e.g., strategic retaliation). For the first time on an overall, formalized basis, the cost of each Defense Department activity has been related to its effectiveness in fulfilling these missions. Alternate systems are presented for top-level consideration in terms of cost and effectiveness analysis. The practical results include "thumbs down" for the RS–70, the Skybolt missile, and the Nike-Zeus antimissile system.

A major charity had been moving along on its natural momentum, doing an effective job in many ways, but not quite sure of just how large it should grow in the future, what new programs it should be undertaking, and what financial and other plans it should be making to ensure its future effectiveness. It has now developed a number of specific subobjectives in light of a definition of its broader objectives. Practical results are taking place in the way of organizational changes, staff recruitment and development, long-range financing plans, and development of new service programs—all based on a general agreement at the policy-making level of what the organization should look like in 1973.

The management of Sears, Roebuck, in speaking of its objectives, says: "The Company sees itself not so much as a catalog merchant or retailer, but as an organized system for efficient and economical distribution, dedicated to serving the public with a broad range of *goods* and *services* [italics added], and to meeting any change in demand." Probably 90 out of 100 large organizations have some stated objectives of this general type. But the difference is that Sears not only states its objectives; it lives by them. In the last ten years the number of mail-order plants has remained steady at 11, and the number of retail stores has increased slightly from 694 to 748 (although many have been modernized and expanded). But the company is now upgrading itself into a style house, as its recent advertising demonstrates. Here are examples of the variety of Sears, Roebuck activities—

- It runs a fleet of 5,000 service and installation trucks.
- Through Allstate it is the largest stock company insurer of automobiles in the country, and fourth largest in the fire and casualty field.
- It is in the life insurance business.
- The Allstate Motor Club and Allstate Tours operate in the travel field.
- It has entered the savings and loan business.
- Homart Development Company recently opened its first shopping center, with a half-dozen others in various stages of planning.
- Sears, Roebuck Acceptance Corp. has about $500 million of installment contracts.

In short, Sears, Roebuck has not occupied itself with perpetuating its existing form. It has arrived at broad objectives and derived a wide and changing range of supporting missions, or subobjectives. All this has led to handsome results, with earnings per share increasing in eight out of the last ten years.

A major drug company has staked out a grand design in the field of human health and well-being. In accordance with this broad objective, the research group has identified some 40 potential and actual program areas—e.g., cardiovascular ailments, fertility control, and cancer. In annual program planning reviews within the research group, scientists and managers go through a series of steps for deriving specific program objectives. They have environmental analysis material on hand—for instance, "If we develop a tranquilizer with such and such characteristics, it will capture X percent of the market." They also have organized information inputs on the long-range needs in the health field (e.g., dermatology). At the same time they have conducted resources analyses so they know their abilities in certain specialized lines of research.

## Choice of Alternatives

The hierarchy of objectives is also valuable in analyzing and choosing alternative courses of action. (This benefit is obviously related to the planning values just discussed, but it deserves separate emphasis.) To use the experience of the drug company again:

> To stimulate thinking about alternative courses of action, management encourages scientists to attend association meetings; invites a considerable number of outside technical consultants—usually university people—to meet with executives; and stresses the study of data from marketing research and the detail sales force.

> Three important questions stand out in the criteria for screening the wide range of alternative subprograms—

1. How important is the proposed program? Importance is usually measured in terms of profit potential.
2. Can we do it? This question is usually related to the availability of skills and knowledge to overcome the technical problems involved.
3. What will it cost? Here the company has what amounts to a cost/effectiveness analysis of alternative programs, much along the lines described earlier in the case of the Department of Defense.

> Of course, the process of exploring alternatives ends with a good deal of reiteration or recycling to cut out nonessentials here, fill out a program there, and to make the total research consistent with a practical budget. In practice, as might be expected, the general program areas do not change radically from year to year. Once a specialized staff and momentum are built up in a given area, a program may last for some time, uncovering new opportunities as time goes along. However, specific detailed projects are changed, and the over-all emphasis in the program also changes as a result of management's approach.

## Management Development

One of the most interesting uses of a framework of objectives is in management development. Most executives are keenly aware that the difference between their organization and other organizations in its field is its personnel. They recognize that the development of its own people is a key issue in the health and success of any enterprise.

Recent theory as well as actual practice in management development has stressed the concept of identifying the objectives of the individual with the objectives of the enterprise. It also stresses making these objectives as specific as possible, and measuring their exact success in meeting them. For example, contrast the effectiveness you might expect in an organization where a supervisor says, "I'm responsible for quality—whatever that means," with effectiveness in an organization where he says:

> I'm responsible for rejects which come off the rotary machines and I've
> agreed on the standard with the Chief Inspector. Each day I get an analysis
> of rejects so I can put things right. At present the General Manager and
> I agree on 2.7 percent rejects as acceptable, but we have a plan to get
> this down to 2.2 percent by next November.[9]

There is ample evidence that this concept of management by objectives and by specific results actually works, and works well. However, the question not always thoroughly explored is, "Are we doing the right thing to begin with?" Possibly the quality control supervisor in the foregoing example is inspecting beautiful products for which there is little demand, for a market where quality is not a key result area, in a situation where the products could better be purchased from the outside, or where the entire company would be better off merged into a larger organization.

If a framework of objectives has been worked out for the whole organization, there is not so much danger of misdirected effort. Top management can be assured that all employees are working toward common purposes which are mutually consistent, appropriately challenging, and realistic in light of both internal and external opportunities and threats. It can be assured that people's potentials are being developed along lines which will increase the effectiveness of the company.

### Organizational Efficiency

It should not be inferred from the foregoing discussion that the formal organization structure should be rearranged to conform closely with objectives in various parts of the company. Rearrangement may or may not be appropriate, depending on the circumstances. For example:

> In the Department of Defense we find that both the B-52 and the
> Polaris submarines are program elements in the Strategic Retaliatory
> Forces. Nevertheless, organizationally they fit into conventional Air Force
> and Navy formats. Support elements of an organization (for instance, the
> payroll department) are frequently organized separately as one distinct
> entity supporting a number of departments or divisions which may have
> widely differing objectives. This is done for the sake of efficiency.
> Non-Linear Systems, Inc., a specialized California instruments manufac-
> turer with 350 employees, has developed a curious form of organization
> which ties in closely with the theory of objectives.[10] The company has a
> president and seven vice presidents, each responsible for an area such
> as innovation, market standing, profitability, or productivity. It shows
> evidence of having excelling results with this system.

However, we must not forget that in business true efficiency—unlike the dictionary definition—is not merely producing a certain result at the lowest cost; worthwhile efficiency is producing a *desired* result at the lowest cost. It is a ratio in which cost is the denominator, and the degree of effectiveness in producing some desired result is the numerator. Thus we can hardly consider efficiency without considering a range of objectives. The cost/effectiveness studies in the Department of Defense and "value analysis" studies at General Electric[11] illustrate the application of such thinking to logical cost reduction and efficiency improvement.

## Conclusion

It is curious that so many discussions of management begin with exhortations to clarify objectives, and then, as if the nature of objectives were well known, proceed to explore some other aspect of the matter at hand. In reality we know very little about the nature of objectives. And it is abundantly clear that we cannot quickly set up some objectives for an enterprise and then proceed on the assumption that they will be meaningful guides to action.

Taking stock of the little knowledge we do possess, we find that we know a few bare essentials. For instance, there are certain minimum tests which an objective, or a set of objectives, should pass. Thus, objectives—

. . . need not begin with the broad grand design of the enterprise, but all objectives in the hierarchy should be consistent with it;

. . . should make the people in the enterprise reach a bit;

. . . should be realistic in terms of (a) the internal resources of the enterprise, and (b) the external opportunities, threats, and constraints;

. . . should take into account the creative conception of a range of alternatives and the relative effectiveness and cost of each;

. . . should be known to each person so that he understands the goals of his own work and how they relate to the broader objectives of the total enterprise;

. . . should be periodically reconsidered and redefined, not only to take account of changing conditions, but for the salutary effect of rethinking the aims of organizational activities.

Objectives, properly developed and applied, can tell us in what paths, new and old, our total undertakings should be moving. They can guide both the day-to-day activities and the personal development of individuals in an organization. If we in management can clarify the objectives of our undertakings by even a small amount, we can greatly increase the effectiveness and efficiency of our businesses.

1. "Marketing Myopia," HBR July-August 1960, p. 45.
2. *Notes on the Theory of Organization* (New York, American Management Association, 1952), pp. 18-19.

3. Ibid., p. 10.
4. *Business Objectives* (Pittsburgh, Carnegie Institute of Technology, unpublished paper, 1962).
5. *Vitality in a Business Enterprise* (New York, McGraw-Hill Book Company, Inc., 1960), pp. 37-38.
6. *Vitality in a Business Enterprise* (New York, McGraw-Hill Book Company, Inc., 1960), pp. 40, 56-58.
7. *The True Believer* (New York, Harper & Brothers, 1951).
8. Stewart Thompson, *Management Creeds and Philosophies*, Research Study No. 32 (New York, 1958).
9. John W. Humble, "Programmitis and Crown Princes," *The Manager*, December 1963, p. 47.
10. See, for example, Arthur H. Kuriloff, "An Experiment in Management, Putting Theory Y to the Test," *Personnel*, November-December 1963, p. 12.
11. See, for example, Hugh McCullough, "New Concepts in Defense Planning, Programming and Budgeting," *The Federal Accountant*, September 1962, p. 70; also L. D. Miles, "Purchasing Must Analyze Values," *Purchasing*, January 4, 1960, p. 65.

# Section 3 Setting Objectives and Planning for Action

**Objectives**

1. To understand the key issues involved in setting objectives.
2. To recognize the importance of including personal development objectives in addition to performance objectives.
3. To improve MBO through effective negotiations of objectives.
4. To become proficient in developing action plans to achieve objectives.

**Figure 6**

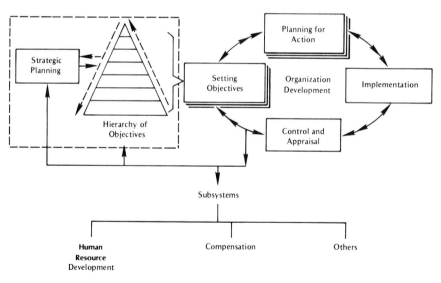

## Setting Objectives and Planning for Action

In the previous section the hierarchy of objectives was introduced. In this part the more specific aspects of goal setting are discussed. Setting objectives appears to be simple, yet it is a complex task fraught with difficulties. It is astounding what happens when managers who have been in their positions for many years are asked to identify their objectives. Many managers are unclear what is expected of them. Moreover, they usually do not know the objectives of the organizational unit to which they contribute, nor do they know the overall objectives of the enterprise.

The selected readings highlight important issues in setting objectives as well as articles that make practical recommendations on how to improve the setting of objectives.

At times there are arguments among authors on whether or not to engage in action planning which is concerned with functions, tasks, and activities necessary to achieve the objectives. Reviewing the pros and cons of action planning, we think that action plans are not necessary for every objective, but they are important for critical and complex objectives. It has been our experience that managers who are introduced to MBO set objectives that are sometimes too high or are based on insufficient information. Through the systematic identification of activities required to achieve the results, it often turns out that the tasks are much more complex than expected. Consequently, objectives can be adjusted to reflect the complexity of the task. In short, action planning is not only an aid to identify and evaluate alternative means to achieve results, but it also facilitates setting of realistic objectives.

The first reading in this section, "Goal Setting: An Important Management Tool," was selected because it focuses on critical issues that will be discussed in greater detail in subsequent articles. For example, the author, Jack Mendleson, points out that setting objectives without action planning is not enough. Furthermore, he draws attention to the critical issue and possible conflicts of tying monetary rewards too closely to performance, a topic further discussed in Section 6.

The article, "Setting Goals in Management by Objectives" by Henry Tosi, John Rizzo, and Stephen Carroll, discusses in great detail the various facets of setting objectives, a process that requires top management support. Moreover, the authors emphasize that goal setting is not an isolated process, but it should be integrated with other key managerial activities.

The next article by William Werther and Heinz Weihrich focuses on the face-to-face interactions between superior and subordinate at the goal setting meeting. This meeting, to be effective, must be carefully planned. Moreover, behavioral science knowledge can be useful when negotiating objectives.

The final article in this section, "How to Get Action into MBO" by Heinz Weihrich, emphasizes the importance of the systematic identification of tasks and activities necessary to achieve objectives. This article makes practical recommendations on how to develop such action plans.

# 1

*Jack L. Mendleson*

# Goal Setting: An Important Management Tool

Currently, many managers believe goal setting is an important tool for the functioning of business organizations. Popular expressions of goal-setting ideas are (1) management by objectives, and (2) management by results. Business managers have translated their strong belief in goal setting into a considerable demand for books and training programs about goal setting and for the services of consultants.

This article explores the following central questions:

Exactly what is goal setting?

Why is it important?

What are the key issues in goal setting, i.e., what are the major areas of disagreement and how, in light of present knowledge, can these disagreements best be resolved?

## What Is Goal Setting?

Manager goal setting is a process of superior subordinate interaction through which work targets or aims are established for the subordinate manager. The work goals established are *current* aims for the individual manager in the performance of his work assignment. These goals apply to a particular period of time.

Goal setting has many variations. The advocates of the concept include leading management theorists behavioral scientists, and practicing managers. The original definition presented above encompasses the several different approaches to goal setting. By reasoning through the key issues below, the manager can determine his own specific approach to this important and often neglected subject. Regardless of the particular approach used, a manager and his superior, to practice goal setting, must define four essential components:

*Verification:* a mutually understood mechanism through which goal attainment can be objectively observed.

Reprinted by permission of the publisher, *Arizona Business*, Vol. 15, No. 5, May 1968, pp. 121-127.

*Feedback:* a set of means through which the superior and subordinate receive information about goal attainment and status of plans to achieve goals.

*Review:* a part of the superior-subordinate interaction in which the parties discuss and evaluate the feedback.

*Recycling:* a final interactive process between superior and subordinate in which goals for the coming period are set.

## Why Is Goal Setting Important?

The discussion of the importance of goal setting to the manager divides into four questions:

What is new about goal setting?

How is goal setting distinct from other management concepts?

What happens without goal setting?

What are the research findings about goal setting?

*What is new about goal setting?* Goal setting is not necessarily the "natural" behavior for managers to follow, despite a commonsense assumption that goal setting is obvious. Wikstrom, in research for the National Industrial Conference Board, summarized the experience of several companies using management by objectives as follows:

> It begs the question to state that managers should know what their responsibilities are, and should be able to develop meaningful targets in carrying out these responsibilities. Experience has shown that even a clear statement of an individual manager's responsibilities does not take the place of a clear statement of the broader objectives toward which his own goals must contribute.
>
> But management by objectives begins with results to be achieved; then the activities necessary for achieving them are decided upon. This is a switch in emphasis that apparently can be very difficult for many managers.[1]

Much the same conclusion emerges from a study in a setting very different from that experienced by American managers. McClelland reports his attempt to develop achievement motivation among managers in underdeveloped nations:

> Much of the success of such a training enterprise depends on getting the man to be specific, realistic, and practical in his goal setting, since he often starts out with general statements like "I want to increase production (or sales) by 20%," or "I want to start a new business." The specific goals he sets are then used as a target against which he can evaluate his progress every six months for two years by filling out a report form. Such record keeping is, of course, simply a method of keeping the goal salient or ever in front of the person, at least for two years.[2]

*How is goal setting distinct?* Several well-known concepts may seem very similar to or overlapping with goal setting. The following observations help to keep goal setting distinct:

1. The ancient notion of a hierarchy of objectives specifies that the overall objectives should be factored into more specific sub-unit objectives. This hierarchy is completely consistent with the present concept of goal setting. What *is* distinct in the new concept is that goal setting specifies a regular, time-specific interaction between superior and subordinate about the goals or objectives.
2. A job description differs in at least two ways from work goals. First, work goals consist of a small number of very important items. Second, work goals apply to a specific time period, while items on a job description are continuing matters of concern. Goal setting often employs the job description as a foundation.
3. In some respects, goal setting serves as a performance appraisal. However, even in situations where goal setting is being practiced, the superior may be called upon to make summary judgments about the subordinate which are separate from the goal setting. Two features distinguish goal setting from the usual practice of appraisal: (a) the essence of goal setting is the interaction between superior and subordinate, while in appraisal, the interaction often occurs *after* the superior has made the important judgments; (b) goal setting more consistently and single-mindedly emphasizes the focusing of efforts toward central purposes, while appraisal often deals with questions of control.

*What happens without goal setting?* It is probably impossible to manage with no goals at all. Yet it is entirely possible to manage without a regularly established goals period and a clear definition of the four goal-setting essentials (verification, feedback, review, and recycling). In the absence of these essentials, several difficulties arise. First, managers often concentrate too much attention upon tasks and means. The means often become ends and become inflexible and inappropriate when conditions change. Schleh explains the difficulty as follows:

> Individuals may easily get out of touch with the central purpose of the enterprise, a process encouraged by the natural inclination to specify the activities that are required of a man instead of the results.[3]

Second, without the goal-setting essentials, "management by drives" often occurs, putting "all emphasis on one phase of the job to the inevitable detriment of everything else."[4]

*What are the research findings?* The author's recent study of eight companies in several different industries demonstrates that specific goal-setting behavior can be measured.[5] In that study, items of behavior, such as the following hold promise of unearthing detailed evidence of the importance of goal setting.

1. A superior-subordinate pair would be said to be practicing a high level of goal setting if they each agreed that the following statements correctly described the subordinate's situation:
   - My boss really wants all of us at my level to understand the goals of his organizational unit and how this unit fits into the total company picture.
   - My boss and I not only regularly put my work goals into writing, but we keep them up to date.

2. A superior-subordinate pair would be said to be practicing a middle level of goal setting if they each agreed that the following statements correctly described the subordinate's situation:
   - I get some specific feedback about my performance, but I need more.
   - Achieving the results my boss expects often requires more of his support than I can get.

3. A superior-subordinate pair would be said to be practicing a low level of goal setting if they each agreed that the following statements correctly described the subordinate's situation.
   - At my organization level we're lucky if we have plans for tomorrow, let alone next week or next month.
   - My boss seems to have only a vague idea of what I'm doing most of the time.

In an earlier study, Raia extensively employed a number of research techniques at the Purex Corporation and discovered that, as a result of Purex's goal-setting program: (1) The degree to which goals were attained tended to improve during the fiscal period. (2) Individual plant performance, in terms of productivity, improved. (3) There was an overall increase in the level of motivation of participants. (4) Communication and mutual understanding between the plants and company headquarters improved as a result of the program.[6]

The General Electric Company has conducted research into performance appraisal and other subjects which are relevant to goal setting. In fact, one of these findings seems to have produced much of the current interest in goal setting and "results-oriented" performance appraisal. It is summarized as follows:

> Appreciable improvements in performance were realized only when specific goals were established with time deadlines and results measures agreed upon. Regardless of how much emphasis the manager gave to an improvement need in the appraisal discussion, if this did not get translated into a specific goal, very little performance improvement was achieved.[7]

This finding was based upon, (1) observation of 84 superior-subordinate pairs in performance appraisal and goal planning discussions, (2) before and after interviews with subordinates; and (3) a follow-up check 12 to 14 weeks after the performance appraisal and goal planning discussions to determine the degree to which performance improvement had been achieved. The finding was consistent with earlier research in other companies, which found that specific goals were necessary for improvement to occur at worker levels.

The General Electric conclusions about goal setting are as follows:

> The most constructive finding of the study was that discussions involving work planning, goal setting, and subsequent reviews of performance, which focused on specific, short-term plans and goals, yielded much greater returns in improved job performance than did comprehensive summary appraisal discussions.[8]

The existing research evidence strongly suggests the importance of goal-setting efforts, both in terms of company-wide and plant-wide programs and in terms of specific interaction between a given superior and subordinate.

## Key Issues in Goal Setting

Because the theory of goal setting, if not the practice, is relatively recent, debate continues on several key issues. The discussion which follows considers five of these issues and attempts to resolve the disagreements in light of present knowledge.

*Objectives only or work planning?* Schleh insists that individual objectives specify only the desired results, not the activities. McNair[9] has echoed Schleh's point, adding that the "targets" should specify "the what, not the how." It may appear, then, that all that is needed is a statement of goals or results and a method of measuring these results.

On the other hand, even the language used in some quarters suggests there is more to the process than merely setting goals, as illustrated by General Electric's "work planning" or "goal planning." The General Electric concept includes, in addition to work goals:

> . . . a strategy for reaching the goals, identification of alternate routes for goal attainment, the identification of resources required to meet the goals ($ budget, manpower, facilities, and information), the identification of tasks necessary for reaching each goal and the time schedule for task completion, measurements to identify progress and achievement, the identification of check points to review progress and make necessary revisions in the plan, and a plan to communicate with those will affect or be affected by the plan's progress.[10]

General Electric's Marion Kellogg rejects the point of view apparently advocated by Schleh, as she comments:

> Just specifying results doesn't do it (i.e., achieve the objectives of Work Planning). Until you've hammered out how you're going to get there, the risk is very high for the (subordinate) manager.[11]

McConkey also goes beyond the idea of merely specifying results. He writes, "Actually, the process of planning to achieve goals is more critical than that of setting the goals."[12] General Electric's study of its Work Planning and Review serves to support and explain McConkey's conclusion:

> The setting of specific goals and performance standards took a relatively small percentage of time. In these sessions, goal setting usually resulted from a problem-solving discussion. In some cases, a goal was stated first, then a lengthy discussion of the problems associated with reaching that goal followed. Although goal setting per se did not get much emphasis, there was considerable emphasis given to the exploration and solution of problems associated with achieving good performance on these goals.[13]

The apparent conflict in concepts can be resolved by taking the broader view; namely, that a fully elaborated goal-setting process *does* involve work planning and considerably more than a mere setting of goals. At the same time Schleh's emphasis on results is instructive, if viewed as the necessary *first* point, rather than the *only* point.

### Emphasis: Short-run or Long-run Goals?

The definite emphasis in theory and practice is upon short-run goals (one year or less). Even "sustaining" or "regular" goals need to be recycled in the short-run period. McConkey writes, "If anyone begins to slip in handling these routine duties, the sustaining objectives become 'leverage'—that is, major objectives for the next period . . ."[14] By inference whether people have not "slipped," the objectives or goals emphasize results which were *not* accomplished before.

While both theorists and practitioners presently emphasize short-run goals, this emphasis causes problems. Dearden presents persuasive case evidence in which "the motivation for short-run improvements can be so strong that serious management errors can result."[15]

It is useful to focus attention *first* upon short-run goals. However, regular attention by superior and subordinate to long-run goals is also needed. In conclusion, given the present state of development of goal setting, the initial and primary *emphasis* should, for best results, be on short-run goals.

## Emphasis: Individual or Group Goals?

Most of the discussion in this paper has dealt with *individual* work goals. However, a rather strong case could be made favoring *group* work goals. Sayles notes two serious dysfunctions of individual goal setting. First, Sayles points out that "looking only at (individual) results encourages subordinates to engage in behavior that may be destructive to organizational relationships."[16] Thus, coordination necessary to meet overall goals may suffer. Second, "such an emphasis encourages excessive competition for scarce resources, such as space, personnel, parts, and maintenance facilities, and leads to neglect of the unmeasured aspects of a job."[17]

It is possible that these dysfunctions could be avoided if group *in addition* to individual goal setting is employed. However, it seems important to at least begin with individual goal setting, thus establishing individual accountability for results. Indeed, the essence of the goal-setting process involves an *individual* subordinate in a dialogue or negotiation with his superior to agree on appropriate aims for that subordinate. Also, the differences in the nature of the work of individuals at the same level limit the use of group goal setting.

The subject of group vs. individual goal setting can be summarized in a few points. First, *individual* work goals seem to serve at least one purpose which group goals cannot—to establish a charter or contract between the individual subordinate and his superior. Second, detailed discussions of group goal setting are scare and are not as well formulated as individual approaches. Third, group goal setting still remains as a possibility. At the present it is best viewed as *complementary* to individual goal setting, not as a replacement. Therefore, a superior and his subordinate are well advised to give first attention to the subordinate's individual work goals. Later attention to group goals may yield further benefits.

## Rewards Tied to Goal Achievement?

Several authorities agree that it is desirable to tie tangible individual rewards to individual goal achievement, if the means to do this can be worked out. Schleh advocates tying results directly to pay. He translates this into the staff area by means of the principle of double credit, or dual accountability:

> Both staff and line should get full credit for any accomplishment of either the staff or the line in the area that the staff is set up to cover.[18]

This dual accountability becomes an important factor in areas of reward such as pay, promotion, and performance appraisal. At one division of Monsanto, for example, "the division is conscious of a new realization, throughout the organization, that there is a direct relationship between the achievement of results and the rewards that are given in the form of salary increases, bonuses, and stock options."[19] Essentially Hughes agrees:

If we reward an employee for establishing a challenging goal and beating it, we are using money as a motivator; however, if we simply hand out money in an automatic way and give increases without relating them clearly to the results achieved, then we are putting it in the category of a dissatisfier . . . If motivation is to come from the work itself, so too must the paycheck.[20]

At the same time, tying rewards closely to goal achievement creates difficulties. Managers recognize these difficulties when they separate the superior-subordinate discussion of needed improvements in the subordinate's work from the discussion of the subordinate's salary and promotability. One General Electric report, for example, employs the heading "What the WP&R Discussions Did Not Cover."[21] First, work planning generally did not include the superior's summary judgment of the subordinate's performance. Second, the subject of salary was seldom mentioned. Third, career planning for the subordinate was not usually discussed. Kay and Hastman recommended that salary and career planning be handled in meetings which are separate from work planning. In another publication Kay, along with Meyer and French, has conceptualized the problem as a "split role" or conflicting role in performance appraisal.[22] In traditional appraisal interviews the superior must play the role of "judge," as he provides a justification for salary action. On the other hand, many appraisal systems have as one of their purposes to achieve improvement in work performance; and this puts the superior in the role of a "counselor."

However, even within various parts of General Electric these concepts have been questioned. Marion Kellogg has expressed dissatisfaction with the conclusions above as she stressed that superiors *must* judge subordinates.[23] Also, other General Electric researchers, Kay and Hastman, in reporting that work planning discussions did not include summary judgments of subordinate performance, noted that "Some subordinates expressed a need for this."[24] It can only be concluded that widespread differences of opinion exist.

In the face of these differences of opinion some workable mechanisms have been devised which actually tie rewards to goal achievement. First, salary increases and promotion decisions may be tied to goal achievement. For example, at General Electric Work Planning (goal setting) is pictured as a "key element" in the compensation system:

(Work planning) . . . provides the manager with current information about individual contribution so that his judgment about development, promotion and salary are sound.[25]

Second, individual development efforts sponsored by one's company (e.g., college courses, seminars, assigned reading programs) may be tied to the individual's goal achievement. Kimberly-Clark reports the installation of "bank accounts" for each individual manager who performs well.[26] Within a broad range of acceptable items of expenditure the individual may use this bank account for his own development. Third, increased freedom or autonomy for the subordinate in his work performance may be used as a reward for goal achievement.

The point, in short, is that rewards for goal attainment *can* be considered part of goal setting, but the specialists disagree. This issue of rewards must be left to the discretion of those who design a particular goal-setting system.

### Role of Personal Goals in Manager Goal Setting

At the present time the strong emphasis in goal setting is upon *work* goals, goals that are immediately relevant to organizational functioning. Very seldom is much emphasis given in the goal-setting interaction to personal goals of the subordinate which are not related to organizational functioning. Yet this does leave the possibility of personal development goals, statements of an individual's aims to improve himself in order to function better for the organization. The Kimberly-Clark program of "bank accounts" previously mentioned is an example of explicit attention to personal development goals.

Odiorne summarizes the thinking of many specialists:

> A manager's personal development goals will usually comprise only a small segment of his total objectives for the goal-setting period.[27]

Odiorne also puts development goals into clearer perspective:

> The establishment of goals for the manager's personal development doesn't imply that his strictly job-centered goals aren't a form of personal development also. In fact, these job-centered goals comprise the manager's major development plan, since they relate to his job performance. Even so, beyond this, there may be personal skills that, if acquired, will make it possible for the man to do his job better, and will stand him in good stead whether he is promoted, or stays in his present position.[28]

This discussion suggests that personal development goals are necessary, because self-insight is not sufficient to assure self-development. Clearly self-development, to Odiorne, is *organizationally relevant* self-development.

Hughes demonstrates more forcefully the need for superior-subordinate interaction about the subordinate's personal goals. His "goal-interaction concept" specifies that "the goals of the organization cannot simply be subdivided and handed to individuals."[29] Hughes elaborates in a way that builds upon the discussion of participation in the earlier section:

> As we have repeatedly said, what is needed is more than participation: the company goals must be turned into another language, another set of symbols, that will be meaningful to the individual.[30]

But the individual subordinate cannot come to understand this language by himself. His supervisor plays a key role: "His role here is essentially that of a mediator between the individual and the organization; that is, he aids in the effective implementation of both the individual and the organizational goal-setting system."[31] This demands that the superior be specifically knowledgeable in both individual and organizational systems and that superior-subordinate interaction occurs.

Finally, Odiorne has compiled a list of activities which might represent personal development goals. Here are three examples from Odiorne's list:

> Attendance at two seminars a year
> Participation in one or two community service activities
> Reading a specific number of management books.[32]

The point of this discussion of personal goals is simply this: Other things equal, explicit interaction about personal goals of the subordinate (including personal *development* goals) strengthens goal-setting efforts.

## Summary

Goal setting is a process of superior-subordinate interaction through which work targets or aims are established for the subordinate manager. The work goals are *current* and apply to a particular period of time.

Goal setting was shown to be important for four primary reasons. First, goal setting is a new approach in that it focuses upon broad, high priority objectives or highly significant results. Second, while goal setting can complement several well-known management concepts, it is distinct from the hierarchy of objectives, the job description, and performance appraisal. Third, without systematic goal setting managers may become overly concerned with tasks and means and manage "by drives." Fourth, the limited research evidence strongly confirms many of the predicted benefits of goal-setting programs and localized efforts.

Five key issues in goal setting were discussed, and the following tentative conclusions were drawn. First, a fully elaborated process of goal setting involves work planning in addition to the mere setting of goals. Second, the present state of developments in goal setting demands that primary emphasis be placed on short-run rather than long-run results. Third, individual goals, rather than group goals, should be given first attention. Fourth, rewards for goal attainments *can* be considered part of goal setting, but the specialists disagree, and the designers of the goal-setting system must decide this issue for themselves. Fifth, explicit interaction about the subordinate's personal goals strengthens goal-setting efforts.

This article has identified several unresolved issues in the theory and practice of goal setting. An obvious conclusion is that more reflective thinking and empirical research is needed. At the same time goal setting has become established as a viable framework within which significant management problems can be solved.

1. Walter S. Wikstrom, "Management by Objectives or Appraisal by Results," *Conference Board Record*, July, 1966.
2. David C. McClelland, "Achievement Motivation Can Be Developed," *Harvard Business Review*, Vol. 43, No. 6, November-December, 1965, p. 14.
3. Edward C. Schleh, *Management by Results: The Dynamics of Profitable Management* (New York: McGraw-Hill Book Co., Inc., 1961), p. 18.
4. Peter F. Drucker, *The Practice of Management* (New York: Harper and Brothers, 1954), p. 128.
5. Jack L. Mendleson, "Manager Goal Setting: An Exploration Into Its Meaning and Measurement," (unpublished Doctoral Dissertation, Department of Management, School of Business Administration, Michigan State University, 1967).
6. Anthony P. Raia, "A Second Look at Management Goals and Controls," *California Management Review*, Summer, 1966, pp. 49-58.
7. Emanuel Kay, et al., "A Study of the Performance Appraisal Interview," March, 1962, (New York: Behavioral Research Service, General Electric Company).
8. Emanuel Kay and Roy Hastman, "An Evaluation of Work Planning and Goal Setting Discussions," March, 1966, (New York: Behavioral Research Service, General Electric Company).
9. Malcolm McNair, Jr. "The American Standard Approach," from a longer article, "Appraisal of Managers and Management Development," *Management Record*, Vol. 23, No. 3, March, 1961, pp. 8-17.
10. Anonymous, "A Composite Description of Work Planning Based Upon Four Departments," a mimeographed paper prepared for internal use at General Electric, undated.
11. Marion S. Kellog, in an interview.
12. Dale D. McConkey, *How to Manage by Results* (New York: American Management Association, 1965). p. 104.
13. Kay and Hastman, *op. cit.*, p. 4.
14. McConkey, *op. cit.*, p. 86. McConkey is describing the program at a Monsanto division.
15. John Dearden, "Limits on Decentralized Profit Responsibility," *Harvard Business Review*, Vol. 40, No. 4, July-August, 1962, p. 87.
16. Leonard R. Sayles, *Managerial Behavior* (New York: McGraw-Hill Book Company, 1964), p. 165.
17. *Ibid.*, p. 165.
18. Schleh, *op. cit.*, p. 211.
19. McConkey, *op. cit.*, p. 86.
20. Charles L. Hughes, *Goal Setting: Key to Individual and Organizational Effectiveness* (New York: American Management Association, 1965), p. 147.
21. Kay and Hastman, *op. cit.*, p. 111.
22. H. H. Meyer, E. Kay, and J. R. P. French, Jr., "Split Roles in Performance Appraisal," *Harvard Business Review*, January February, 1965, pp. 123-29.
23. Marion Kellogg, in an interview with the author.
24. Kay and Hastman, *op. cit.*, p. 111.
25. Anon., Work Planning Bulletin 9B, "What About Pay?" An internal publication of the Employee Compensation Service and Individual Development Methods Service, General Electric Company, December 14, 1965, pp. 3-4.

26. David Wilkerson, "A Results-Oriented Development Plan," *The Conference Board Record*, March, 1966, pp. 40-45.
27. Odiorne, *op cit.*, p. 136
28. *Ibid.*, p. 127.
29. Hughes, *op. cit.*, p. 92.
30. *Ibid.*, p. 120.
31. *Ibid.*, p. 117.
32. Odiorne, *op. cit.*, p. 137.

# 2
# Setting Goals in Management by Objectives

Henry L. Tosi
John R. Rizzo
Stephen J. Carroll

Management by objectives (MBO) is a process in which members of complex organizations, working in conjunction with one another, identify common goals and coordinate their efforts toward achieving them. It emphasizes the future and change, since an objective or goal is an end state, or a condition to be achieved or have in effect at some future time. The emphasis is on where the organization is going—the what and the how of its intended accomplishments. Objectives can be thought of as statements of purpose and direction, formalized into a system of management. They may be long-range or short-range. They may be general, to provide direction to an entire organization, or they may be highly specific to provide detailed direction for a given individual.

One purpose of MBO is to facilitate the derivation of specific from general objectives, seeing to it that objectives at all levels in the organization are meaningfully located structurally and linked to each other. Sets of objectives for an organizational unit are the bases which determine its activities. **A set of objectives for an individual determines his job,** and can be thought of as a different way to provide a job description. Once objectives are determined and assumed by organizational units and by individuals, it is possible to work out the means or performance required for accomplishing the objectives. Methods of achieving objectives, resources required, timing, interactions with others, control, and evaluation must have continuing attention.

**Objectives may or may not require change.** The goal or end-state may be one of insuring that no change occurs—for example, an important recurring organizational operation. However, the emphasis still remains on change and the future, and "no change" conditions can be thought of as making finer change discriminations in the management process. However, MBO is deemed most appropriate in situations where activities tend not to be recurring or repetitious, where change toward new or improved conditions is sought. Typically, these would be innovative endeavors, problem-solving situations, improvements, and personal development.

**Objectives may originate at any point in the organization structure.** Quite naturally, they should be derived from the general purposes of the organization, and consistent with its philosophy, policies ,and plans. It is beyond the scope of this paper to discuss the details of policy formulation and planning. Rather, it is recognized that these activities take place and that the setting of objectives can, and often does, occur in concern and consonance with them. For example, plans can specify the phasing and timing of organizational operations, out of which are derived objectives for those involved in implementing them. Objectives are not considered as substitutes for plans, but rather as a basis for developing them. Stating objectives accomplishes the following:

1. Document expectations in superior-subordinate relationship regarding what is to be done and the level of attainment for the period covered by the goal.
2. Provide members with a firmer base for developing and integrating plans and personal and departmental activity.
3. Serve as the basis for feedback and evaluation of subordinates' performance.
4. Provide for coordination and timing of individual and unit activities.
5. Draw attention to the need for control of key organizational functions.
6. Provide a basis for work-related rewards as opposed to personality-based systems.
7. Emphasize change, improvement, and growth of the organization and the individual.

## Objectives as Means-End Distinctions

The formulation of objectives throughout an organization represents a kind of means-end analysis, which is an attempt to factor general requirements into specific activities. Means-end analysis starts "with the general goal to be achieved, (2) discovering a set of means, very generally specified, for accomplishing this goal, (3) taking each of these means, in turn, as a new sub-goal and discovering a more detailed set of means for achieving it, etc."[1]

MBO is predicated on this concept. It is assumed that a means-end analysis can occur with a degree of precision and accuracy. The end represents a condition or situation that is desired, a purpose to be achieved. Here, the concept of *end* is equated with *goal* or *objective*. Objectives may represent required inputs to other sectors of the organization. They may be specific achievement levels, such as product costs, sales volume and so on. They may also be completed projects. For instance, the market research department may seek to complete a sales forecast by a particular date so the production facilities may be properly coordinated with market demands. Objectives, or end states, are attained through the performance of some activity. These activities are the *means* to achieve the *end*. It is important to distinguish between ends and means in the use of the "objectives approach" since there are implications for measurement and assessment which will be discussed later in the paper.

It is obvious that a malfunction or break in such a process may lead to major problems in implementing management by objectives. It is for this reason that commitment, effort, support, and use by top management is critical at all levels to obtain consensus of objectives, cooperation in achievement, and the use of objectives as criteria for evaluation. But there are some problems in doing this. This paper is directed toward these: stating objectives, areas they should cover, the question of measurement, as well as some suggestions for dealing with them.

## The Objective

The objectives for any position should reflect the means-end distinction discussed earlier. The first critical phase of objectives-setting is the statement which describes the end state sought. It should be:

- Clear, concise and unambiguous.
- Accurate in terms of the true end-state or condition sought.
- Consistent with policies, procedures, and plans as they apply to the unit.
- Within the competence of the man, or represent a reasonable learning and developmental experience for him.
- Interesting, motivating, and/or challenging whenever possible.

**Some examples of goal statements** might be written as: increase sales by 10 percent; reduce manufacturing costs by 5 percent; reduce customer complaints; increase sales by 5 percent by December 1; increase quality within a 5 percent increase in production control costs; develop understanding and implementation of computer techniques among subordinates.

Notice that these goal statements have at least two key components. First, each clearly suggests an *area of activity* in which accomplishment occurs. Second, some clearly specify a level of achievement, the quantity or deadlines to be met. We will refer to the desired level of achievement as *performance level*. The need for this distinction is obvious. It indicates the evaluation criterion by specifying the *level* or the condition which should exist. This has clear implications for both measurement and appraisal. Before discussing these implications, however, a more detailed examination of the scope and types of objectives in the MBO process is required.

**Scope and type of objectives.** It would be difficult to conceive of developing objectives for a manager which would cover each and every area of responsibility. The structure of most jobs is simply too complex. Yet once objectives are set for a position, they should comprise the major description of the job, and their achievement in light of what is known about total job requirements should be assessed. A sense of interference or conflict between objectives and other job requirements should be prevented.

Two major types of objectives may be delineated: *performance* objectives and *personal development* objectives.[2] *Performance objectives* refer mainly to those goals and activities that relate to the individual's position assignment. *Personal development* goals have to do with increasing the individual's skills, competence, or potential. Delineating types of objectives in this manner, more importantly, allows for an assessment of how MBO is being used and what emphases are deriving from it. For instance:

- Once all objectives are set for a person, a basis exists to ensure that there is a "balance" of different types, that he is problem solving, developing, and maintaining critical functions.
- Some estimates can be made regarding the importance of objectives and consequences of failure to achieve them. For example, a man who fails on a difficult creative objective should not be evaluated the same as one who fails to maintain a critical recurring operation.

**Performance objectives.** This type is derived directly from the job assignment, from the major areas of responsibility and activity of the individual that he must sustain or manage. Among them would be the maintenance of recurring or routine activities, the solving of problems, or the creation of innovative ideas, products, services, and the like. Some of these may take on the form of special activities or projects not normally part of the job. That is, even though they are part of the normal job requirements, they are goals which may take on special importance for a number of reasons—emergencies, changes in priorities, or simply management decisions.

A special activity for one position may be routine for another. A special project goal for a lower-level manager might be a routine goal for his boss. Developing a computer-based information system for personnel records may be a highly creative objective for the personnel department, yet should probably be considered a routine goal for a systems analysis group.

**Discretionary areas and other problems.** By its very nature, organization imposes restrictions on individuals. The structure of an organization defines legitimate areas of influence and decision making for an individual. Specialization and definition of function tend to limit decisions and activities to those defined for the incumbent.

If the objectives process is intended to, and does, facilitate subordinate participation and involvement, we must recognize the implicit nature of power. A lower-level manager cannot *legitimately* influence goal levels and action plans in areas in which he has no discretion, unless he has the *approval of his superior*. Therefore, it is necessary to spell out areas in which the subordinate has some latitude so that he knows what his decision limits are. Otherwise he may be misled into believing that he can participate in departmental and organizational decisions which have been defined, either procedurally or by managerial fiat, as being outside his discretion area. When you expect to participate and then cannot, negative consequences may occur. It is for this reason that it is important to determine and *communicate to the subordinate* what these discretion areas are.

One way to define discretion areas is to determine whether an individual should influence means or ends. If the activity operates primarily across the boundaries of the organization and is affected by conditions beyond its control, then the individual charged with performing it may be in a better position to determine both the goals (or ends) and the most appropriate manner to achieve them. For instance, the marketing executives in constant touch with the external environment are in a better position to determine possible sales penetration and programs than others in the organization. However, not having discretion over goal levels should not preclude involvement in goal setting. Here the MBO process should focus on developing the best *means* (later called action plans) for goal attainment.

High levels of skill and technology required in a particular function may make the specialist better able than a nontechnical person to assess what can be done in a technical field. Thus, he should be involved in determining goal levels, as well as in carrying out activities. This is not to suggest that organizational constraints and requirements be entirely removed. Budget limitations, sales quotas, and production requirements are boundaries or restrictions which may not be removed but may have to be made more flexible.

If performance levels are set, for any reason, at higher organization levels, then there is little option but to focus on the determination of the "best" activities to achieve these levels. Internal definition of goal levels will most probably be for activities which function primarily within the boundaries of the organization. The assumption, of course, is that the one defining the objective, or level, is either competent to do so or must because of its critical importance.

An important limitation on discretion is organizational level. The lower the organizational level, the more and more narrow the zone of a manager's discretion. That is, the manager at the lower levels is responsible for fewer, more specific, and more measurable activities and can commit smaller quantities of resources than those at higher levels.[3]

Another factor which causes variation in the discretion range for a particular job is the changing competency levels of the incumbent. A person learning a job may need more guidance from the superior. However, as his skills increase, the superior may spend less time since the subordinate can capably handle more activities and make more decisions. The objectives approach, incidentally, may help the superior make assessments of the subordinate's competence to expand the decision area. As a subordinate becomes more successful in achieving goals, additional and more challenging goals within the parameters of the job could be added. When the incumbent can perform these adequately, then consideration should be given to possible promotion and transfer.

What about those decision areas beyond the discretion limits? We are not suggesting that the subordinate should have no part in these decisions. His role may be contributing information and assistance, such as providing inputs to the decision-making process of the superior which the superior may choose to accept or reject. But this type of activity must be differentiated from *goal setting participation,* in which the individual *has something to say about the final shape and form* of the goals and activities. However, discretion boundaries are not rigid. While a particular decision may fall within the discretion range under normal circumstances, emergencies might develop which would result in the decision being made by the boss. These conditions cannot be foreseen, and consequently not planned for.

## Personal Development Objectives

First, it is important to stress that these must be based on problems or deficiencies, current or anticipated, in areas such as improvements in technical skills or interpersonal problems. They may also be directed at developing one for movement within the organization. The critical nature of these objectives lies in their potential as means to combat obsolescence under a rapid expansion of knowledge, to prepare people for increased responsibility, and to overcome problems in organizational interactions.

Setting development goals is probably more difficult than setting performance goals, since they are personal in nature and, as such, must be handled with care and tact. This difficulty may be avoided by simply not setting them. It could be argued that they should be avoided since they are an intrusion into the individual's privacy by the boss or the organization. However, when perceived personal limitations hinder effective performance, the problem must be treated.

Thus, if at any time the superior believes an individual's limitations stand clearly in the way of the unit's goal achievement, it should be made known to the individual. He may not be aware that he is creating problems and would gladly change—if he knew. Many technically competent people have been relieved from positions because of human problems they ostensibly create. Many might have been retained had they only known that problems existed or were developing.

Personal development objectives should be a basic part of the MBO program, *when there is a need for them*. But, if they are included only to meet formal program requirements and are not problem-based, little value will obtain. Then personal improvement goals will probably be general and ambiguous, tenable only if the organization wishes to invest in "education for education's sake." For other than a philosophical or value-based justification, personal development should attack deficiencies related to performance, containing specific action proposals for solving the problems. This may be done in the following manner.

*Pinpoint a problem area.* Parties involved in goal setting should continually be alert to negative incidents resulting from personal incapacities. The boss is in a particularly important position for recognizing problems. When situations occur which he believes are due to either personal or technical limitations, he should be aware of who was involved, and make some determination of the cause of these problems. Other individuals in the unit may bring problems to the fore. Those with whom an individual interacts may be in a reasonably good position to judge his technical competence or to determine when problems are due to his behavior. If colleagues are continually complaining about another person, additional investigation into the problem is warranted. Perhaps the most important source of these negative incidents is the subordinate himself. He may be very aware of problems in which he is involved and by discussing them may determine those in which he has been the primary cause.

These negative incidents should be relatively significant in effect and frequency and not simply a single event that has caused some notice to be taken. This does not mean, however, that an important incident which occurs one time should be overlooked if it suggests serious deficiencies.

There are at least three areas in which personal development objectives should be set.

• **Improve interpersonal relations.** Inability to maintain reasonably effective working relationships may be due to a person's lack of awareness or his inability to cooperate. This may arise from personality deficiencies or simple lack of awareness of his impact upon others. He may be unable to recognize that he is precipitating problems.

• **Improve current skills.** A manager may be, for instance, unable to prepare a budget or to engage in research because he has not had adequate training in these areas or because his training is not up to date. His general performance may be acceptable, but his skills should be improved.

• **Prepare for advancement.** Another possibility covers either technical or human skills required for different or higher level positions. These are truly developmental goals which focus on preparation for advancement. There are many ways in which they may be achieved. In some cases the individual may be given advanced work assignments; in others, they may be achieved by exposure in training situations to new concepts. In any event, they represent a *potential* problem area.

*Assess the causes of the problem.* Once it has been established that a problem exists, the cause needs to be determined. Causes should be sought jointly, a result of investigation and discussion by both the superior and subordinate after both have thought of possible causes.

The possible causes of problems may be grouped into three general categories:

• **Procedures and Structure.** The structure of the organization itself may induce disturbances. Interpersonal conflict may develop because of the interdependence of work activities. For instance, if formal requirements cause a delay in information transmission, those who need it may develop negative attitudes and feelings.

• **Others with whom an individual must work.** Problems with subordinates or managerial peers of the goal setter may be caused by personality incompatibility or lack of certain technical skills. While this may represent an important cause of problems, it is too easy to blame negative incidents on others.

• **The Person Himself.** The *individual* may have habits and characteristics which are not congruent with those of subordinates or colleagues. Or, he may lack the technical skills requisite to carry out certain responsibilities.

Attempting to define problems and causes facilitates converting development objectives into achievable goals. Like other objectives, they can be general (attend a sensitivity training course or role-playing seminar), or more specific (attend XYZ course in financial planning, use PERT techniques on Project X).

Self-improvement goals may be designed to improve current performance, or may be specifically intended to develop skills required at higher levels, or in different jobs (where it may be impossible to describe the end state of affairs to be achieved because success can be determined only in the future, or in other positions).

For development objectives it is necessary simply to rely upon the determination that the action plan has been carried out and that the individual has learned something. Suppose, for instance, that a development goal for an engineer destined to be a supervisor read as follows: "To meet with members of the financial, marketing, and production groups in order to learn how product release schedules affect their areas." Currently, he may have to know little about this since he may now have little impact on product release schedules. The question is "How do you know that the activity produced the desired learning?" You don't. At some point in time, the superior, who presumably has some knowledge in the goal area, should discuss the results of the meeting with the subordinate, emphasizing particularly the important points that should have been learned. If this is done the subordinate will have the learning experience of the meeting and the reinforcement from discussion.

There is obviously no way to determine if these activities will improve the current, or future, performance of the manager. Managerial judgment is important here. We must simply assume that the superior is able to work with the subordinate to define activities of value in future work assignments.

Finally, it should be clear that performance and development objectives may well be derived from and related to management training and development efforts. These efforts must account for current organizational problems and future needs, and treat development as an integrated organization-wide effort. MBO should therefore be integrally tied to them.

## Performance Required: The Action Plan

Some of the problems inherent in MBO can be overcome by stating and discussing the specifics of the performance required to accomplish an objective. Earlier, the differentiation of means and ends was stressed. The goal statements reflected the ends: here, the performance or "action plan" refers to the means to accomplish an objective. It describes the manner in which it is to be attained. These means reflect alternatives which lead to the desired end and performance level.

The action plan may be brief statements, but it should summarize what is to be done. The action plan for a complex activity should be broken down into major subprograms and should represent the "best" alternative, of possibly many, which would achieve the goal level. The action plan provides an initial basis for a total action program for the individual or department. These action plans might be stated in the following manner:

• **For the sales increase**—develop more penetration in a particular market area by increasing the number of calls to dealers there.

• **For the reduced manufacturing costs**—analyze the overtime activities and costs and schedule more work during regular hours.

Subordinates may base their own action plans on those developed by their manager, using his plan to guide their own roles in the unit's effort. Thus, clear differentiation of means from ends can facilitate lower-level use of the objectives process.

Including both means and ends permits comparing performance with some criteria and determining if events occurred which are presumed to lead to a desired outcome. It is important to recognize the distinction between measuring an objective and determining if an event has occurred. If we are unable to quantify or specify the goal level adequately, then we simply *assume that the desired goal level will be achieved* if a particular event or set of activities takes place. For example, while it is very difficult to measure if a manager is developing the talents of subordinates by means of any hard criteria, we can determine if he has provided them with development opportunities. If they have participated in seminars, attended meetings, or gone off to school, it may be *assumed* that the development activity is being properly conducted.

Some further benefits and opportunities provided by adequate attention to an action plan are as follows:

1. Aids in search for better, more efficient methods of accomplishing the objective.
2. Provides an opportunity to test the feasibility of accomplishing the objective as stated.
3. Develops a sounder basis to estimate time or cost required and deadline for accomplishment.
4. Examines the nature and degree of reliance on other people in the organization toward coordination and support needed.
5. Uncovers anticipated snags or barriers to accomplishment.
6. Determines resources (manpower, equipment, supplies, facilities) required to accomplish the objective.
7. Facilitates control if the performance is well specified and agreed upon; reporting need only occur when problems arise in implementing. This is a form of planning ahead; when plans are sufficiently complete, only deviations from it need be communicated.
8. Identifies areas in which the superior can provide support and assistance.
9. Facilitates the delegation process.

*Determine coordinating requirements and contingencies.* Successful achievement or failure of an objective may depend upon the contribution and performance of other individuals or departments. Therefore, since they may be extremely critical to successful performance, they must be considered.

Some contingencies apply to all objectives and need not be documented on each. For example, delays in the availability of resources, change in support or priorities from higher management, equipment failures, delayed information or approval, and the like, which are unplanned, should relieve some responsibility for objective accomplishment.

Other contingencies, specific to the objective, should be discussed. Among these might be inadequate authority of the subordinate, lack of policy covering aspects of the objective, possible failure to gain other's cooperation, known delays in the system, and so on. Once these are uncovered, several actions are possible:

• Reexamination of the objective (e.g., alteration of a deadline) when and if the contingency occurs.

• Commitment of the superior to aid by overcoming or preventing the contingency.

• Revision of the performance required to accomplish the objective.

• Establishment of a new objective. If a contingency is serious enough, an objective aimed at overcoming the problem may be justified.

## Measurement and Appraisal

Management by objectives carried with it most of the familiar difficulties and complications of measurement and appraisal processes. Its emphasis on performance, as opposed to personality traits or criteria presumed related to performance, makes it potentially more effective. But this potential cannot be realized unless measurement and appraisal are reasonably valid, reliable, objective, and equitable.

**Means, ends and evaluation.** Performance evaluations should rarely be based only on whether or not the objective was accomplished, or on the sheer number accomplished. They should include:

1. Quantitative aspects. (Was cost reduced 5 percent as planned?)
2. Qualitative aspects. (Have good relations been established with Department X? Has an evaluation technique been established?)
3. Deadline considerations. (Was the deadline beaten? Was it met?)
4. Proper allocation of time to given objectives.
5. Type and difficulty of objectives.
6. Creativity in overcoming obstacles.
7. Additional objectives suggested or undertaken.
8. Efficient use of resources.
9. Use of good management practices in accomplishing objectives (cost reduction, delegation, good planning, etc.)
10. Coordinative and cooperative behavior; avoidance of conflict-inducing or unethical practices, etc.

Evaluation and measurement, therefore, require considering both means and ends, being concerned with both the objective (number, type, difficulty, etc.) and the means to its achievement (cost, cooperativeness, time consumed, etc.). Unless this is done, an important opportunity to communicate expectations, feedback performance results, and setting effective goals may be lost. It must be fully understood that evaluation has obvious links to action plans, as well as to desired end states.

**Further consideration in measurement.** Some goals lend themselves more easily than others to measurement—scrap rates, production costs, sales volume, and other "hard" measures. These measures pertain most to lower organizational levels and to areas such as production, marketing, or other major functional activities of the organization and least to most staff and specialist units. The measurement problem often reduced to finding the appropriate, agreed-upon criterion for each objective, realizing that some will apply to many situations while others are unique to a single objective.

We have already detailed the distinction between performance and personal development objectives. Another distinction relevant to the measurement problem is the difference between routine and special project objectives. Clasifying objectives according to these types permits some important refinements in evaluation and control. By examining the nature of the mix of objectives for a set of positions it is possible to determine any or all of the following:

- The extent to which each individual has some personal development objectives.
- That sufficient problem-solving or innovative activities were forthcoming in units where they might be required.
- The priorities for performance or personal development objectives.

*Routine objectives* are basic to the job, a core part of the job description. How should they be measured? The most appropriate method for evaluating if an individual has achieved them is first to insure that he is aware of these activities and required levels. The manager must tell the subordinate—early in the relationship—what the activities of the job are and what the desired level of performance is. Evaluation should not occur after a period of service unless there has been previous discussion of criteria.

At the same time that the criteria are being specified, acceptable tolerance limits should be developed. Measurement of the routine should be a major part of the objectives process, yet it should be of most concern *when performance falls outside acceptable levels.* Essentially, we are proposing that minimum performance levels be set for routine activities. Therefore, evaluation of routine goals is *by exception,* or when these standards are not met. Naturally, the ability to manage by exception demands good plans or clear standards from which exceptions can be specified in advance. Odiorne cites the following example:

> The paymaster, for example, may report that his routine duties cluster around getting the weekly payroll out every Friday. It is agreed that the measure of exception will be zero—in other words, the boss should expect

no exceptions to the diligent performance of this routine duty. Thus, the failure any week to produce the payroll on Friday will be considered an exception that calls for explanation by the subordinate. If the cause were reasonably under his control or could have been averted by extra care or effort, the absence of the payroll will be considered a failure on the part of the subordinate.[4]

**What about superior performance?** When a subordinate frequently exceeds the performance levels, the manager should let him know that his outstanding performance has been noticed. Positive feedback should occur, especially to let the individual know when he is performing his major job responsibilities exceptionally well.

Generally, routine job responsibilities or goals are expressed as job standards, or other "hard" performance measures. Although appraisal and evaluation essentially compare performance to the standard, this may be relatively short sighted and suboptimal. Recall that the manager should also evaluate the activities or the manner in which performance was carried out. Often costs may be reduced by foregoing other expenditures, which may have negative long-run effects. There can be substantial distortions of behavior when only quantitative criteria are used in measurement.

*Problem-solving, special project,* or *creative objectives* are more difficult to quantify than the essentially routine. If the ends are truly creative, determining an adequate performance level may necessarily rely on intuitive judgment. Since innovation and invention are needed in their very formulation, we cannot generally measure results in these areas adequately, or directly. It is usually possible, however, to judge if an activity has been performed appropriately even though the ends, or the performance levels, are neither quantifiable nor measurable. Furthermore, constraints may be set on the activities. We can assess that they have occurred by some specific point in time or that a specific dollar amount has been expended. Thus, we are not only concerned with whether or not events have occurred, but also within some tolerance limit such as of target dates, budget constraints, or a quality assessment by the manager. It becomes possible under these conditions to establish review points, thus giving attention to the outcomes of activities when they occur. Deliberation on these outcomes can serve to re-evaluate both objectives and means. Thus changes are possible, and both flexibility and control are assured where they appear to be most needed—where predictions, plans, and standards could not be specified or articulated in advance.

**Deadlines and budget constraints** can be strictly specified in some cases and not in others. A great deal depends on:

- The importance of the objective.
- The ability to determine the time or costs required in performance.

- Whether or not written plans or objectives of other people require coordinated completion dates.
- The amount of time and money the subordinate will spend on the particular objective under discussion.
- The predictability of problems or barriers to accomplishment.

Discussing these constraints allows greater understanding between superiors and subordinates and establishes their use in evaluation. Expectations become known; realities can be tested. Deadlines and costs should be viewed as "negotiable," and should be reasonably and rationally arrived at whenever possible. Deadlines especially should not be set simply to insure that action is initiated.

We wish to re-emphasize the importance of this criterion problem. A fundamental requirement for MBO is the development and use of sound criteria for evaluation, appraisal, and feedback. This is critical to achieve meaningful changes in behavior. "Hard" criteria must be used with extreme care. They are best viewed as ends or levels; they indicate nothing about attaining either. "Soft" criteria involve not a particular level of achievement, but determination that an event or condition has or has not occurred. These soft criteria are a vital and fundamental part of MBO. Without them, the approach cannot be well implemented.

To some managers, the development and communication of goals comes naturally. There are those who are able intuitively to determine and specify appropriate measures, criteria, goals, and the most satisfactory methods for achieving them. They innately sense what must be observed and measured and communicate this effectively to subordinates. This, of course, is the behavior which management by objectives seeks to develop and reinforce.

## Summary

Research and experience strongly support the relationship between the degree of a subordinate's acceptance of the objectives approach and his perception of its support and reinforcement from top management.[5] Organization support is critical for two reasons.

- Top management may be an important reference group for lower level managers. Ambitious employees are likely to emulate managerial behavior. They identify with the top management and act similarly. If top management uses a particular method of managing, lower level managers are likely to use it also.
- Consistent factoring and communication of goals to lower organizational levels is necessary. The general objective of the organization must be continually broken down into smaller and smaller units. The boss must learn what is expected, must communicate this to his subordi-

nates, and must work with them to achieve these objectives. If this process breaks down at any point, then the whole approach is difficult to use.

Objectives must be written down for the entire organization, but the degree of detail and precision cannot easily be specified. This may be a matter for organizational policy and procedure, or it may be determined by mutual superior-subordinate agreement. However this is resolved, the varied aspects of objectives-setting should be attended to, discussed, and resolved as fully as possible to benefit from the MBO process.

Most important is that the approach must be intrinsically built into the job of managing. It must be related to other organizational processes and procedures, such as budgeting. It should be fundamentally incorporated into planning and development activities. It should be one of the major inputs to the performance appraisal and evaluation process. If not, it is likely that unless a manager intuitively uses this approach, it is easier to do other things. There are costs involved in MBO. There must be some value or payoff which managers can recognize; otherwise they will view it as a waste of time.

1. J. March and H. Simon, *Organizations*. New York: Wiley, 1958, p. 191.
2. These categories are similar to those proposed by Odiorne. See his *Management by Objectives*. New York: Pitman, 1964, especially Chapters 7, 8, and 9.
3. H. Tosi and S. Carroll, "Some Structural Factors Related to Goal Influence in the Management by Objectives Process," *Business Topics* (Spring 1969), 45-50.
4. Odiorne, p. 104.
5. H. Tosi and S. Carroll, "Managerial Reactions to Management by Objectives," *Academy of Management Journal* (December 1968), 415-426.

William B. Werther, Jr.
Heinz Weihrich

# 3
# Refining MBO
# Through Negotiations

Shortcomings of other management philosophies have led many practitioners to embrace the management by objectives (MBO) approach. The widespread and growing popularity of MBO is explained by its orientation: MBO focuses upon results and is performance based. Unlike other management appraisal systems that often concentrate on personality and conformity traits, MBO requires the manager to concentrate on the most critical item: objectives used as targets toward which activities are directed.

Most management systems that do not adhere to MBO precepts suffer because identifiable goals are missing. This forces managers to judge the performance of subordinates on subjective, rather than objective, criteria. In the terms of transactional analysis, superior-subordinate interactions more closely resemble interactions—where the subordinate is given a more equal role—are too few. Moreover, unfair treatment is more likely in subjective performance appraisal because the superior's personal biases can enter into the evaluation. Even when the assessment of performance is free of biases, it tends to be work—not results—oriented. The central question becomes: "How hard are my people working?" On the other hand, MBO focuses upon a different and more important question: "What are we accomplishing?" Although the difference may appear subtle, the distinction between activity and results is significant.

In using objectives as the focus of control, however, they become the primary determinant of organizational viability. If the manager directs resources towards the wrong targets or fails to clearly establish the goals, efforts may be wasted or even counterproductive. Resources are misdirected; frictions and frustrations are generated; and, future performance suffers.

When poor performance eventuates, the flow of rewards diminishes or fails to materialize. The implicit or explicit agreement that hard work

William B. Werther and Heinz Weihrich, "Refining MBO Through Negotiations," *MSU Business Topics*. Summer 1975, pp. 53-59. Reprinted by permission of the publisher, Division of Research, Graduate School of Business Administration, Michigan State University.

will be rewarded becomes null and void since the hard work failed to produce meaningful organizational gains. The result of breaking this psychological contract is lower motivation, increased frustration, and reduced morale. Thus, misguided objectives not only lead to poor performance, but they may perpetuate poor performance in the future.

For organizations to remain viable they must identify and achieve their objectives. To do this, it is necessary to understand the framework in which the objectives are used. An examination of the MBO approach will serve to place objectives in perspective before discussing the process of negotiating these goals with subordinates.

## The MBO Framework

To explain MBO is not easy. It is like happiness: it is different things to different people. Some view it as a form of appraisal; others consider it as a system of managing.[1] We take the latter view, but focus our attention in this article on one of the most critical aspects of MBO: the negotiation of objectives.

MBO is a process in which activities are consciously directed toward defined goals. The superior and subordinate jointly identify the objectives. That is, both are actively involved in the process. This usually necessitates a review and definition of responsibilities in terms of end results. Verifiable objectives then become the standards against which performance is measured. Consequently, the evaluation of the contribution made by each individual and organizational unit towards the overall goals of the company is facilitated.

The most fundamental aspects of MBO involve:

- *setting verifiable objectives,*
- *directing activities toward the achievement of the objectives,* and
- *evaluating actual performance against the objectives.*

Although these steps may appear simple, the process itself can be complex. Organizational issues, human relations problems, and even societal considerations can be involved. Offsetting such potential difficulties are the considerable benefits associated with the MBO process.

## Benefits of MBO

An examination of the benefits attributed to MBO provides insight into widespread success of this management technique. Although they differ from company to company, the following benefits are typical of successfully setting objectives:

1. **MBO emphasizes results rather than activities.** It is possible to be extremely busy (doing unnecessary tasks) without achieving results. In MBO, activities are directed toward defined ends.
2. **MBO facilitates the identification of conflicts between objectives.** Conflicts may arise within the individual (choosing among alternatives), between and among individuals (interpersonal conflicts), organizational units, and the organization and its environment.
3. **MBO helps to integrate individual needs and organizational objectives.** During the negotiation of objectives, individual needs can be translated into personal development objectives.
4. **MBO facilitates coordination of individual efforts and the activities of organizational units toward common overall company objectives.**
5. **MBO provides verifiable standards against which performance can be measured thus providing feedback.** People have a need to know how well they are doing.
6. **MBO makes explicit important aspects of the psychological contract.** For example, it reinforces commitment of the individual to contribute to organizational goals; the organization commits itself to treat the employee fairly in respect to just wages, nondiscrimination, and so on.
7. **MBO makes self-control possible.** If the subordinate agrees to verifiable goals, he knows whether he achieved them. Self-control leads to self-improvement. The subordinate will recognize his needs for improvement in weak areas; moreover, he can improve and grow by building on his strengths.
8. **Effective negotiation using MBO concepts facilitates interaction between superior and subordinate that is based on the maturity of both.** It involves gathering objective information, and making intelligent decisions based on this information. Thus, the emphasis is not *who* is right, but *what* is right based on reality testing.

Despite the many advantages of negotiating objectives within the MBO framework, it must be understood that these advantages can only be gained through the sometimes arduous and always intricate task of establishing the MBO program in each individual situation.

## Difficulties in Negotiating Objectives

The first step in the MBO process, setting objectives, is often the most difficult part of MBO. To facilitate effective negotiation of objectives, participants need to be aware of problems such as the following:

1. **A choice may have to be made among goals that are in conflict.** For example, layoffs require a decision between profit maximization and employment stability.

2. **In selecting a specified goal, other goals may have to be foregone.** For example, limited resources may preclude an organization from pursuing two attractive investments concurrently.
3. **Organizational objectives and individual needs may be in conflict; in fact, some think that they are inherently incompatible.** MBO, properly practiced, facilitates the integration of personal and organizational goals.
4. **A vertical integration of objectives of the superior and subordinate may be hindered by insufficient communication.** However, there is considerable evidence that MBO facilitates communication because it forces the superior and subordinate to agree on objectives, ideally through bilateral negotiation on an adult level.
5. **Conflict in horizontal objectives may be created through functional orientation of individuals.** A credit manager wanting to reduce bad debts may do this by restrictive credit terms, not fully recognizing the resulting decrease in sales. On the other hand, the sales manager may want a liberal credit policy to boost his sales without being too concerned about the risk of default. Thus, by pursuing their own objectives, the credit and the sales manager are working against each others' objectives. MBO must reconcile these goal conflicts.
6. **Interdependence of organizational units makes it difficult to renegotiate objectives because a change of one objective often requires changes in other parts of the system.** It must be recognized that organizations consist of interwoven networks of goals. Changes in one set of goals can occur only with careful planning. Nevertheless, changed environmental conditions may make new goals a mandatory undertaking. MBO is not static. It is a flexible managerial system that can adapt to changes in the internal and external environment.
7. **Selecting areas that are major determinants for the success of the company requires a great deal of analysis of the managerial system.** Even if the critical points are identified, determining the proper goal level requires honest negotiation. Objectives that are set too high result in nonachievement, and cause frustration. Objections set too low, provide no challenge. Objectives should provide some challenge, but they should also be attainable.

Each of these potential pitfalls is serious, but the most difficult part of setting objectives is in the interrelationship between the superior and subordinate during negotiation of objectives. It involves unequal power relationships that may inhibit communication and create other undesirable consequences. Even experienced managers find the process of actually negotiating objectives to be arduous. Yet, no dimension of MBO is as crucial as the face-to-face encounter between subordinate and superior.

## Negotiating Objectives

Implementation of MBO is fraught with difficulties; even after the hurdles to a successful implementation are overcome, additional refinements are necessary to ensure future benefits from MBO[2]. Whether implementing or refining an MBO program, a critical task is to actually set targets with subordinates in a network of objectives. Establishing the right target is essential; otherwise, organizational resources are ineffectively deployed. However, the manager must astutely evaluate an array of possible goals in order to select an optimal mix. Since these new objectives introduce changes into the work environment, the manager must then consider the behavioral implications surrounding change. Only after evaluating potential objectives and weighing the implications can he actually negotiate periodic changes in the targets of the MBO program.

It is clear, therefore, that to establish objectives under an MBO approach, analytical, behavioral, and negotiating skills are required by the manager irrespective of his organizational position—whether he is supervisor, middle manager, or executive.

The characteristics of objectives are varied. They take on unique dimensions in each organization; in fact, they change from division to division within organizations. Even so, some general considerations exist whenever there is an attempt to establish explicit objectives.

### Analytical Considerations

Of utmost importance is the selection of the right objectives; although this should be obvious, too often measurable objectives are pursued to the detriment of more subjective, but equally important, targets. The criterion is to evaluate each meaningful objective in light of its contribution to the department's and the organization's overall goals, strategy, and purpose. Those targets that hold the potential for the greatest positive or negative impact on performance are the most significant objectives.

Once the right goals are identified, their priorities should be determined. In evaluating priorities, thought must again be given to the potential contribution of each target to the larger concerns of strategy and purpose. The interdependency among objectives cannot be overlooked. For example, if the objective of reducing labor turnover is ignored, the higher order objectives of improving productivity and quality may not be achieved.

To facilitate the selection of major objectives requires both a top-down *and* bottom-up approach. Only with each organizational level setting objectives in a systematic fashion (from top to bottom) can continuity occur. Then, a bottom-up approach is employed to develop commitment through participation. In effect, the hierarchy of managers becomes a means-end chain where each subobjective contributes to some explicit objective; each objective then contributes to still more important goals. Thus, the goal setting process works both ways: top management provides the direction of the company and lower level managers set objectives that support the overall plan.

New or modified objectives represent change. Appropriate attention must be given to the emotional implications of change, or the change itself may be resented or resisted. Although behavioral scientists have made significant strides in recent years, there is no panacea for resistance to change; but, resistance can be minimized.

## Behavioral Considerations

Before dealing with potential resistance to change, the practitioner should take a positive view. The needs of each involved individual must be contemplated to provide a means by which these personal needs can be integrated into the achievement of organizational objectives. That is, the reward structure should be triggered by the accomplishment of desired objectives and it should concurrently satisfy personal needs.

Resistance to change stems in large part from a fear of failure; to overcome resistance the manager must remove or lessen this fear. Positive action is required from the manager to give the subordinate reassurances and the information necessary to understand how the change will affect him. Moreover, he must be given the proper tools.

Reassurances, obviously, may take many forms. Comparing planned assignments with past successes is an excellent technique. Not only does it reassure the employee, it sets an implicit expectation of similar performance on new assignments. Since most people strive to live up to the favorable image held of them by others, this technique serves a motivational role too.

Participation in the determination of objectives and their priorities also helps because this process gives insight into the reasons for the target. Equipped with such knowledge, the individual is better able to tackle the fear that often emanates from the unknown. Moreover, exploring the issue in consultation with a superior solidifies the implicit bargain of commitment and reinforces positive behavior. In turn, such supportive interactions further open communications between the parties.

But reassurances in the absence of the requisite authority are meaningless. The manager must think about the implications of the objectives; he must agree with each subordinate about what authority and responsibilities are associated with the assignment. Too frequently objectives are not achieved because the manager assumes the employee knows the new authority and responsibility limits. They should be explicitly stated. Similarly, other changes in the subordinate's resources should be communicated.

With a realistic assessment of the objectives, their priorities, and the behavioral implications of change, the manager must now draw on his negotiating skills.

### Negotiating Considerations

Although selection of the right objectives and evaluation of the behavioral implications are essential, no aspect is more consequential—or more poorly understood—than the actual negotiation process. While common guidelines exist for all forms of negotiations, negotiating objectives with subordinates differs from vendor-vendee and labor-management bargaining. When dealing with a subordinate, it is clearly a win-win session. That is, both sides should gain. The manager wants commitment to objectives by the subordinate; the worker wants recognition and respect for his abilities. These are mutually compatible.

What is not compatible is a parental orientation on the behalf of the superior. Talking down to the employee and telling him what to do is not negotiating; such an attitude demeans the subordinate to the role of order taker. This interaction pattern might be appropriate under some circumstances, but it does not build commitment to objectives nor does it recognize the employee as a mature human being.

Since commitment and open communications are essential to establishing objectives, the manager must endeavor to make the goal-setting session positively reinforcing. Only through positive feedback can an employee's self-image be maintained at a high level. With this "can-do" attitude fueled by high expectations on both sides of the table, the worker will be operating closer to his ability—provided, of course, that positive reinforcement is forthcoming at other times also.

To complement the fundamentals of negotiations, there are numerous goal-setting techniques. These tactics are important for two reasons. First, the face-to-face setting of objectives with each subordinate is the most difficult aspect of operationalizing an MBO program. Second, it is difficult because few managers have had any training in such negotiations. Their negotiating experience—when it exists at all—is almost always of the win-lose variety.

## Negotiations Tactics

Tactics, however, are not a substitute for careful evaluation of objectives and the impact of change. Instead, tactics are a supplement to such planning and should be based upon the fundamental assumptions already examined. Some of the more helpful tactical considerations also provide further insight into the negotiation/goal-setting process.

*Privacy.* Developing specific objectives with individual workers may concern sensitive areas. One employee may see other co-workers as a constraint that he is reluctant to discuss. The manager is more apt to detect, and the employee is more apt to overcome, his reluctance if the meeting is held in private.

*No interruptions.* Setting objectives with workers is very likely the single most important activity a manager performs. Constant—even occasional—interruptions indicate that the cause of the interruption is more important than the objectives being discussed. Moreover, these disturbances may make the subordinate feel that he should end the session quickly (by not asking questions, for example) so his boss can get on to more important matters. What could be more important than setting objectives?

*Advance arrangements.* Little is to be gained by a "surprise" discussion of objectives. The subordinate should be consulted to establish a mutually agreed upon time for the meeting. The purpose of the upcoming session should also be known. This will enable both parties to give prior thought to the necessary goals. The appointment should be kept; a postponement subtracts from the perceived importance of the meeting.

*Duration.* Time is a manager's most valuable resource. Nevertheless, the goal-setting session should be conducted informally and in an unhurried manner. A quick meeting may save time initially. If the time saved, however, is at the expense of understanding, the cost may prove prohibitive.

*Body language.* Many managers believe body language to be unscientific trickery. Consider, however, the feelings communicated when the superior sits with his arms folded and an inscrutable look on his face. The typical reaction of most subordinates would be: "He sure wasn't very receptive."

The meeting between subordinate and superior should be conducted with the courtesy and spirit of a conference with a peer or the chairman of the board. When the subordinate enters the office, the superior should stand up and greet him with a handshake and a smile. He should close the door and put aside whatever work is in process. An ashtray should be offered if the subordinate smokes. The superior should assume a relaxed, even casual, position and begin with a comment or two favorable to the subordinate. In short, the use of physical gestures can put the employee at ease. It may take a minute or two to do these things, but they do facilitate more open communications.

*Participation.* A meeting is not a lecture. Involvement by the subordinate is necessary if a sincere commitment is to be established. If the subordinate appears hesitant or reluctant to communicate at any time, an affirmative nod of the head and a smile followed by silence on the manager's behalf will often cause the worker to volunteer more information. This procedure is especially effective near the end of the session after the employee has initially responded to a question like: "Is there anything I can do to assist you to achieve these targets?"

If a topic seems overly threatening, it should be set aside with the suggestion that both parties think about it and meet again to explore the issue further. It must be clearly understood that the postponement is so both parties may consider the point. The delay is not intended to table the issue; the follow-up meeting should be as soon as possible. However, the postponement can be successfully used to maintain the open and cooperative atmosphere in the goal setting session.

*Resistance.* Soliciting employee feedback gives the manager an opportunity to uncover sources of resistance. Recognizing resistance is important because it is either an indication of some logical error by the manager in assessing desired objectives or a clue to some underlying concern of the worker. When resistance occurs, the manager should reflect upon both possibilities; if the objectives seem appropriate, then it is probable that the resistance is emotionally based. Examples of emotional resistance include displacement (blaming inability on others), rationalization (offering excuses disguised as reasons for past, present, or future failures), or even subtle comments ("I'll try," or "I'll do my best"). Each of these reactions should be viewed as an indication of the employee's uncertainty—about his ability or his understanding of the goals. Further nondirective exploration of the goals or the employee's feelings is demanded by such situations.

*Conciliation.* Be conciliatory. If disagreement arises over an item, an "either-or" stance should be avoided. Focus instead upon those areas of agreement. A compromise may be advantageous; an eager willingness to pursue several goals may be cooled by the manager's insistence on some issue.

*Realistic goals.* Even the most capable performer cannot do everything. If there are too many objectives, some will not be achieved; if standards are set too high, they become frustrating and demotivating even if a limited number of objectives are being pursued. Further, targets should be set in verifiable terms. Usually this means measurable in some manner that leaves no question as to whether the objectives have been achieved. Obviously, objectives should not be selected simply because they are quantifiable. Subjective goals, especially those that provide overall direction, can be equally important. If goals are independently verifiable, however, the employee can better judge his performance, and the accuracy of subsequent evaluations is less likely to be questioned. Thus, from a tactical view, realistic goals should be limited in number, with obtainable standards, and (if possible) objectively measurable.

*Written objectives.* After the goal-setting session, the objectives should be written down and reviewed with the subordinate. This procedure has three benefits. First, it assures agreement as to the goals to be achieved;

standards, timeframes, and the basis for evaluation should be included. Second, the written document can be used to compare objectives with subsequent performance. Third, and equally important, it requires at least one follow-up meeting between the superior and subordinate.

*Follow-up sessions.* MBO and the subprocess of goal setting are not substitutes for managerial leadership. The manager must still plan, organize, and control. To effectively control requires follow-up sessions. These may be extremely short; but whatever length, they show the superior's continued concern and allow positive feedback to the employee. Moreover, follow-up sessions provide an opportunity for raising questions in a positive, nonthreatening atmosphere.

## Conclusion

Management by Objectives represents the most widely accepted approach to management. Some firms have had years—even decades—of experience with this technique. Yet, persistent difficulties still exist.

No aspect of MBO is more significant or more fraught with pitfalls than the actual negotiation of goals with subordinates on a face-to-face basis. Analytical, behavioral, and negotiating skills are required. Before discussing goals with subordinates, the leader must evaluate objectives in light of their potential contribution to the organization's purpose and strategy. Within that framework, priorities can be established. However, organizational priorities represent only half of the picture. To be truly successful demands that thought be given to behavioral considerations: the subordinates' needs. Without such consideration, resistance to change is apt to rob the MBO process of its effectiveness.

Only after the analytical and behavioral implications of objectives have been evaluated is it appropriate to actually negotiate new targets with subordinates. This negotiation process must be based upon win-win or positive-sum philosophy. That is, successful negotiations can proceed only under the assumption that effective leadership involves an integration of employees *and* organizational needs. If goals are to be pursued at the cost of subordinate needs, resistance most certainly will be encountered, and the MBO program will be less effective.

Beyond a win-win strategy, negotiations must occur on an adult-adult plane surrounded by high expectations and positive reinforcement. Only in an atmosphere of mutual respect and support will maximum effort be forthcoming. With careful preparation and a positive environment, there are numerous techniques that can be utilized to facilitate effective nego tiations. Though uninterrupted privacy is necessary, the most important tactics involve common agreement upon realistic goals that are clearly communicated in writing. No matter how carefully each step is thought through, if the objectives are poorly communicated, all previous efforts are wasted. Subordinate activities will be misdirected. Therefore, follow-up sessions by the leader are mandatory to assure objectives are clearly understood. Failure to conduct follow-up sessions is a failure of leadership. Such shortcomings undermine the sincerity of the negotiation process and the success of the MBO approach.

1. Heinz Weihrich, *A Study of the Integration of Management by Objectives with Key Managerial Activities and the Relationship to Selected Effectiveness Measures* (Ph.D. diss., Graduate School of Management, University of California, Los Angeles, 1973).
2. William E. Reif, "Implementing MBO: A Change Strategy," *Arizona Business,* November 1974, pp. 17-23.

Heinz Weihrich

# 4
# Getting Action into MBO

Objectives are the ends toward which activities should be directed. But, what does one find in practice? An organizational analysis too often reveals that activities are duplicated, are unnecessary, or contribute little to objectives. Moreover, it may be found that some important activities are not performed at all, simply because nobody in the organization feels responsible for it. Therefore, a more systematic approach to planning for action is necessary to make MBO more effective. The purpose of this article is to bring action into MBO. Besides an overview of action planning, specific approaches—the use of the key result area matrix and the key task matrix—will be the focal points of this discussion.

Objectives are a starting point in the managerial process. The action plan is concerned with *what* key functions, tasks, and activities must be carried out to achieve the objectives. Moreover, it has to be decided *how* to reach the objectives most effectively and efficiently because in almost all situations alternative courses of action can be taken. Since timing is critical in the management process, it has to be decided *when* things must be done. Finally, unless it is stated *who* is going to do the tasks, they will not get done.

There are those who maintain that the manager should only be concerned with setting objectives, and not with activities. There is, of course, some merit to this position; because a very active person doing the wrong things does not contribute to the objectives of the organization. On the other hand, it has been my experience that action planning—especially when it pertains to objectives that require a complex program—is not only necessary for determining the important activities, but it also facilitates goal setting itself. For example, one of the criteria for good objectives is that they are reasonable, achievable, and realistic. In consulting I found during goal setting sessions that managers set objectives that did not meet these criteria. To test important objectives, it was necessary to go through the process of action planning, listing the necessary activities and estimating the time as well as costs and resources required to carry

Reprinted by permission of the publisher, *Journal of Systems Management,* November, 1977.

them out. Based on this analysis—which was essentially an action plan—objectives could be set that were challenging, yet realistic.

Action plans not only facilitate setting of objectives, but they result in other *benefits* as well. First, they force the manager to look for and test several alternatives available to achieve the objectives. Second, the necessary activities are identified and can be grouped in the most effective and efficient manner based on the available human and material resources. Third, responsibilities are determined and authority is delegated congruent with the responsibilities. Fourth, during the action planning process, potential problems are uncovered and steps can be taken to prevent their occurrence. Fifth, resource requirements and costs are estimated. Sixth, time schedules are established that facilitate realistic time frames for objectives and plans.

## The Action Planning Process

During the goal setting process it becomes evident that for some objectives a simple statement of what is to be accomplished is not sufficient. Consequently, an action plan has to be developed. The following eight steps—which will fit most situations—facilitate this process:

1. Identify the end results. This is really a part of the goal setting process. It is restated here to emphasize that activities must contribute to the achievement of objectives.
2. Determine important functions, tasks, and activities necessary to achieve the end results. If the list of activities is too long, it would be useful to group the activities.
3. Provide for vertical and horizontal integration of groups and individuals.
4. Identify the key tasks and activities for individual positions.
5. Define roles, authority, and responsibility for each individual position.
6. Schedule the time needed for major activities and coordinate them into a time network. Adjust, if necessary, the objectives.
7. Determine the adequacy of human, financial, and other resources necessary to achieve the objectives and to carry out the activities.
8. Review the action plans and see if they are congruent with the objectives.

These steps provide a useful framework, but it must be understood that they do not always follow the above sequential order. For example, when setting objectives, it may at that time become necessary to determine the time dimensions of critical events. Therefore, the steps should not be followed rigidly, but rather with flexibility to fit the particular situation.

## Key Result Area Matrix

In a comprehensive MBO system, as suggested here, the organizational aims can be viewed as a hierarchy. More specifically, the socioeconomic purpose of the organization results in a mission statement, which, in turn, leads to long-range and strategic objectives, more specific overall objectives, division objectives, department and unit objectives, and finally individual objectives (Figure 7). We will focus first on the more specific overall objectives with attention given to the objectives in the key result areas (KRA). Later, the determination of specific responsibilities will be discussed in connection with the key task matrix.

### Overall Key Result Area Objectives
Organizations, as suggested by Drucker, have several objectives.
> Objectives are needed in every area where performance and results directly and vitally affect the survival and prosperity of the business (Drucker, 1954).

Although there is no unanimous opinion about which areas are key result areas, the following list contains some of the more important ones for business organizations: (1) profitability, (2) markets, (3) products, (4) productivity, (5) financial and physical resources, (6) innovation and research, (7) human resource development, (8) organization development, and (9) social responsibility.

During the objective setting process, objectives are established in these areas. The task, then, becomes to identify the contributions of individuals to the KRA, which can be done through the overall Key Result Area matrix.

### KRA Matrix Analysis
The KRA matrix indicates the areas in which performance is of vital importance (Figure 8 is an illustration). On top of the form, horizontally, key managerial positions are listed. People in these positions make major contributions to the KRA. In the cells, check marks are inserted to indicate who contributes to KRA. At this point, the specifics of their contributions are not yet clearly determined.

### Process of Determining Individual Contributions
There are several ways of determining the contributions of individuals. We will focus on one approach—a group approach—which I found useful in my consulting work. Top management, in collaboration with key executives, identifies the KRA or the objectives in these areas; these are then discussed with the management team. Each manager of the team states whether he can contribute to the specific KRA. Contributions are marked by a check (✔) in the matrix, which indicates that the individual

**Figure 7**
Hierarchy of Objectives.

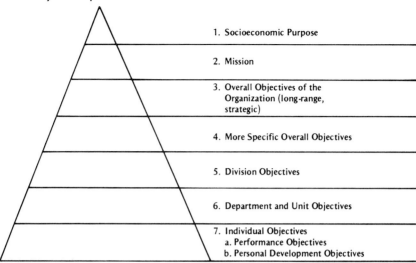

1. Socioeconomic Purpose

2. Mission

3. Overall Objectives of the Organization (long-range, strategic)

4. More Specific Overall Objectives

5. Division Objectives

6. Department and Unit Objectives

7. Individual Objectives
   a. Performance Objectives
   b. Personal Development Objectives

manager sets *his* objectives in a way that will contribute to the KRA. An "x" is used to indicate no major contribution to the KRA. It should be noted, however, that Figure 8 is an illustration only. The specific contributions of the functional departments to KRA may differ in specific companies.

In the KRA matrix (Figure 8), the Key Result Areas are indicated only by key words or phrases. The top executive, of course, has to be more specific in what he really wants to be accomplished. There are two approaches he can take. *First*, he may state in general terms, what the organization expects to accomplish. Then, other members of the management team are asked how they can contribute to the KRA. Key Result Areas are communicated throughout the organization. Consequently, through the bottom-up approach, specific overall objectives can then be set in the KRA, based on the inputs from lower level managers. In other words, top management gives broad direction and provides the framework, but the setting of the more specific objectives is *primarily a bottom-up approach.* Using this approach might reveal that the overall objectives in the KRA may be set higher than if they were stated initially in concrete terms by top management. But some superiors could feel uncomfortable with this approach, thinking that they have abdicated their responsibility by letting lower levels tell them what can be achieved.

The *second* approach is for top managment to develop rather specific objectives in the KRA, with of course, the inputs and participation of other managers. An example may be: "To increase the market share of product Y by 10 percent by December 31, 1979." These objectives are

**Figure 8**
Relating Key Results to Manager's Responsibilities—Illustration Only.

| Key Result Areas \ Management Position | President | Research and Development | Engineering | Production | Quality Control | Marketing Sales | Finance | Personnel | Other: | Other: |
|---|---|---|---|---|---|---|---|---|---|---|
| 1. Profitability | ✓ | ✓ | ✓ | ✓ | ✓ | ✓ | ✓ | ✓ | | |
| 2. Markets | ✓ | ✓ | ✓ | ✓ | x | ✓ | x | ✓ | | |
| 3. Products | ✓ | ✓ | ✓ | ✓ | ✓ | ✓ | x | x | | |
| 4. Productivity | ✓ | ✓ | ✓ | ✓ | ✓ | ✓ | ✓ | ✓ | | |
| 5. Financial and physical resources | ✓ | x | x | ✓ | x | ✓ | ✓ | x | | |
| 6. Innovation and research | | | | | | | | | | |
| 7. Human resource development | | | | | | | | | | |
| 8. Organization development | | | | | | | | | | |
| 9. Social responsibility | | | | | | | | | | |

then communicated to lower levels of the organization. Each manager—and even nonmanagers may be involved—in turn sets his own objective, congruent with the objectives of the higher organizational unit. So this *primarily top-down approach*—with rather specific overall objectives—is followed by the bottom-up approach. Top management then reviews the objectives derived through the upward flow and makes, if necessary, changes in the overall objectives of the organization.

The practicing manager, of course, wants to know whether he should use the first approach, stating the KRA in general (but not too vague) terms, or if he should determine the overall objectives through collaboration with his top management team and state them in rather specific terms.

The answer to this question depends on the organization, the existing managerial philosophy, the organizational climate, and the task requirements. Whatever approach is taken, however, it must be a two-way process: Top-down *and* bottom-up. The difference is that in one case more emphasis is on the *top-down* and less emphasis on the bottom-up approach. In the other case, stress is placed on the *bottom-up flow* of objectives after the overall objectives have been broadly outlined or stated as a KRA.

## Key Task Matrix

In the KRA matrix the important areas in which performance is of vital importance were identified. The checkmarks indicate how individuals see their contributions in respect to the KRA. Although this is an excellent beginning in determining the specific responsibilities, further refinements may be needed. In the following discussion of the matrix, there is frequent use of the term "Key Tasks" (KT); it includes both the broader concept of key functions, and the more specific key activities.

Organizations are complex and usually several members contribute to joint results. The analytical tool we want to use is the key task matrix.

### Principal Aspects of the Matrix

In order to achieve the objectives, functions, tasks, and activities have to be carried out. A separate Key Tasks Matrix (KTM) form is used for selected objectives (Figure 9); the major functions, tasks, and activities are listed in the first vertical column. Relationships with positions are determined only after there is general agreement on what has to be done. On the top of the form, key positions are listed. The people in these positions are members of the team that may be involved in achieving the objectives.

The forms, completed with tasks and activities, are distributed to team members. Individually, they are asked to indicate how they see their relationship to the specific tasks and activities by inserting a symbol in the respective boxes intersecting the listed tasks and their own position. The code system developed and tested by Melcher will be used here:

A. *General Responsibility*—The individual guides and directs the execution of the function through the person delegated operating responsibility.

B. *Operating Responsibility*—The individual is directly responsible for the execution of the function.

C. *Specific Responsibility*—The individual is responsible for executing a specific or limited portion of the function.

# Figure 9
## Key Task Matrix (KTM)—Illustration Only.

Objective: *To develop and introduce at least one new product and generate $200 million in sales by December 31, 1977*

Prepared:
Approved:

| No. | Key Functions, Tasks, Activities | President | VP Marketing | Sales Mgr | VP Mfg | Production Manager | Research and Development | Engineering | Quality Control | VP Industrial Relations | Etc. | Comments |
|---|---|---|---|---|---|---|---|---|---|---|---|---|
| 1 | To explore ideas and product needs | A | B | C | D | E | C | E | | | | |
| 2 | To screen the ideas and appraise them for their potential values to the Co. | A | B | C | D | D | C | C | E | | | |
| 3 | Make a business analysis | A | B | C | E | E | C | | | | | |
| 4 | To develop the product | A | D | D | C | C | C | B | D | F | | |
| 5 | To test the new product | A | B | C | C | C | C | F | C | | | |
| 6 | Commercialize the product | A | C | B | C | C | C | | C | F | | |
| | | | | | | | | | | | | |
| | | | | | | | | | | | | |
| | | | | | | | | | | | | |
| | | | | | | | | | | | | |

*Responsibility Codes:*

| A = General responsibility | B = Operating responsibility | C = Specific responsibility | D = Must be consulted |
|---|---|---|---|
| E = May be consulted | F = Must be notified | G = Must approve | |

D. *Must Be Consulted*—The individual, if the decision affects his area, must be called upon before any decision is made or approval is granted, to advise or relate information, but not to make the decision or grant approval.

E. *May Be Consulted*—The individual may be called upon to relate information, render advice or make recommendations.

F. *Must Be Notified*—The individual must be notified of action that has been taken.

G. *Must Approve*—The individual (other than persons holding general and operating responsibility) must approve or disapprove.

Individuals who indicate *Operating Responsibility*, are also asked to state how they see the responsibility of other team members in respect to the particular task. In other words, if a manager thinks that he has an operating responsibility, he has to identify working relationships of other team members for the activity by inserting the appropriate responsibility symbols in the matrix.

The forms, completed by each team member, are then analyzed—usually by a consultant—to determine overlaps and underlaps of responsibility as well as other conflicts. Overlap of responsibility means that more than one person has the same responsibility for a particular task. On the other hand, underlap means nobody feels responsible for a task, and there is a high probability that this task will not be carried out. So, the process of completing the KT matrix forces each member of the team to think through his own responsibilities as well as those of others. Moreover, it requires managers to communicate with each other. Those involved in organization development know that communication is one of the major problems in organizations, and the KT analysis helps to overcome it. Figure 9, a partially completed form, is an illustration only, the specific responsibilities will differ for the individual companies.

**Process of Conflict Resolution**

Inevitably, responsibility conflicts will be discovered during the analysis of the KT matrix. How should they be resolved? There may be delicate situations where the superior and the respective subordinates have to resolve the conflicts in one-to-one meetings. However, in the proper organizational atmosphere, it is generally advisable to discuss the findings of the KT analysis in group meetings. During such a discussion, a perceptive consultant will also often discover problems that go beyond specific responsibilities; for example, problems that may involve attitudes of team members toward each other, which inhibit the functioning of the group. This information can be useful for building effective work teams.

In conclusion, the KT matrix, with the primary components of (1) key functions, tasks, and activities, (2) positions of team members, and

(3) responsibility relationships, is a useful tool for bringing action into the MBO process. It facilitates the identification of tasks, the determination of responsibilities, and the execution of controls. It is a beneficial but time-consuming process and therefore should be used with discretion.

### Authority Delegation

With the objectives set, the key functions and tasks identified and assigned, it may become necessary to redefine the authority associated with the positions. Authority, the right to command, should be sufficient to accomplish the stated objectives and to carry out the required activities. It is, therefore, important that authority is reviewed, clearly understood, and communicated to all who need to know.

## Summary

Objectives give the company direction. But objectives—especially those that require complex programs—need to be supported by an action plan.

To get action into the plans, key result areas (KRA) must be identified and related to managerial positions; the KRA matrix is a useful tool facilitating this process. The contributions of the individuals in these positions are thus identified; this enables each person to set his own objectives directly contributing to the KRA. The process of setting objectives must be a two-way approach: top-down and bottom up. Which one of the two should be emphasized depends on the particular situation; but neither can be ignored.

Handling responsibilities pertaining to the key functions, tasks and activities is greatly facilitated by the key task (KT) matrix. In this matrix, the kinds of responsibilities for specific tasks and activities are identified and related to managerial positions. Finally, authority, which should be congruent with responsibilities, should be reviewed and, if necessary, redefined.

Management by Objectives has proved over the years to be one of the most effective approaches to management. But objectives alone are in many cases not enough. Therefore, action planning, the often ignored aspect, when added to good objectives, offers a propitious means for achieving them.

## References

Drucker, Peter F. *The Practice of Management.* New York: Harper & Brothers, Publishers, 1954.

Melcher, Robert D. "Roles and Relationships: Clarifying the Manager's Job." *Personnel,* 44, 3 (May-June, 1967), 33-41.

Weihrich, Heinz. *A Study of the Integration of Management by Objectives with Key Managerial Activities and the Relationship to Selected Effectiveness Measures.* Unpublished doctoral dissertation, University of California, Los Angeles, 1973.

# 4 Implementation of MBO and Organization Development

**Objectives**
1. To recognize important factors that facilitate and hinder the implementation of MBO.
2. To gain insights into implementation from experiences of different enterprises.
3. To become aware of political issues that hinder effective implementation.
4. To understand the relationship between MBO and the managerial grid.

**Figure 10**

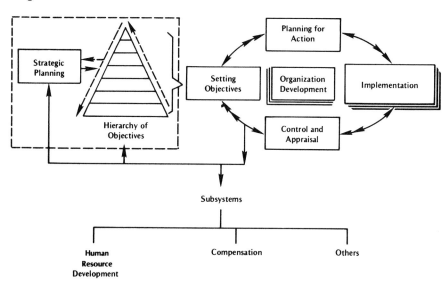

## Implementation of MBO and Organization Development

MBO to be effective requires both, a systematic preparation for implementation and due recognition of behavioral aspects of individuals involved in the change. Our MBO systems model shows that Organization Development (OD) facilitates the steps of setting objectives, planning for action, implementing MBO, and control as well as appraisal. But in a comprehensive MBO system, OD would also be used to develop the strategic plan and the hierarchy of objectives. OD and the implementation phase of MBO are both concerned with a planned approach to change; both give due consideration of the human aspects of managing, and both aim to make the total organization more effective.

The first article "Implementation—The Guts of MBO" by Dale McConkey was selected because it raises some important questions an organization should ask even before deciding whether to use MBO. Also the installation of MBO requires a systematic analysis. One should be aware of so-called MBO experts with an attitude of "I have the solution—what is the problem?" Instead, MBO must be tailored to fit the organizational needs and requirements.

The second article in this section, "Avoiding the Pitfalls of the MBO Trap" by John Humble, gives illustrations of companies' experiences with MBO. Moreover, Humble is an advocate of the use of an MBO advisor, who usually is trained by a consultant and who should be a highly respected person with considerable business experience. Finally, to be effectively implemented, MBO must consider the personal needs of individuals who will be affected by the program.

Most of the writings describe how MBO has been implemented in large companies. But Jack Mendleson in "Personal Targets for Effective Management" shows how a small real estate office implemented MBO.

Few people will disagree about the soundness of the MBO concepts. So, why does MBO fail at times? George S. Odiorne in his article, "The Politics of Implementing MBO," provides some answers.

The last article in this section, "Effective Management by Objectives through the Grid" by Heinz Weihrich, shows the application of the Grid approach to MBO. The Managerial Grid, developed and popularized by Robert R. Blake and Jane S. Mouton, has long been recognized as an important Organization Development (OD) tool. The Grid suggests that the concern for people and the concern for the task are not mutually exclusive, rather they are complementary. This article shows that the various positions on the Grid—with different degrees of concerns for people and the task—have important implications for the MBO processes of (1) setting objectives, (2) planning for action, (3) implementation, and (4) control and appraisal.

# 1
# Implementation—
# The Guts of MBO

During the last 15 years the growth of Management by Objectives (MBO) has been both rapid and widespread. Its growth as a system of managing has blanketed the United States, Canada, and England and has made a not insignificant impact on the Continent and as far away as Japan where its impact ranges from major companies like Sony, the electronics complex, to the mayor's office of the city of Sapporo.

Also, MBO has been applied to every conceivable type of organization; capital and consumer goods companies; service organizations such as banks, schools, and hospitals; nonprofit organizations such as Junior Achievement of the United States; military and government entities; law enforcement agencies; and retailing operations. It has reached its most widespread application in manufacturing and sales type organizations. Its growth rate in the past five years has been especially spectacular.

Applications of MBO within these organizations include its use as a total system of managing—using it as they do as the basis and vehicle for planning, organizing, delegating, directing, controlling, evaluating performance, coaching and developing, compensating, and motivating. Others use it for only limited purposes, e.g. evaluating performance and planning.

## Not All Successes

This widespread adoption and the multifaceted applications have not been all successes. Certain of them have been resounding successes. The success of others is questionable. Still others have been outright failures. Why?

Almost invariably the answer lies in the manner in which the system was implemented and especially in the preimplementation phase. A study of the implementation methods as related to later success indicates a high degree of correlation in over 300 different MBO programs. The organizations which understood the full import of MBO and took the time and effort required to implement it properly have enjoyed the

Reprinted by permission of the publisher, S.A.M. Advanced Management, July 1972, © 1972 by Society for Advancement of Management.

maximum fruits of the system. Those which devoted only minimal time and effort to implementation have enjoyed success only commensurate with their efforts.

The organizations which endeavored to adopt and copy the system out of hand, and overnight, have usually failed. The strongest support for these conclusions is that not one single company studied, which had properly implemented the system in the first instance, has ever discontinued using it as its *primary* approach to management. Certainly, these organizations have modified and amended their systems as experience was gained, but the basic MBO system is still intact and being vigorously pursued. Thus, it becomes of paramount importance to define "implementation" and to set forth its key components. Of equal importance is a complete understanding of the prerequisites which management must meet before it begins to implement the system.

There remains little question but what the MBO system has received numerous black eyes which it did not deserve. Almost all of these black eyes should have been visited upon the managers who tried to adopt it without being competent to do so. Contrary to belief in some quarters, MBO is not a simple system. It has many principles, many nuances—some subtle, some overt—many virtues, and many pitfalls. All must be understood, appreciated, and practiced by the manager who would apply it successfully.

## Before the Implementation

Much of the success of implementation should be based on a major decision which must always precede implementation; namely, do we really understand what MBO is all about and do we want to adopt it in our company? Too many organizations, much to their later regret, have moved right into implementation without having made this decision effectively. The chief executive officer and, hopefully, his senior officers will complete an exhaustive analysis before making this decision. This analysis will include securing definitive answers to several critical questions which include:

1. Do we really understand the full import of MBO as it would affect our organization? Do we understand how it operates, its strengths, its pitfalls?
2. Is it right for our organization—are we willing to devote the time and effort (especially on the part of the chief executive) to make it effective (probably a minimum of three years to reach 85% effectiveness)?
3. Are we ready for it? Have we met the three major prerequisites—proper management atmosphere, organizational clarity, and an effec-

tive management information system? If not, can we meet them before implementation?

4. Is this the better timing? Are operations so unstable presently that there would be an excessive number of distractions from the concerted effort which is required? Will sufficient executive and managerial time be available? Would another period be better?

5. Why do we want it, what will it do for our organization? Various aids are available to assist in this analysis phase. They include—again, as a very minimum—the following:

   A. *Reading*—Several excellent books are available, written by recognized professionals, but check out the person before buying the book. Those books which include actual case studies of company experiences are especially valuable as the companies discussed can serve as the basis for further investigation as suggested in ( B ), below. Time spent on researching and preparing a bibliography will be well worthwhile.

   B. *Experience of Other Organizations*—Properly undertaken, this phase will provide the better basis for making a decision. Ask penetrating questions of at least six organizations which have practiced MBO for at least three years and insist on full answers. Are they really practicing MBO or claiming to for window dressing? What have been their successes and failures? What impact did it have on their management group and overall company performance? For what purposes do they use MBO? What conditions prevailed in the company? Would they do it all over again?

   C. *Outside Counsel*—Finally, bring in competent ( *repeat* competent ) outside help on an *ad hoc* basis to answer questions and provide guides and checkpoints for your decision.

The ultimate question which must be answered is:

Are you certain of what you are getting involved in and are you fully committed to making MBO work in your organization?

Only if this question can be answered in the affirmative, without reservation, should an organization move to the implementation stage.

## The Implementation

The three most common approaches to implementation of MBO are set forth below:

1. *One Level At A Time*—In this approach, the implementation begins at the top and MBO is implemented one ( or two sometimes ) level at at time, usually with six months to a year intervening between each

level. Example: During the first year only the president and his senior officers work with MBO; a year later the next level—major departments—start working with MBO; the remaining levels are covered in succeeding years. This is the middle ground approach and the one more commonly followed.

2. *One Department Only*—One department or division is selected as a pilot project, usually for a minimum of one year. The experience of this unit is used as the basis for determining whether or not MBO will be adopted in the rest of the organization and, if so, which of the other two approaches will be used. This is the most cautious approach.

3. *All At Once*—All levels of management are treated as a total unit and implementation for all begins and proceeds concurrently—generally with all levels attending the same meetings and indoctrination sessions. This is the most optimistic approach.

As Approach 1, *One Level At A Time*, is recommended by the preponderance of experience, it will be used in the remainder of this article when discussing the highlights of indoctrinating managers.[1]

Implementation for each level is divided roughly into two periods of six months each—the first period consists of indoctrination and getting ready to operate, the second six months is devoted to actually operating under MBO on a "dry run" basis.

The controlling rationale, especially during the first six months, should be to take small bites and digest each one completely before proceeding to the next. This is the foundation laying stage and, much like constructing a building, a sound total structure cannot be built on a sloppy foundation.

*Stage 1, Getting Ready.* This stage should cover both MBO as a system and the writing of effective objectives. An objective should never be written until the writer understands the system in which the objective operates. Violation of this premise almost invariably results in noncoordinated objectives written in a vacuum and which are carried out in isolation rather than as a proportionate part of the departmental and company objectives. Both the system and objectives are covered by a combination of reading assignments, discussion groups, workshop sessions, and coaching by competent leaders.

After about two to three months of this indoctrination, managers usually are prepared to start writing simple objectives. Emphasis should be devoted to getting managers accustomed to, and comfortable working with, objectives and the place of their objectives in the total scheme of things—not in writing the most perfect possible objectives. This can come later.

During the ensuing three months, the intent is to have each manager write increasingly complex objectives, each writing followed by an evaluation and coaching session, until he has become fairly adept at structuring meaningful, measurable objectives. Finally, he recommends a group of objectives on which he will operate and be measured during the second six months—the "dry run" phase.

*Stage 2, Operating Under Objectives.* It is made clear to each manager that he is operating under MBO on a "dry run" basis during these six months and that his future will not sink or swim based on his results. He is still undergoing training and indoctrination.

A feedback method is established to measure his performance against each of his objectives. Both he and his superior receive copies. Half way through this stage the manager and his superior hold a formal review (just as they will do in the future for each quarter of the year) to evaluate progress toward objectives, discuss any variances, and review the validity of the objectives for the remainder of the period. Necessary revisions are made to plans and objectives.

A similar review takes place three months later (at the end of the full year) and if managers are found capable, they begin actually operating under all facets of MBO. The implementation then moves down to the next level of management and similar indoctrination is provided for them. The process continues until all levels are covered and the total management group has become a part of MBO.

The importance of effective communications is emphasized during this transition from one stage to another. If the fact that MBO is being adopted is treated as a deep, dark secret, the levels of management which have yet to be covered will likely build up fear and distrust of the system. Managers at all levels should be acquainted with the fact that MBO is being adopted, including any timetable, the reasons why (purpose), and the part they will play in the system. Progress reports should be issued periodically and senior managers encouraged to brief their managers from time to time as the installation unfolds.

## After the Implementation

No one has yet made a "bug free" or perfect installation. Nor will they! Sick dogs only get sicker unless they are treated.

Therefore ,the final phase of implementation takes place after implementation and goes on forever to one degree or another. It is comprised of continually evaluating the system for effectiveness and making the necessary revisions and improvements commensurate with experience gained.

Major departures from the original system are better handled by periodic educational meetings like those held when the system was first implemented. The quarterly progress review sessions also are an excellent, on-going means for evaluating the system itself and making improvements.

Much of MBO is a state of mind—a way of doing things better and emphasizing continual improvement. Minds aren't changed overnight and neither will MBO be effective overnight.

## Caveat Emptor

One note of caution is appropriate for those executives who may require outside assistance when implementing. The rapid growth of MBO has brought with it the usual camp followers, soothsayers, and peddlers of magic. They take the form of consultants, business educators, and educational management associations. A week seldom passes but what another one publicly declares himself to be an expert in MBO. And, their ranks continue to grow, swelled as they are by the unqualified who read a few books on the subject, attend a session or two, and then hang up their shingles. Of such stuff experts and instant—but short lived—heroes are made.

Those who may consider outside help would be well advised to seek definitive answers to the following questions before retaining assistance:

1. Has he had at least five years of experience working with all phases of MBO? Hopefully he will have been a key manager operating in an organization which practiced MBO.
2. Has he made at least one full scale MBO installation and then lived with it for a minimum of three years?
3. Does his experience include all phases of MBO treated as a total management system or has he worked primarily with one or two facets of the total system, e.g., planning and/or evaluation of performance? The specialist is like a duck out of water when trying to advise on the many aspects of an initial installation.
4. Did he get the bulk of his knowledge from practical experience or is he quoting from a book or some quoter of quoters?
5. Does he talk practical, operating language or does he fill the air with definitions and high priced terms? Does he preach or practice?
6. Can he give specific examples as to how each phase of MBO works?
7. Will he give you an introduction to the subject and a thick report of recommendations, along with a big bill, and then leave or will he stay and work with you through the implementation stage by stage? The former should be avoided at all costs.
8. Is he knowledgeable when applying MBO to staff jobs or is his experience confined to applications to line jobs—where the application is much easier.

9. Can he cite some of his work where MBO hasn't been 100% effective? If he's had the requisite experience, he's had a few of these.
10. Is he trying to peddle a large number of forms and paperwork? Does he insist that all forms must be used exactly as recommended? Excessive paperwork is a major weakness of MBO and too many forms usually indicate a person who is more skilled in method than analysis. MBO requires an analytical mind.
11. Is he worth at least the $500 a day he should be charging? A qualified practitioner is worth this. If he's not charging and earning it, then he's probably the wrong man.

## Conclusion

The wealth of experience of the countless, diverse organizations which have embraced MBO dictates several conclusions which should be of benefit to those who may be considering installing an MBO system, to those who have just begun, and equally, if belatedly, to those which profess to practice MBO but wonder why they aren't. These conclusions may be summarized as follows:

1. In the hands of a competent management, MBO can be a potent vehicle for improving individual managerial productivity and total organization performance.
2. The number of installations has exceeded by far the amount of preparatory work.
3. Many of the later weaknesses can be traced back to the lack of proper implementation earlier.
4. The later success of MBO is directly proportional to the thoroughness of implementation.
5. The analysis preceding the decision whether or not to adopt MBO is of paramount importance especially in determining the degree of commitment on the part of management.
6. Implementation is time consuming, laborious, and often frustrating, but well worthwhile.
7. While the actual implementation stage is highly important, the actions which precede and follow this stage are equally important.
8. Only the more successful organizations practicing MBO have appreciated that implementation is the real guts of MBO.

1. For a detailed presentation of implementation see Dale D. McConkey, *How to Manage by Results,* Revised Edition, American Management Association, New York, 1967.

# 2
# Avoiding the Pitfalls
# of the MBO Trap

Although the use of management by objectives is accelerating in America and Europe, some critics are finding fault with the system. Indeed, a minority of managers feel disillusioned by the MBO approach.

The problems, however, are not with the system itself but with the incomplete or faulty applications of it. I shall try to suggest some ways of avoiding the most common mistakes.

Management by objectives was first coined by Peter Drucker back in 1955. In *The Practice of Management*, he wrote:

> What the business enterprise needs is a principle of management that will give full scope to individual strength and responsibility and at the same time give common direction of vision and effort, establish teamwork and harmonise the goals of the individual with the common weal. The only principle that can do this is Management by Objectives and self-control.

In the fifteen years that have passed since Drucker wrote these words we have got into substantial difficulties when we have strayed from the breadth and wider implications of this definition.

*At its best, management by objectives is a system that integrates the company's goals of profit and growth with the manager's needs to contribute and develop himself personally.* It is not a new wonder tool that can replace intelligent or sensitive leadership, and its misuse has probably caused more harm than good in the past few years.

Harry Levinson in one of the latest issues of the *Harvard Business Review* points out one of the major pitfalls of MBO. It fails, he says, to take into account the deeper emotional roots of a manager's motivation. The MBO process puts the manager in the same position as the rat in a psychologist's laboratory maze. The rat performs in a certain way to get the food; if he fails to perform, the experimenter starves the rat until he wants the food and learns to perform correctly. Says Harry Levinson:

> Management by objectives differs only in that it permits the man himself to determine his own bait from a limited range of choices. Having done so, the MBO process assumes that he will (a) work hard to get it,

Reprinted by permission of the publisher, *European Business*, Vol. 27, Autumn 1970, pp. 13-20.

(b) be pushed internally by reason of his commitment, and (c) make himself responsible to his organization for doing so.

In fairness to most managers, they certainly try, but not without increasing resentment and complaint for feeling like rats in a maze, guilt for not paying attention to those parts of the job not in their objectives, and passive resistance to the mounting pressure for ever-higher goals.

Levinson's criticisms are valid for narrowly conceived MBO programmes.

## The Manager's Secret Personal Goals

While management is only too ready to try to define the goals of the company, it often ignores the deeply-held personal goals of the manager himself. If the system is going to be management by objectives, some of them had better be *his* objectives. What does he want to do with his life? Where does he want to go? What will make him feel good about himself? What does he want to be able to look back on when he has expended his unrecoverable years?

Some feel that these are personal questions that have nothing to do with business. However, to try to ignore these deeply-felt needs is just a delusion, and any MBO system introduced without a concern for the answers to these questions will no doubt be heading towards failure.

But even when these priorities have been given their due, MBO programmes can fail to live up to their expectations. Very often this is because they were not introduced with the full support and understanding of the top management group. Indeed, management by objectives *must* involve all the executive managers of a company in a very direct way. Not only must they be involved in defining and rethinking their own objectives and the strategic purpose of the business, but they must also be receptive to comments, criticisms and suggestions from their subordinates.

Any attempt to introduce management by objectives "quietly"—for example, using it as only a part of a management development programme—is doomed to failure.

When the American company General Mills introduced an objectives-based performance appraisal programme in 1954, its initiative lay mainly with corporate personnel staff and its orientation was to personal development. Executive managers realized that individual improvement goals were unrelated to the overall business objectives and therefore not really meaningful.

After six years, the programme was dropped, and a new MBO approach was developed by the top executive group themselves. They saw MBO primarily as a valuable way to improve results through integrated planning and control. Personnel growth and development is a valuable

**The Essential Features of
Management by Objectives**

Management by objectives requires certain basic steps on the part of management. Any MBO system must include:

1. Reviewing critically and restating the company's strategic and tactical **plans.**
2. Clarifying with each manager his key results and performance standards and gaining his contribution and commitment to these. The relationship between each manager must be fully understood so that teamwork is facilitated.
3. Establishing rigorous **procedures for control** and self-control of progress. This will always include performance and potential review.
4. Establishing imaginative **Management Development Programmes,** including training plans, selection, salary and succession plans.
5. Finally, providing conditions in which these results can be achieved. This means a supportive climate of opinion, **effective organization structure,** and sound management control information.

A real programme of management by objectives is an integrating force in three ways. It brings together company planning and control with management development programmes. If these two do not support one another, neither can succeed.

It also bridges the growing gap between two great schools of management thought today: the quantitative school, which in effect says, "if you can't measure it, it doesn't exist," and the behavioral school, which is concerned with vital human factors such as motivation, teamwork, achievement and opportunities for growth.

MBO seeks to take from both these schools of thought the most practical methods and perceptions and build them into a total programme.

Finally, it makes a significant contribution to the establishment of an integrated management information system.

---

by-product since General Mills now regards MBO not so much as a programme as an approach to managing.

The senior management team should not approach MBO blissfully unaware of its demands on them. They should expect to attend briefing seminars, do some background reading, visit companies experienced in introducing MBO and thoroughly understand what the programme will involve.

Furthermore, it is unrealistic to believe that there is only *one* way to introduce management by objectives into a company. So much depends on the present situation. If, for example, a creative strategic plan, supported by operational plans covering even unit levels, already exists, it is possible to move in at unit level. Management by objectives can be used primarily as a tool to get these objectives into action through individual managers and teams of managers. On the other hand, management by objectives can also be adopted primarily to diagnose whether the organization structure is effective.

One company, the Société Photosia in France, introduced its MBO system in a two-fold manner. Firstly, the executives were given briefings in a series of seminars. They then set about defining their objectives for the company. A questionnaire was sent out to other members of the management team who had participated in the seminar. By asking for completely frank and honest answers, they cleared the air of problems of communication, delegation of authority and other potential friction points. For example, they found middle managers resented being given insufficient information or receiving data too late.

As a result, the top managers did some honest soul searching and tried to remedy the problems they had found. They also went over the objectives they had set up for the four years with their subordinates: the marketing manager, sales manager, the head of the Paris sales office, the head of the sales office for outside of Paris, the head of the marketing research office, the budget office, and so on.

Each time, the *general* objectives were used to define *specific* objectives for each manager. At each level there was feedback between the superior and the subordinate, bringing modifications along the way. The introduction of MBO at Photosia acted as a revealer of bad habits and ways of thinking and acting.

*Adopting MBO forces people to communicate and, what is important, should remind them of the human side of management.*

## Guidelines to Minimizing Problems

To minimize problems a large organization should do some pilot work before launching a total company-wide programme. Thus a group of high quality advisers can be trained and a tailor-made programme drawn up to suit the special needs of the business.

However, management by objectives should never be introduced horizontally at a single level of management. For example, the attempt to apply management by objectives at a supervisor level alone is certain to fail. As we have seen with Photosia, the right sequence is usually for the board to clear its mind on company objectives and then communicate them down the line. The disadvantage, though, is that the board cannot make its best decisions in isolation and the ideas and perceptions of managers must be tapped and communicated up to the board. When this dialogue is carried out sincerely, "both parties" learn from one another.

Clearly the MBO work is not complete until it has embraced the full range of objectives from top to bottom of the business. However, in practice, to insist that nothing can be done unless the main board itself makes a start may sometimes be naive. It can happen that operational managers are so heavily loaded with day-to-day work that they literally do not have the time to think ahead. Some crude work in setting unit objectives and in improving the performance of individual managers at a non-strategic level may be a necessary starting point.

When managers start showing signs of improvement, more time and better control over their immediate problems should result. It is then possible to do some really worthwhile work for the future. This short-term effort, moreover, is also a training and educational period. Later, when a company's strategic goals are well expressed, they can be communicated to a group of managers who already understand how to define their own objectives and who are committed to change. In this way, the process of planning, control and personal development becomes much more self-sustaining.

Consider this example of a launching sequence.

When Mr. J. Gulliver took over as chief executive of Fine Fare, a major British supermarket group, the company's profit was poor with no trend towards improvement. Policies and objectives were ill-defined. Control of the 320 supermarkets was over centralized, staff morale was poor and labour turnover high.

The first action taken was to review the company's strategy: each business sector was required to meet set financial criteria, unprofitable assets were pruned and working capital and cash flow policies established. Marketing policies were also reviewed and a manpower audit made. This alone saved the group £ 100,000. With strategy clear, Mr. Lynn Owen, Director of Trading Operations, set out primary objectives:

- to stop current trading loss position during the first six months and during the second six months to reach break-even. This required a 10% increase in current gross sales turnover whilst maintaining gross profit margins.

- to improve staff morale and weld its members into a team.

Detailed MBO methods were then used to express these objectives right down the line. A pilot project in one store led to a 65% sales increase in six months: all stores then adopted the method. Every manager has a job performance target sheet and in addition to normal management review there are four programme review meetings each year.

Thus at Fine Fare MBO started with a fundamental review of corporate strategy and the establishment of primary objectives; these were expressed through an improved organization structure with the *involvement and development of all the managers.* Incidentally, Mr. Gulliver reported recently that this work had in four years increased Fine Fare sales from 75 m. to 147 m.; reversed "no profits" into 4.75 m. profits; changed the return on capital invested from nil to 31%, and developed a management team with the will to continue this total strategy through the 70s.

## Sacrificing Men Who Cannot Be Spared

Another pitfall managements fall into is thinking that the MBO programme will take care of itself. Most successful management by objectives programmes have required an adviser* or team of advisers in order to help executive managers get the project moving. In fact, a recent survey by the British Industrial Society, covering some 19 firms which had been successfully using MBO for one year or more, indicated that all of them considered that there was need for an adviser.

If the adviser is of the highest quality and a man respected within the company, then top management has done more to convey its *real* belief in the programme than any formal written communication or presentation at a meeting. Willingness to sacrifice the time of a man who "cannot be spared" is the best testimony of the seriousness of intent of top management.

The adviser must be very thoroughly trained since he has two critical roles to play. *He must communicate the growing body of knowledge about the techniques, methods and know-how of management by objectives to managers.* This is an educational role. And he must *facilitate changes in the relationships between people* and help to establish a constructive climate of opinion for success. This is a social role, in which the adviser is acting as a change agent.

Here, the main problems, apart from selecting the wrong type of man, are advisers who become over-enthusiastic and do too much work personally; or becomes mechanistic in issuing forms and procedures inherited from another company or from a textbook. Advisers should normally be seen as people who launch a programme and the justification for continuing the appointment, even in a large group, must be most carefully considered. Lasting success arises when the work is so built into the normal process of executive management that little or no specialist support is required.

Mr. D. K. Van Houten, General Manager of K.L.M., Royal Dutch Airlines which introduced MBO into its worldwide field organization (with a work force of 13,000 people operating in 70 countries), points out that the adviser's ". . . catalyst role is of great importance in helping

---

*Editor's note: Mr. Humble speaks of an adviser in the British sense. In the United States we would speak of a consultant, whether internal or external.

managers to make this fresh appraisal of their objectives and their performance. It follows that the people assigned to this work, whether from inside or outside the business, must be of high quality and maturity and thoroughly trained in the latest techniques." The adviser must secure the positive participation of line management at every stage. As Mr. Van Houten concludes, "Attitudes cannot just be changed overnight and time, patience and persistent counselling may be necessary if lasting benefit is to be obtained."

## Cynicism About Another "Quack Programme"

However, even supposing the adviser understands his job and the board backs the programme 100%, there will be problems if management down the line is not fully briefed on what management by objectives stands for in a total sense, as well as the detailed mechanics.

On the face of it MBO looks incredibly simple. Many managers assume that they already know what is expected of them and that they already have effective standards and control procedures. *They are often cynical about a programme which purports to help them to do these obvious things better.* So the briefing must be done personally, patiently and imaginatively by senior management, as well as by the advisers. The way in which management by objectives integrates with existing systems in the business must be explained; otherwise it may appear to managers that an extra management system is being superimposed on one that already exists.

One major industrial concern in South Africa, disappointed with the progress of its MBO programme, wanted to find out why many managers resisted the work in spite of top management's briefing and explicit support. An attitude survey showed fundamental reasons for this resistance:

• the business was highly profitable. Managers were not self-critical and said complacently, "Things are going well. Why change?"

• good managers welcomed precise and challenging targets. Poor managers were justifiably insecure at the prospect of their inadequacy being revealed.

• managers had no confidence that top management would persist with MBO. They had past experience of new techniques and methods being introduced and their fading away unnoticed in a year or two.

Furthermore, managers who are asked to set their own objectives and therefore tell the truth about standards must be able to trust their superiors fully. When the briefing comes about, superiors must create a climate of confidence.

An essential discipline of management by objectives is the attempt to quantify precisely what one is trying to achieve, individually and as a company. Generalized statements such as "we will increase our sales next year" give way to statements such as "we will increase our penetration of the French market by 4% by July 1971 with products a, b and c."

Even in areas where at first sight it is difficult to find any standards at all, some progress can be made. For example, "keep the company pension plan under review" can after analysis lead to the statement, "by the end of 1970 make a proposal to the managing director of the company for a pension programme that will provide benefits which equal or exceed those offered in this area but with no increase in cost to employees or the company."

This insistence on quantification and measurable results is essential. However, a good MBO programme also recognizes that there are *some* objectives which as yet, with our limited information, can be stated only in qualitative or subjective terms. This may not be desirable, but it is as well to recognize areas which cannot be measured rather than to rely on inadequate measurable data. If one chooses the wrong quantitative standard then one can have dedicated effort going in the wrong direction. Consider the Veterans Administration in the U.S.A. referred to by Peter Drucker in *The Age of Discontinuity:*

"It may sound plausible to measure the effectiveness of a mental hospital by how well its beds—a scarce and expensive commodity—are utilized. Yet a study of the mental hospitals of the Veterans Administration brought out that this yardstick means mental patients being kept in the hospital—which, therapeutically, is about the worst thing that can be done to them. Clearly, however, lack of utilization, that is empty beds, would also not be the right yardstick. How does one then measure whether a mental hospital is doing a good job within the wretched limits of our knowledge of mental diseases?"

Clearly a company working in MBO has a delicate middle path to tread. On the one hand, it must insist on thinking through every key task and every important objective and spelling out as precisely and quantitatively as possible the result to be achieved. On the other, *a detailed spelling out of objectives may only complicate the task of reaching them. Specific statements give the opposition an opportunity to organize its defenses.* Suppose, for example, that a president is convinced that his company must phase out of the principal business it has been in for 35 years!

## Limitations of Long-Range Planning

Many companies are stimulated by their MBO programme to make their first Long-Range Plan, and all the evidence shows that this is a fruitful piece of work. For example, the first attempt to plan long-term brings an integrating and unifying power to the group of managers at the top of the business. It is a catalyst of radical change rather than a minor improvement of the existing situation. It creates an attitude of mind focused more on tomorrow's opportunities than yesterday's mistakes. Certainly it facilitates communications up, down and across the business, and compels serious thought about the correct sequence and methods of business planning from top to bottom in the organization.

However, Long-Range Planning and its contribution can be overstated. It is not a substitute for an entrepreneur; it is not a magic and final answer, but rather a series of answers which are by a cascade approach constantly refined and improved. It certainly isn't easy work, and at some stages of company growth—for example, rapidly exploiting an unexpected opportunity—the full sequence may be inappropriate in its complete form for all companies.

A problem often raised by companies is, "Should objectives be changed if circumstances change during the planning period?" Obviously, this reflects a fear that to make a plan is to create inflexibility. In our experience, a well-based plan with the assumptions clearly stated and agreed is in fact a foundation for flexibility. When urgent decisions and changes have to be made, those involved start off with a common basis of knowledge and understanding and, therefore, perceptive and rapid change is facilitated. However, unless there are really significant changes in the premises on which the original plans were based, it is unwise to make too many changes. After all, the challenge for managers when the going gets rough is not to give up, but to find other means of reaching the agreed goal.

## Linking the Company's Objectives with the Individual Manager's Results

Another problem to avoid is having each employee pursue his goal without taking into account the overall objectives of the company.

Photosia found, for instance, that its sales and service departments, which formerly worked closely together, were suffering from lack of communication. What had happened was that after the introduction of MBO, the sales department had its set of objectives and no longer felt concerned about what occurred after the sale. Each one, they felt, should take care of his own objectives and not worry about his neighbour. To remedy the situation, management was obliged to set joint objectives shared by both departments.

The MBO system must ensure that individual managers' objectives mesh not only with their colleagues' objectives but also with total company goals.

An executive at Honeywell, Inc., interviewed by the National Industrial Conference Board, said, "There are two things that might almost be considered fundamental creeds at Honeywell: decentralized management is needed to make Honeywell work and management by objectives is needed to make decentralization work."

And to make MBO work there must be two elements: the *Key Results Analysis and the Job Improvement Plan.* Some companies believe that all that is required is to establish a series of personal objectives for achievement in a defined period. These selected areas are obviously chosen for their improvement potential, and managers are motivated to achieve these limited goals.

The problem arises when they achieve these goals by neglecting other important areas of the job. Success in the limited areas is defeated by losses elsewhere. However, if the manager is thoroughly instilled with the idea of the total success of the job, he loses grasp on *priorities.* Which area, he may ask himself, needs improvement? It is to handle this problem that the Job Improvement Plan concept exists.

The two work in tandem. The Key Results Analysis serves as the basis of achievement for the total job. The Job Improvement Plan highlights the key tasks that require an improved performance.

*The review of the manager's performance* (and the review of his potential) are two other touchy areas of MBO.

In a major study of six British companies it was revealed that with most manager appraisal schemes,

- appraisers are reluctant to appraise,
- interviewers are even more reluctant to interview,
- the follow-up is inadequate. Reports carry little or no weight when transfers, promotion or training are considered.

If the MBO system is fully applied, the number of problems in this field should be reduced. Discussions usually improve because they are based substantially on agreed and, as far as possible, quantified goals.

In addition, fewer ugly surprises should occur at review meetings. Review is not an isolated event once a year but rather an additional occasion for taking a total view of results and resetting objectives. This total review supports an on-going, day-to-day, week-to-week management review.

Potential review often creates problems because it is poorly handled. It is a subjective area and common sense and discretion must be used in discussions with the manager. Very often some things should *not* be discussed at all. His superior should handle this delicate subject in conjunction with a staff expert such as the personnel manager. Only thus can the manager's potential be put into context with the openings and career possibilities available throughout the firm.

The personnel manager should be able to help in another field of MBO: *training.* No doubt everyone in a management line-up is *for* training. Yet how many times do companies run management training courses for, say, their middle managers only to stifle the enthusiasm generated when it runs counter to the practices of top management?

Or how often are the training opportunities incomplete? The manager's supervisor may frequently fail to identify from the Performance and Potential Reviews the range and kind of training needed for his subordinate. In many cases he just doesn't know what facilities are available.

It is also easy to get sidetracked into concentrating on only *management* training.

In many cases, particularly at the middle and lower levels, success as a manager requires an up-to-date technical knowledge. The overconcern with management training may lead to the neglect of identification of technical and administrative training needs.

## The Invasion by Unwieldy, Useless Control/Information Systems

The whole concept of management by objectives involves a deep consideration of control and information systems. They are required to provide focus of attention and feedback on the progress of key business and personal objectives. It is not surprising, however, that a number of companies run into problems with their control systems.

Usually this arises because they do not make a thorough analysis of the total control pattern. They improve separate pieces of information without looking at the relationship between the various parts. Even more dangerous is to focus attention—through control information—on unimportant matters.

An American-owned cattle-feed manufacturing business based in Europe did exactly this. It developed an extremely tight control over labour-staffing levels, utilization, and so on, while keeping its control information on material cost and yield primitive. Yet labour costs represented 12% of selling price and materials over 50%.

Another problem is that *additional controls are added without the company giving itself the discipline of removing a number of existing ones*. Thus there is extra confusion and a proliferation of paperwork. A management by objectives programme should reduce the amount of existing control information whilst concentrating control patterns on the vital results areas.

Having ironed out all of the above problems, management may be tempted to sit back and take it easy. It will have forgotten another important aspect: *maintaining momentum*.

Certainly, there seems to be an extraordinary human capacity to convert the most exciting, vital and dynamic concepts of management into dreary, mechanistic routines. Without imaginative plans to prevent this, MBO can deteriorate over a period of time.

As Brian Viner, Director of Viners Ltd., once said of his experience of management by objectives:

> Even where this concept of management has been completely built into the business and apparently accepted, it does need constant leadership to ensure that it is kept up to the mark.

One important way to maintain vitality is to keep the system under constant review. Paperwork, for example, which was essential as an educational tool in the early stages of the programme, might well be discarded once everybody has the habit of managing in this way.

Colt Heating & Ventilation is a privately-owned company employing 800 people in Britain, Holland, Belgium, and Germany; it introduced MBO in 1966. Significant benefits followed, including a streamlined organization structure, better delegation, a long-range business plan and financial benefits of over £ 100,000 per annum. However, a critical review of the MBO system showed certain weaknesses:

* too many performance standards for each job,
* too much paperwork,
* too much time in job reviews looking to the past,
* not enough initiative for change being maintained at middle levels of management.

Paperwork was drastically simplified and every manager has his results, controls, review and improvement plans on two pieces of paper. These are kept in a pocket diary for ease of regular use.

All managers have been trained to prepare for review meetings, and as the General Sales Manager comments:

> Already we have a greater desire to participate fully. We have resolved to devote no more than 25% of our job review time to looking back and 75% to looking forward. The benefits are enormous.

## Conclusion

Management by objectives will create its own problems in the long run if it is not treated as an approach which must grow and develop organically to meet the changing needs of the business. This growth should not be haphazard. It must be planned and led by the top management team, and treated as just as important as developing new markets and new production facilities.

Avoiding the pitfalls of the MBO trap demands constant watching of the way the system is functioning. Is there proper communication from the lower levels of the company on up? Is the system being kept flexible?

Are the objectives of both the company *and* its managers being kept flexible? Are the objectives of both the company and its managers being taken into account?

MBO is a two-sided system—one side technical, the other human. They are closely related and putting the emphasis on one as opposed to another is bound to lead to failure. Concentrating on performance goals or production levels and forgetting about the delegation of authority, the dialogue, the individual's development and fulfillment is the surest way to fall headlong into the pit.

# 3

*Jack L. Mendleson*

# Personal Targets
# for Effective Management

The manager of men* faces two central problems:

- how can he make decisions and supervise in such a manner that he achieves the results for which he is charged?
- at the same time, how can he maintain and develop his unit to achieve "bigger and better things" through time?

These two problems are faced by all managers in business, government, and education. The problems apply to top-, middle-, and first-level managers.

To work out these problems successfully, the manager must differentiate carefully among the individuals reporting to him. The perceptive manager realizes that: (1) capacity to perform an assigned task varies widely from one individual to the next; and (2) each individual brings to the organization a unique mix of strengths and weaknesses.

Individual goal setting (IGS) is one means of differentiating among individuals. IGS—both a technique and philosophy—takes the individual at his present stage of development. Then, through a continuous goal-setting process, the successful individual gradually learns to handle more responsibility and freedom.

What is IGS? A method and philosophy for establishing *work goals* for individual contributors for a specific target date. Work goals are aims or results. Each work goal is a clear statement of what a man wants to do and when he wants to do it.

Why bother? IGS provides a workable connection for corporate planning and control, results-oriented performance appraisal, management and employee development, and systems of rewards for performance. IGS builds a two-way street, an operational way of fusing organizational goals and individual contributor's needs. This two-way street encourages: (1) management by exception; and (2) the growth of each individual toward self-direction at a pace which is reasonable for that individual.

Who sets the goals? Ideally every person who contributes to the re-

Reprinted by permission of the publisher, *Canadian Business Magazine,* Vol. 43, No. 1, January 1970, pp. 54-58.
*Editor's note: I should have said "people." J.L.M.

sults of his organization sets goals for his own work with the help of his boss. In organizations where goal setting has not received much thought, it is best to start with top managers and involve contributors in IGS from the top downward, level by level, period after period.

How often are goals set? Once every operating period. The length of the period varies from one organization to the next. The operating period is the time in which significant progress toward operating results can reasonably be expected. This may be one month, a quarter, or six months. Ordinarily one year is too long.

How are the goals set? The contributor reviews the planned contribution of his operating unit to the objectives of the overall organization. He also reviews, by means of his job description, his own continuing assignment. From this review he defines his major *responsibilities.* Then he writes a letter to his boss. This letter states: (1) the individual's work *goals* for the operating period; and (2) the way in which his progress toward goals can be seen (indicators). Then the contributor and his boss discuss this RIG (responsibilities, indicators, and goals) in a face-to-face meeting. The contributor can expect to make changes in his original ideas the first few times around. As a result of the dialogue the contributor and his boss reach agreement about reasonable goals.

The agreement defines good performance by the contributor. If no agreement is reached, the two of them continue the dialogue. Nothing is more important to the organization than this agreement. Can a contributor be too busy "getting there" to determine where he wants to go? The agreement, once reached, is a two-way commitment. The subordinate commits himself to the goals and the superior commits himself to helping as needed. This commitment is confirmed by a memo written by the subordinate addressed to the superior. The contributor and his boss each keep a copy and send a third one to a central person (such as the personnel director). At the end of the operating period the contributor and his boss meet again and review the progress toward achieving the goals. Following the review new goals are set for the next period. The new goal setting might be called recycling..

In summary, how are the goals set? (1) The contributor defines his RIG. (2) The contributor and his boss discuss this RIG, modify it where necessary, and eventually reach an agreement. (3) This agreement is confirmed by memo. (4) At the end of the period the contributor and his boss review the progress toward goals, using the memo as the standard. Then they set new goals for the next period as summarized in the table on the following page.

Is this all there is to it? No. This is a workable procedure, used every day by some of America's most successful corporations. But IGS is also a state of mind, a focus upon human effectiveness as a means of profitable operation and human satisfaction.

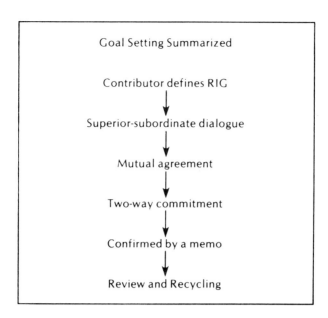

Goal Setting Summarized

Contributor defines RIG

↓

Superior-subordinate dialogue

↓

Mutual agreement

↓

Two-way commitment

↓

Confirmed by a memo

↓

Review and Recycling

Is IGS new? No, the basic ideas are ancient. IGS is closely akin to management by objectives and management by results. Hopefully IGS is the most understandable way of viewing recent developments at the frontiers of management research and practice. IGS is analogous to jogging. Just as there is nothing new about running or the need for exercise, there is nothing new about the need for objectives or goals and the need for the superior-subordinate understanding. But the new formulations—IGS and jogging—provide a systematic approach confirmed by substantial research.

## Applying IGS in a Real Estate Office

After about a year of successful operation working alone as an independent realtor in a large metropolitan area, Phil Criss decided to hire a sales force to help him sell residential real estate. Phil felt this move was necessary in order to become more "visible" to people who were new in the area. He had also discovered that potential customers had more confidence in large real estate offices than in the one-man office operated from the realtor's home. Therefore, Phil leased an office in a thriving shopping center and over a period of a few months hired six people to sell real estate. Three of the six worked part-time only. All six work entirely on commission. The office pays for the expenses of newspaper advertising, "for sale" signs, and all office expenses, including the services of a full-time secretary.

Phil began with the idea of establishing a "big happy family" of sales people. The sales people were to have considerable freedom in deciding when to work and virtually complete freedom in methods of sales operation. Phil planned to intervene only in the "closing" of sale, a rather technical matter with important legal considerations for both buyer and seller.

Apparently Phil began the expansion program with the notion that each sales person would try to maximize his income from commissions.

## Problems Involved in Application

Pat Williams, a married woman with children of school age, has sold part-time for six months. Apparently her main reason for taking the job was to keep occupied and to meet interesting people. Her sales record shows that she is very ineffective. Most of her successful contacts with customers were made during the one day a week when she had "floor time." (During a salesman's floor time all the walk-in and call-in business go to that salesman.) Pat was reluctant to go out of the office and "beat the bushes" as Phil would have preferred. Even worse, if a customer inquired about a particular home or particular region that was unavailable, Pat would politely say, "Sorry we couldn't help you." She did not suggest other fairly obvious possibilities. When the potential customer walked out he would seldom be seen again.

Roscoe Shepp, another salesman, liked to hang around the office a lot and tell potential customers his latest jokes. Roscoe felt it was important to kid the customer to establish rapport. The customers did not particularly appreciate this approach. Phil believed that Roscoe wasted a lot of time which could be spent talking business and actually showing properties. Phil felt certain that Roscoe could improve his mediocre sales record with a more business-oriented approach.

Roland Ellis caused more concern than any of the others. Roland retired from his previous company at an early age with a substantial pension. Despite his lack of previous sales experience he has become an excellent salesman in his six months with the Criss Agency. At the end of the first quarter Phil noticed that Roland was on the way to selling one million dollars worth of property in the year. Phil remarked to Roland, "You're making it! Keep it up and you'll do a million dollars of business this year." Roland quickly calculated his commission on one million dollars of sales, discovered the commission income plus his pension would put him in too high an income tax bracket, and took two weeks vacation. Unfortunately this sudden vacation came just at the time when Phil was hospitalized for a minor operation.

## The Specific Application of IGS

To begin to remedy these problems the author suggested to Phil that he:

1. have each individual salesman submit a goals letter quarterly.
2. sit down with each individual and review and modify the goals set. Over time certain policies will be established. Some levels of sales will be too low to be adequate goals. Through time the RIG will be established.
3. at the end of the quarter, review progress toward goals. In the case of inadequate performers the discussion could center around work plans for the next period (i.e., just how can the goals for the next period be met? What new sales approaches might work?)

By means of these three steps Phil can:

1. Help Pat and Roscoe see the large investment the agency makes in each of them. Then Phil may be able to suggest to each of them reasonable goals and reasonable levels of improvement from one period to the next. Phil may also be able to suggest improved approaches to contacting and dealing with clients. Finally, if either Pat or Roscoe cannot achieve a reasonable level of performance within two or three periods, Phil can begin encouraging them to look for other work. At the point where Phil decides an inadequate performer has been given a "fair chance" Phil can establish minimum conditions (level of sales) necessary for continuing the performer's "floor time."
2. Help Roland see that high sales is not necessarily a sufficient measure of success from the agency's point of view. Obviously Phil needs to establish vacation policies which, if violated, will lead to later penalties in floor time. On the positive side, Phil can offer the top-selling salesman his choice of floor time and "feature spots" in the advertising. Roland still may decide to limit his total earnings, but at least Phil will have made a more concerted effort to reward the performance.

(Obviously a more detailed analysis is needed. Phil needs to study the individual salesman very carefully to discover just what they do find rewarding.)

## The Observed Values of IGS

Listed above are a few valuable applications of IGS in a particular real estate agency situation. Individual Goal Setting offers Phil the chance to correct his people's mistaken notions of how much one can "get away with" at the agency. At the same time satisfactory performers retain the appropriate areas of freedom and the possibility of earning truly meaningful rewards for successful goal attainment. At the time of this writing Phil was grappling with the IGS ideas and was confident that they could be easily applied in the next few months.

## Applying IGS in Larger, More Complex Organizations

The real estate organization just described was small and organizationally simple, with only one level of supervision and no development of staff or supporting functions. In more complex organizations many additional forces come into play which may distract individuals from their basic performances, their basic goals in the organization. Goal setting as outlined in Table 1 really helps overcome the distractions! But the whole subject becomes somewhat more complicated in the more complicated organization.

## Kinds of Goals to Aim For

In his book *Management by Objectives,* George Odiorne, an outstanding proponent of goal setting, tells us there are four kinds of goals. First, routine or regular duties constitute results that the organization must have, and that can be measured by exception. Second, problem-solving goals typically are the central issue in goal setting; the organization needs to have results in problem solving, and results can be assessed by solutions within the time promised. Third, creative or innovative goals are nice to have, and can be measured by stages of completion. Finally, personal development goals must be established if the organization is to retain its best members in the long-run.

## Functional Components of IGS

Another helpful way of viewing goal setting is by breaking the subject down into its functional components. Through lengthy research six content categories have been established:

1.  Goal characteristics. The general category is illustrated by this statement: "My boss and I not only regularly put my work goals into writing, but we also keep them up-to-date." If the manager agrees with this statement, this contributes to the conclusion that the performer and his boss are setting goals in conjunction to a large extent.
2.  Feedback and accountability. Here is a negative item in this category. "It's only when there's an emergency 'upstairs' that I get any indication how I'm doing, and then it's usually negative." If the manager agrees, this contributes to the conclusion he and his boss are not really setting goals to any great extent.

3. Measurement or verification and standards and par. Here is a verification statement near the high end of the scale: "I have verifiable work goals; I mean, at the date agreed upon, my boss can tell readily how close I've come to accomplishing my goals."
4. Paths to goals and path facilitation. Here is a middle-range example: "Sometimes my boss asks me just how I plan to reach my work goals, and sometimes he doesn't."
5. Career development; personal preferences; subordinate autonomy. Here is another "half-way" example: "My boss will sit down and talk about my long-term career goals if I push him hard enough."
6. Relation of goal attainment to individual rewards. Here is an item at the low end of the scale: "At my organization level, about equal percentage increases in salary generally go to everybody whenever increases are passed out."

## Summary and Conclusion of Project and Theory

Goal setting is the process of establishing individual work goals—aims or results—for a specific time period. Superior and subordinate must agree, but the initiating responsibility lies in the hands of the individual.

The importance of individual goal setting should be clear. The logic is persuasive—RIG, dialogue, agreement, two-way commitment. The real estate illustration points up the possibilities in the small, simple organization. The discussion of components shows what must be done in the more complex organization.

Three basic principles underlie this article. First, to perform well, the individual must know what is expected of him. Goal setting adds to his knowledge. Second, to perform better than before, an individual must receive definite quick feedback about past performance. The goal setting review provides this feedback. Third, to improve and continue to improve, an individual must receive assistance as he needs it. The two-way commitment of goal setting helps assure this assistance.

George S. Odiorne

# 4

# The Politics
# of Implementing MBO

It is not likely today that many managers will object to management by objectives as a concept or philosophy. The question of available alternatives seems unanswerable in the face of such an eminently logical developmental system. Why, then, do people seem to have reservations about committing themselves to it? Why, indeed, do some find it impossible to make it work, while others report great success in its application and enthusiasm for its effects?

One of the major reasons for the failure of MBO in many organizations is that those in charge fail to recognize the political character of the implementation process. MBO is indeed logical and systematic, but it also must deal with a number of factors, including power and authority, the organization form, and the values and expectations of people. The MBO implementer, therefore, must recognize the reality of political constraints and manage them during the process of implementation.

If he fails to do so, MBO may start off with a flourish but gradually fade away; begin well, reach a certain level, and stall; or start well but produce a dramatic failure and be dropped, becoming a taboo subject thereafter. Success, on the other hand, results when MBO begins at a sound level of acceptance, gains from its own successes, continues to flourish and expand its influence and contributions, and is widely appreciated and supported.

Case studies of successful and unsuccessful implementation plans show that there are three major avenues currently used for implementation of MBO and that all three must be modified by political constraints characteristic of every organization. This article will briefly illustrate the three approaches, and then describe the political considerations that must guide them.

Reprinted by permission of the publisher, *Business Horizons*, Vol. 17, No. 3, June 1974, pp. 13-22.

## Three Approaches (Figure 11)

Methods of implementing MBO may rely on the use of raw power and direct orders, persuasion, or education. Case studies indicate that no one route is best; instead, analysis of the organizational climate and the situation will indicate the best approach—one alone or perhaps a combination of all of them. A specific set of steps in linear form would be highly desirable, but such a method would probably miss the mark and lead to an implementation that fails in one or more respects.

### Authoritarian Directives

It is an article of faith, supported by some research evidence, that the installation of MBO must start at the top. In part, such a beginning is justified. The purpose of the business flows down and the methods of getting there flow up. The strategies of the business are chosen by persons with high-level responsibility, whereas the operational objectives are the responsibility of lower levels. This might lead to the conclusion that the power of the higher-ranks must be invoked to direct implementation. This approach, which Joseph Juran has labeled the "king's ear" approach, is founded upon the assumption that if the staff man can get the president's car and cause him to issue the right directives everybody below him will obey. The concept is that of the self-executing order, a rare phenomenon.

**Figure 11**
The Three Approaches and the Political Constraints.

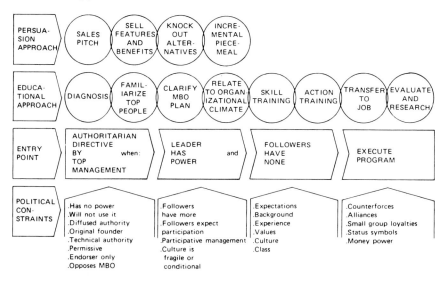

Behavioral scientists deplore such autocratic methods but they are used in some organizations where tight technical organization and discipline are the mode of operation. Where the following conditions exist in the organization, such authoritarian methods will indeed work:

> The leader has absolute power and is willing to use it.
>
> The followers need the leader more than he needs them, because he has knowledge, skills, or resources which they need but that he can withhold.
>
> The followers have lived under unexplained orders for some time, perhaps for their entire working lifetime, and have learned to expect them, even when the subject is MBO.
>
> The situation requires autocratic orders. The leader is expected to state his orders quickly and clearly if he is in charge of a ship at sea in a storm, a plane in distress, or a temporary work force.

Under proper circumstances, autocratic implementation of MBO has been successful. This is not to say that all situations demand it; many are not suitable for autocracy—the college faculty or the volunteer group, for example. The major limitations of the use of force to implement MBO lie in the situation in which it is applied. Where the boss has no power or has power and will not use it, the followers expect to be consulted and have something important to withhold (and will do so). Under these circumstances, the authoritarian directive will produce counter-responses that block MBO.

### Persuasion

One reason for the failure of MBO to achieve its full potential has been the misguided reliance upon persuasion as a means of implementation. The guru or inspirational speaker comes to a meeting of management and through horatory lectures persuades everyone that MBO will be beneficial. Persuasion methods ordinarily can be distinguished by their content.

*First,* they appear to be balanced, that is, they explain all of the advantages of MBO, then turn and judiciously explain the disadvantages of not managing by objectives. This is clearly an advocacy approach designed to persuade. *Second,* features and benefits are grist for the persuader's mill. A description of the features and a discussion of the usefulness of each are persuasive tactics.

Third, in this debater's form of persuasion, all of the alternatives for solving some chronic problems are noted. Then each is knocked out in turn, excepting the MBO solution. The *fourth* form of persuasion, incrementalism, is probably the most risky. It consists of starting with a simple segment of the whole program and selling it. "You simply sit down once a year with all of your subordinates, and talk to them about their objectives" would be an incremental approach. Many instances of MBO failure have been caused by incrementalism in the introduction. The concept began as a change in the company performance appraisal system or as a salary review plan, but lost favor when the full implications of the time and effort demanded were realized.

Persuasion is the favorite method of hortatory speakers and consultants. It is detested and avoided by academics who would prefer an approach that relies almost wholly upon education, particularly in the underlying theory. As a complete method of installation, it obviously leads to disillusionment. Yet it has a useful part in implementation in the early stages, if only to get people to submit to education.

## Educational Programs

One of the more successful patterns for installing an MBO program is a continuous educational effort which teaches the concepts, philosophy, and procedures of MBO in detail. As a training subject, MBO has many excellent features.

> Training should produce behavior change, and training in MBO is measurable. It can be readily determined of the training worked: Did the trainees set objectives or didn't they?

> The quality of the results can be noted clearly. The course may suggest, for example, that a manager should establish three classes of objectives. The effect on the manager can be checked by examining sample goals statements.

> MBO comprises a sound basis for relating training to the job. Some training sessions require students to set objectives on their job as part of the course; they learn by doing what they are being taught.

> MBO provides a vehicle for teaching more general management education. It can be the framework for teaching motivational methods, management functions (organizing, planning, and controlling), and such interpersonal skills as coaching, counseling, and listening.

> MBO can teach interpersonal skills that can be applied on the job, rather than skills which the boss will not permit or endorse when the trainee returns to the desk or plant floor. This is especially true if the boss attends the session or is used as a trainer.

> MBO can reinforce company objectives rather than become, as it does in many behavioral courses, an internal reform movement to overcome the organization's autocratic or bureaucratic tendencies or to produce some new kind of organizational form.

> MBO is capable of maintaining a high level of trainee interest, since it deals with the real world of work and world problems, and with interpersonal and group relations problems.

> Conceptually, it is easy to learn, for MBO training courses ask people to "talk shop"; they have a tendency to do this whether they are in training or not. Except for courses in which the trainers have worked hard at obscuring the obvious, the language is operational and practical.

The basic framework of MBO permits it to take a behavioral or logical systems direction without appearing contradictory or mutually exclusive. This means that it can appeal to the personnel and training men in the organization, as well as to the engineer, controllers, and dollar-centered managers.

Both insiders and outsiders can be used as trainers. The insiders have more knowledge of the business and can deal with real world problems, and the outsiders can be briefed sufficiently to relate to the world of the trainee.

## The Politics of Implementation

The constraint of organizational politics is a formidable barrier to implementation. Unless it is taken into account, it will outweigh the logical and behavioral efforts that go into directing, persuading, or educating people to accept a new management system. Several political factors must be considered.

### The Power Structure

An often overlooked political factor affecting the implementation of MBO is the power structure of the organization. MBO is rightly seen as having the potential for shifting the locus of power inside the organization, and accordingly will meet political resistance from those who might be affected adversely.

The resistance of such persons as corporate attorneys or other executive staff members is frequently rooted in the probability of shifting power. A person who has developed a strong personal relationship with the top officers, in which they draw upon his counsel in all sorts of matters other than law or his specialty, is clearly threatened by systematic management. In one large firm, the corporate purchasing director had performed numerous personal favors for the president and his family, and had attained the status of a family favorite. When MBO was suggested, this family retainer saw immediately that his status could be threatened and he greeted the proposal with a flurry of cluckings and exceptions. He noted its flaws and limitations, insisted that it was nothing new, and adopted other delaying and obstructive tactics familiar to the MBO administrator.

In another firm it was the tax manager who headed up the political resistance movement against MBO. The manager had helped the family with the controlling interest to minimize their personal estate taxes over the years, and he hoped to retain his personal position of favor.

### The Diffusion of Authority

In many modern corporations there has been a blurring of the decision-making power. Starting at the top, where the charismatic leader or dynamic chief has been supplanted by "the office of the president" generally occupied by two or three men, it is difficult to identify a single channel for decisions. This has some advantage in gaining acceptance for decisions, but it also generates political maneuvering in order to get objectives decided upon. In other organizations, the key committees of the board may produce some mutually exclusive objectives which they are pushing. These require some political tacking and hauling in order to make a particular position dominant.

In government, of course, the basic motivator of the system and its servants is political power, and the diffusion of power is well understood by most of the people who share in it. The cabinet member knows the bureau chiefs ostensibly under his control can lobby their congressman to protect a job or program. A letter from the congressman can always sway the bureaucrat. At the same time, the large departmental public relations departments in government can swing public opinion to press congressmen for increased space or increased military and welfare appropriations.

Such a political climate requires more patience, continuous effort, and persuasion to get a management style change such as MBO into effect. Even some trading of favors and arm twisting may be necessary.

### The Fragility of Participation

Even in those organizations where participation of the lower levels has been designated as the mode of operation, it is possible that it can be withdrawn. Where the possibilities of power exist, there is a possibility that power once withheld will be reasserted.

Take the case of the governor of a state who was enthused about MBO and employed a participative style of management. He delegated extensively and pressed decisions down to the lowest possible level. This produced high morale at lower levels. But the governor left office and his successor immediately suspended all of the mechanics of participative management and centralized everything in his office. In the process, he declared his support of MBO, but in fact he killed it by locating total control in his office.

Similar experiences have been found where a humanistic president of a corporation installed a participative MBO program. Upon his retirement a four-star general assumed his office and promptly applied autocratic controls. He eliminated certain policy committees, scuttled meetings which had been the major vehicle for MBO, and ordered the appraisal form abandoned and training programs stopped. The reason he did so was plausible. The company had been in market trouble, and a lax style of MBO had made the corporation an easygoing but unprofitable place. After a turnaround, he retired. Major promotions were made from within, the earlier participative management style of MBO was restored, and the results were excellent.

It is a hard political fact about organizations, public and private, that MBO which is inextricably tied to participative management may be damaged if an autocratic boss gets on top. MBO which is top down and somewhat autocratic to begin with suffers no such setback. On the other hand, it never had the developmental and humanistic benefits of participative management in the first place.

---

"It is a hard political fact . . . that MBO which is inextricably tied to participative management may be damaged if an autocratic boss gets on top. MBO which is top down . . . "suffers no such setback.."

---

## The Problem of Countermoves

A strong move to produce an MBO program that would change the behavior of people or the arrangement of the organization and how it does its work can be counted on to produce an equal and opposite reaction somewhere. It may be expressed by scoffing; by wisecracks; by acronyms for MBO ("Massive Bowel Obstruction" or "Mr. Big's Obsession" to name two); or by overintellectualizing the obvious.

In other cases, the reaction produces some fairly stiff fights, scuffles, and corporate infighting. This is not peculiar to MBO, but is characteristic of political response to changes that will shuffle the power structure and power alignments in the organization. Changes in cost accounting or market research, a new salary system, or simply reassignment of parking places will trigger the counterresponse.

Predicting the reaction and pinpointing its source is one of the arts of the organization politician. He is then able to take corrective, remedial, or ameliorative action before the problem arises. In some instances, he finds these sources of reaction by testing his idea in tentative form, sending out position papers and holding discussions in order to elicit such responses. If the trouble spots surface after installation, they can be patched up through trading, arm twisting, or muscle, or by changing the program.

Even though most politically aware persons realize the advantages of option *b* over option *a*, it is often impossible to get complete support. Therefore, the need to modify and amend the MBO program after it is underway, for example in the second go-around, should be considered one of the political realities. Running roughshod over those who would resist a new idea not only stiffens the backbone of the resistors, but makes all changes less likely to be accepted.

## Unit Loyalty

An often overlooked rule of allegiance is that people center their loyalties around the smallest unit of which they are a member rather than the overall organization. The basic unit for the soldier is his squad, not the armed forces or the free world. It is the engineering project for the engineer, rather than the entire firm. The personnel expert is often more centered in his staff department's goals than the corporation's.

This fact has great significance for implementing MBO. It means that the objectives must be related to this man, this job, in this unit, this year. Expecting people to be motivated by grand designs and overall global strategies is unrealistic and contrary to political realities.

In one large oil company, the MBO program met poor acceptance in the engineering and development departments, even though it was a smashing success in the refinery and the marketing department. The resistance in the two departments was not only embarrassing, but threatened to weaken the program in other areas as well. A wise MBO administrator suggested a conference in which the people in engineering designed their own MBO system, with special salmon-colored forms and a different kind of calendar of events. The program immediately began to operate smoothly.

Diversity in applications of the MBO program may be necessary for the political reasons of unit loyalty. Permitting variances in details, in application, in timing, and in sequencing of events may assist implementation.

## The Individualists

One of the greatest potential sources of political opposition to an MBO program is the uniformity and conformity imposed by some systems. When the MBO program is seen as a set of forms to be filed—a cookbook set of procedures—it will run into individuals who resist.

The reasons lie in the value systems of technical, managerial, and professional people, who possess primarily middle-class values. They are most often the educated professionals, although a degree or college experience is not necessarily the sole criterion. People without degrees who have associated with such persons at work have often acquired their values. They cherish their own professional individuality, and while an objective observer might see this individuality as insignificant, it has an important bearing upon the behavior of the person. The desire to participate in decisions is strongly held by the middle-class employee, and denial of the wish will produce political effort contrary to the whole idea.

Sometimes the individualists will object to the name of a program. Some of the best MBO programs have found it necessary to adopt another label, calling it "goals management" or permitting major subunits to use their own names or acronyms. The fetish of maintaining a single unified program with a common label, often adhered to by corporate staffs, can work to the disadvantage of the program.

The image of being "unprofessional" or requiring unprofessional behavior can be the kiss of death to any kind of new procedure. The unexplained and seemingly pointless order or the cold memo not accompanied by a dialogue increase the likelihood that the program will be seen as an indignity or as unprofessional.

This perception can be extended to the specifics of the standards of performance which are produced from the goals-setting process installed. If it seems to be enforcing conformity and attacking present eccentricities, the whole program becomes suspect.

One of the major features of MBO which makes it politically palatable to professionals is that it is indifferent to activities but is deeply concerned about output. This assurance of the protection of individual idiosyncracies is important to professionals.

**Status Symbols**
Attention must be paid to the effect of the new system on the present structure of status in the organization. Status symbols are the subtle indicators of a person's standing in relation to others.

In some instances, there are the physical symbols of office, such as uniforms, desks, office fittings, parking places, and the like. In other instances, more probable in an MBO program, it will be the reduction in influence or authority for some, as the center of decision making moves to a lower level. In one bank where MBO was installed, the power to make certain equipment purchase decisions was delegated. Yet when the new equipment arrived the president was shocked. "My feelings were hurt that they hadn't consulted me," he reported later.

Social and status significance is attached also to certain prerequisites or roles. If an MBO system robs a person of such status symbols as authority to conduct the annual performance review or to award raises, resistance from the deprived can be expected. He is, in his own mind, forced to downgrade, depreciate, or even attack MBO. However, the true reasons for the opposition will not be revealed.

Such an attack is not conducted openly, of course, for the losses would appear to be a trivial, and perhaps even an immature, reason for attacking something as logical as MBO. Thus the attack will be couched in terms that are eminently logical and rational in language, even though the basis is far from being rational.

**Organization Form**
Among the more sophisticated approaches to political maneuvering to get an MBO system in operation is that of organizational planning. Decentralization, for example, is ostensibly an organizational structure change, but it also forces MBO into being. Decentralization is also a political action, for it represents a shifting of power within the organiza-

tion. It is a blending of the bureaucratic form with centralized control, described by Max Weber, with the humanistic form in which lower level persons make more independent decisions, described by Joseph Litterer.

The dispersal of profit responsibility in many places simply makes it impossible for the top executive to control all the activities of all of the subordinate profit centers. Accordingly, the higher level of management must satisfy its domineering tendencies by defining results expected and measuring those results, meanwhile keeping its hands off the operations. This is far less a matter of being persuaded of the virtues of delegation and participative management than a simple inability to see everything. When you run out of eyes, hours, and ability to see everything, you are naturally required to manage by objectives whether you like it or not.

Such exemplary managerial practices are likely to develop in organizations like conglomerates where the new units have been acquired in one bite. It is especially imperative when the acquired company was purchased on some kind of payout plan over the years, with strict contractual arrangements allowing the founding management to retain their positions as long as profits are satisfactory. Far better than a sophisticated training program is an installment method of acquiring new firms which promote MBO; the result is almost inescapably MBO. The idea, for example, that a corporate president can manage 100 divisions autocratically rather than by objectives is, on the face of it, impossible.

MBO also results in firms that are nationally dispersed (the Prudential Insurance Company, for example) with all but a few managerial functions distributed among the five or six large regional offices, each with a complete functional staff. The bank with 350 branches will probably manage them by objectives, even if it does not realize it is doing so. The alternative is an exorbitant computerized management information system (MIS) and communications system. It is far more economical and sensible to find good men, place them in jobs, get them committed to objectives, and control them by exceptions.

On the other hand, a centralized organization form with functional departments usually means that the MBO program is a form of artificial or arbitrary choice. Bosses who are in the same room or even the same building with all of their employees may declare that MBO is their official style. However, they often are playing house with the employees, and in fact do not manage by objectives at all, even when they talk a great MBO game.

### The Effect of Alliances

Two or three divisions or departments, connected by a network of alliances, joint programs, mutual support, and interdependencies, can make or break an MBO program at will. The credit and sales departments, which share the task of keeping receivables under control, can make a shambles of capital management goals or they can make achievement seem effortless and natural. The industrial engineering department can team up with production to make MBO easy or difficult.

Alliances can be formed among groups that fear they would be weakened, and their joint resistance will benefit both. Hospitals are replete with examples of groups which might ordinarily find themselves in competition but are instead joined in coalitions in the face of threatening objectives. The surgeons and medical staffs competing for personal and technician time will stand together against the administrator whose objective is to reduce technician costs.

Take the case of the controller who was committed to a computerized management information system. It was his intent to have an on-line, real-time, alpha-numeric tube in every manager's office. Thus, he would have daily—even hourly—control over every important input or resource to be employed in every part of the business. The personnel department at the same time was pushing MBO, suggesting delegation, freedom of action, and goals management rather than control of detailed activity.

In another office, the corporate attorney had built up a "Merlin the magician" relationship with the president. The counsel was in and out of the president's office, reporting little stories and advising on all sorts of things. He too recognized MBO as a threat to his position as high counselor. He teamed up with the controller to condemn MBO as a spurious and probably risky adventure that was probably not fully thought through and perhaps basically unsound—if not downright illegal. MBO never stood a chance. Power is not something voluntarily relinquished, and those who have it may see MBO as a shifting of power downward, and will accordingly employ alliances and political power to fend it off.

**Money Is Power**
Those who control money or produce it in large amounts have power and can sway all kinds of decisions. In one large electronics firm with ten divisions, one division produced 80 percent of the profit. The general manager of that division had far greater power over corporate policy than his rank would indicate. If he disagreed with or could not use a corporate policy, he would simply ignore it. Because he produced most of the profit, he was sometimes gently admonished but never severely crimped.

Such a power center is able to block new programs which do not suit its mode of operation. On the other hand, if the general manager of such a center can be persuaded or educated to adopt MBO it will probably become a corporate-wide system.

In other instances, it is a single function. Marketing is king in many firms where the "marketing concept" determines the basic strategic goals. In others, it is the technology center or the financial group. In highly unionized firms, the labor relations manager will have considerable influence, and often determines whether MBO will be given a hearing, to say nothing of its being implemented. Power is often rooted in the ability to affect revenues, expenses, or pricing.

## Dealing with Conservatism

Kenneth Boulding has pointed out that change agents, liberals, and innovators are often characterized by high intensity behavior, while conservators and persons opposed to change are low intensity in behavior. The change-oriented person may have to be dramatic, shrill, strident, persuasive, and even flamboyant to get a full hearing. The best response for the conservative is to lower his voice and be rational, cautious, and meticulous.

It is the strategy of conservatism and calmness to propose that the change be examined in detail, that it be tried only in part, and that perhaps certain aspects have not been fully revealed. In the face of such a strategy of delay and obfuscation, the change agent must act with skill. He may upon occasion take the organization by storm. If he persuades the top man, gets his directive from on high, and proceeds with a vigorous combination of advocacy and education to build a plurality in the organization, he may get his way.

The true merits of education as a vehicle for change are seen here. The conservative critic can thus be isolated and quietly permitted to change his mind without engaging in high intensity tactics, for it should be realized that the strength of a counter-movement is often related to the intensity of the attack on the status quo.

In some instances, the value of the outsider is that he can provide the decisive voice of change to break the deadlock of inertia created by the low intensity opponent. When the outsider is gone, then the less intense movements can begin. Once the silence has been broken, the insider MBO advocate can restore quiet, deplore the excesses which he himself introduced, and quietly proceed with his educational and persuasive efforts.

MBO has failed in many organizations because those in charge ignored the political considerations included in the implementation. MBO is logical, systematic, and so on, but it must deal with various problems and influences. This does not mean that politics is contrary to the management systems known as MBO, and that where politics enters changes and a new system cannot be expected to flourish.

Political behavior itself has purposes, and goals are the beginning point of politics as well as of business or administration. It does require, however, that the MBO implementer must not ignore political realities, and that his choice of methods of implementation must discriminate among alternative approaches, and that the political constraints are realities which must be managed.

# 5

# Effective Management by Objectives Through the Grid

There are few management approaches that have stimulated as much interest as Management by Objectives (MBO). Similarly, the Managerial Grid—an effective way of developing managers—has been adopted widely by many companies not only in the United States, but also abroad. The question, naturally, arises whether MBO and the Grid have anything in common. After all, both are concerned with effective management. Even more important—and practical—is to raise the question *could the Grid facilitate the implementation of MBO?* I suggest that the answer is a resounding "Yes"; to support this, is the purpose of this article.

Management by Objectives, like happiness, means different things to different people. To some, it is an appraisal tool. To others, it is a means of integrating individual objectives with those of the organization. More recently, MBO is viewed as a system of managing that integrates many key managerial activities. In short, it is a way of managing (Weihrich, 1973). For this discussion the most useful approach is to focus on the steps of the MBO process, which involve: (1) Setting Objectives, (2) Developing Action Plans, (3) Implementation, and (4) Controlling Organizational Performance and Appraising Individual Results (see Figure 12). These steps will be used as the framework of this article after clarification of some Grid concepts.

Blake and Mouton suggest that the concern for people and the concern for production are not mutually exclusive, rather they are complementary. The optimizing manager, therefore will have a great concern for production as well as for people. Unfortunately, few managers measure up to this ideal model as will be seen in the discussion below. Yet every manager has a discernable style. It is assumed that a manager, identifying his style and its implications, is proceeding toward improving not only himself, but also the organization. The tool that facilitates this process is the Managerial Grid.[1]

The Grid simply is a chart with two nine-point scales ranging from 1 to 9. The horizontal scale represents concern for productivity; the vertical

Reprinted by permission of the publisher, *Manage Magazine*, September-October, 1976, pp. 8-11.

**Figure 12**
Steps in the MBO Process.

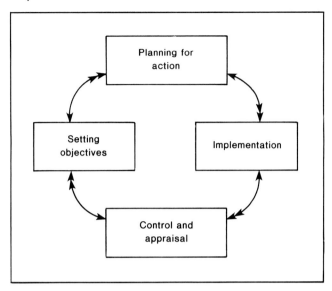

scale pertains to concern for people. Scale value 1 is a low concern (for production or people) and 9 represents a high concern. In theory, then, there are 81 possible positions. However, we will focus only on four extreme positions to illustrate their probable relationships with the MBO process; these are summarized in Table 1.

## MBO and the Grid

MBO is a process that actively involves the manager and his subordinates. Each individual's style of managing will have a profound impact on the various steps of managing by objectives.

### Step 1: Setting Objectives
One of the most difficult aspects of MBO is setting objectives that are measurable and giving direction to individual and organized efforts. Although this step appears simple, it is a task that requires a clarification of the organizational and individual aims, how they are coordinated, and the effects of working together in an organized fashion. How, then, will this task be carried out by managers using different styles? Let's explore this.

    1. **Task Management (9, 1).** This manager, with a high concern for the task (scale value 9) and a low concern for people (scale value 1),

would probably set the objectives for his subordinates. He would not provide subordinates with opportunities to think about their own jobs or let them participate in setting their own objectives. In fact, he most likely sees authority as the only means of determining the goals of those reporting to him. He sees humanistic aspects as a hindrance to getting things done. Consequently, the set of objectives pertains to performance only and does not include personal development goals.[2]

2. **Country Club Management (1, 9).** This manager has a low concern for production, but a high concern for people. Thus, his emphasis is on a harmonious relationship with subordinates because he assumes that happy workers will be productive. Unfortunately, not enough attention will be given to performance goals. Personal objectives, therefore, may be more emphasized than production goals.

3. **Impoverished Management (1, 1).** A manager with this style, one could argue, does not manage at all. With a minimum concern for production and people, things do not get done. No goals are set; no direction of organizational effort is indicated; no communication exists between the manager and subordinate. Consequently, nobody feels that he makes a contribution to the aims of the organization.

4. **Team Management (9, 9).** The manager adopting this managerial style has maximum concern for production as well as people. It is indeed the aim of Grid training to bring managers closer to this model. This manager will set for himself challenging, yet attainable objectives. But his objectives are not set in isolation, rather they are coordinated with efforts of other organizational units.

Subordinates participate in setting their own objectives which pertain not only to performance, but also include personal development. Consequently, there is a high degree of congruency between organizational and individual objectives, as illustrated in Figure 13, with the shaded area indicating the high degree of integration. Although the primary responsibility for setting objectives rests with the subordinates, they feel free to elicit assistance and information from their manager who is regarded as a coach and advisor. This, in turn, facilitates concerted action. Organizational members pull in the same direction, making a substantial contribution to the aims of the organization, which, in turn, results in effective performance. In short, the integrated efforts result in synergy, and the total effect is more than the sum of individual effort.

**Step 2: Planning for Action**

Objectives give direction to individual and organized efforts. At times this is not enough; plans for action to achieve these ends need to be

**Table 1**
Relationships Between MBO and Grid Positions

| MBO Process / Grid Positions | 9.1 Task Management | 1.9 Country Club Management | 1.1 Impoverished Management | 9.9 Team Management |
|---|---|---|---|---|
| 1. Setting Objectives | Superior sets objectives for subordinates. Little participation. Emphasis on authority. No personal development goals. | Emphasis on harmonious relationships. Low concern for performance objectives. | No goals are set. No direction. No communication. Individuals make minimum contributions to organizations. | Manager sets challenging, yet attainable objectives. Subordinates set their performance and personal development objectives. Organizational and personal objectives are congruent. Coordination of objectives. Synergistic effect. |
| 2. Developing Action Plans | Superior determines tasks. Limited alternatives evaluated. Coordination problems due to lack of participation. Manager very directive. | Tasks not clearly identified. Not conducive to analysis of alternatives. No coordinated time schedule. Responsibility unclear. | No action planning. | Systematic identification of tasks and alternatives. Analysis of different courses of action. Active participation. Effective coordination. Acceptance of responsibility. |
| 3. Implementation | Superior defines MBO program. Extensive use of manuals, forms, and procedures. Following directions. Rigid mechanistic program. Little participation. Underlying philosophy not understood. | No coordinated effort. Superior does provide little leadership. Everyone implements MBO as he sees fit. | MBO does not get implemented. No commitment to MBO. | People actively involved in the process. Frequent and open communication. Manager as a coach. Organization as an interlocking system. |

| 4. Control and Appraisal | Control from top. Standards may be inappropriate. Little self-appraisal. Superior makes evaluation. | Little control. Appraisal not taken seriously. Insufficient accountability. No accurate feedback from superior. | Without standards no control possible. Appraisal neglected. No feedback. | Critical control points established. Analysis of deviations. Problem solving attitude. Self-appraisal. Looking toward the future. Improvement plans. Superior as helper. |
|---|---|---|---|---|

**Figure 13**
Congruency of Objectives in Team Management.

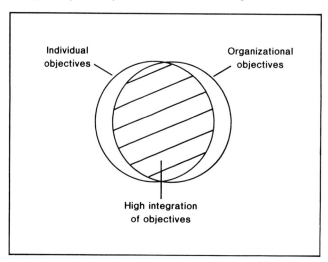

developed. Basically, this requires determining *what* has to be done, *how* it is to be done, *when* it is to be done, and, finally, *who* is going to do it. The process of action planning will differ depending on the style the manager uses.

1. **Task Management** (9, 1). The superior sees as his prerogative—and, perhaps, responsibility—the determination of what must be done to achieve the objectives. Little input is elicited from subordinates. Moreover, only few alternative courses of action are considered. Further, because of the lack of participation, problems in coordination may surface. The manager rather clearly establishes who is going to do what; the result may be clearly defined job descriptions.

2. **Country Club Management** (1, 9). This managerial style is not conducive to effective management. Tasks necessary to achieve objectives are not clearly identified. In addition, there is no systematic analysis of alternative courses of action, nor evaluation of their effectiveness; courses of action are selected by chance rather than by careful evaluation. Similarly, the time schedule for the various activities lacks coordination. Everybody works to suit his fancy. Responsibilities for carrying out the tasks are unclear with the result that nobody assumes responsibility for irksome activities.

3. **Impoverished Management** (1, 1). This managerial style — with minimum concern for production and people—results very simply in no action plan at all. In fact, it is a style that does not deserve to be called "managerial."

4. **Team Management (9, 9).** In contrast to the foregoing, the manager who embraces this approach has maximum concern for production and people. Tasks and activities are systematically identified. The environment is conducive to the evaluation of many alternatives; and the selection of the best alternative (or alternatives) is based on effective teamwork with inputs from many organizational members, especially those who are affected by the decisions. This, in turn, facilitates the timing of the activities and results in concerted action. The manager and his subordinates do not attempt to shirk responsibilities; they welcome them. Consequently, they feel accountable for their actions. At the same time, there is a clear realization that it is teamwork that brings results.

## Step 3: Implementation

Objectives and plans are of little value unless they result in action and are implemented. The style adopted by managers will substantially influence the way plans and the MBO program are put into action.

1. **Task Management (9, 1).** The primary concern of management is to get things done and to get them done efficiently. Human aspects are ignored in this process. The superior will allow little, if any, participation by subordinates. Thus, there is considerable resistance to MBO. The program often is implemented by extensive reliance on a manual with strict procedures. Instead of a flexible approach tailored to organizational demands, subordinates fill out many forms to meet procedural requirements. MBO, therefore, may become a rigid, mechanistic program that lacks real commitment by the participants. Since the underlying philosophy of MBO—stressing self-control and self-development—is not understood, MBO is considered an imposition by upper management.

2. **Country Club Management (1, 9).** This managerial style emphasizes concern for people, but not production. Consequently, management does not exert the necessary leadership to implement MBO which does, in fact, necessitate a new way of managing. Moreover, the objectives and action plans of various managers are not coordinated and everyone applies MBO as he sees fit.

3. **Impoverished Management (1, 1).** With minimum concern for production and people MBO never really gets implemented. At best, the manager may go through the motion of the MBO requirements to retain his job, but there is no commitment to MBO. Implementation would require a behavioral change, which would be too uncomfortable to the manager.

4. **Team Management (9, 9).** This managerial style, with a high concern for production and people, is most conducive to an effective imple-

mentation. During all phases of the MBO process, people are not only prepared for MBO, but they are active participants. Thus, there is a great deal of commitment to objectives and action plans, with a minimum amount of resistance. There is also frequent and open communication among managers to identify factors that may hinder the effectiveness of the team. The superior is considered a coach helping subordinates to achieve their objectives. Finally, the efforts of individuals and organizational units are coordinated to form an interlocking system.

## Step 4: Control and Appraisal

Control refers here to monitoring organizational performance, and appraisal pertains to the evaluation of individual results. Both have in common the setting of standards, measuring performance against these standards, and taking corrective action.

1. **Task Management (9, 1).** The manager adhering to this managerial style will rather closely control the performance of his department and his subordinates. Consequently, there is little opportunity for self-appraisal. Because of limited participation, the developed standards may be inappropriate, yet they are used as a benchmark for measurement. By using the autocratic approach, the superior arbitrarily makes the evaluation of his subordinates, giving them minimum opportunities for self-evaluation.

2. **Country Club Management (1, 9).** This manager, in order not to hurt the feelings of subordinates, does not exercise control. Appraisal— although conducted in a friendly atmosphere—is not taken very seriously. As a consequence, subordinates do not feel accountable for results. Also, the lack of leadership does not give subordinates a clear indication of their performance because of insufficient feedback from the manager.

3. **Impoverished Management (1, 1).** No verifiable objectives exist; without them performance cannot be measured. The function of control and appraisal is simply neglected.

4. **Team Management (9, 9).** The high concern for production as well as people is conducive to effective control and appraisal. Control standards are established at critical points. The analysis of performance is done with the intention of finding the causes of undesirable deviation, instead of finding fault. Rather than an appraisal by the boss judging performance critically or benevolently, there is more self-appraisal by the subordinates. A problem solving attitude prevails that not only views past performance, but also—and even more so—focuses on the future. From the past, one can learn; the future, one can influence. Therefore, considerable effort is expended to improve organizational and individual performance. In all, the atmosphere is positive and the superior is viewed as a helper or coach rather than a judge.

## Summary and Conclusion

The purpose of this article was to show—although provisionally—the relationships between two very successful approaches to management: Management by Objectives and the Managerial Grid.

The managerial style does have a considerable, and probably decisive, effect on the way the steps in the MBO process are carried out. A high concern for production with a low concern for people does not give sufficient attention to the important human variables. On the other hand, a high concern for people with a neglect of production does not result in optimum performance. Concern for neither production nor people results in minimum performance.

To be effective, a high degree of concern for production as well as people is needed. In such an environment objectives are challenging, yet attainable; organizational demands and individual needs are integrated; tasks and activities are coordinated for optimum results, and the organization becomes an interlocking system with open communication and frequent, accurate feedback.

During the last few decades environmental changes have required new values, with new demands on the manager that call for more creative approaches to management. MBO and the Grid are two of these approaches; each, especially if combined, has the potential to meet these new needs. The essential first step toward personal and managerial effectiveness is to examine one's own managerial style as applied to the steps in MBO. The Grid facilitates this process. Should we not get on with this job?

1. The discussion of the Managerial Grid is based on Blake and Mouton.
2. The terms "objectives" and "goals" will be used interchangeably.

# Section 5   Control and Appraisal

**Objectives**

1. To understand the basic control process and to recognize that the best controls are those that prevent undesirable deviations from occurring.
2. To understand the relationship between MBO and budgeting.
3. To become aware of the pitfalls in appraisal and to develop steps to avoid them.
4. To improve the interaction between superior and subordinate through the application of Transactional Analysis.
5. To make appraisal effective by evaluating managers against performance objectives and the way managers carry out their managerial functions.

**Figure 14**

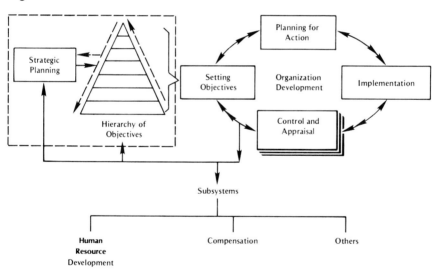

## Control and Appraisal

In previous sections it was shown that the development of strategies and hierarchy of objectives are essential parts of a comprehensive MBO system. The more detailed steps in the MBO process involve the establishment of specific goals, the development of action plans, and the recognition of the human aspects in the implementation of MBO. The articles in this section discuss the next step in the MBO process: controlling organizational performance and appraising individual results.

*Control* means that managers establish standards, measure organization performance against these standards, and take actions to correct undesirable deviation.

*Appraisal,* of course, is a kind of control. The focus of the readings is on the evaluation of a person's performance and the human aspects involved in the appraisal process. As will be recalled from an earlier article by Peter Drucker, the emphasis in MBO is on self-control and self-evaluation. Obviously, immediate superiors play an important role in appraising their subordinates. Sometimes the next higher level manager is also involved in reviewing the performance of persons two levels below in the organizational hierarchy. More recently, group appraisals and peer reviews have also been used to supplement the appraisal by the superior of the subordinates.

The first article, by Harold Koontz and Robert W. Bradspies, "Managing Through Feedforward Control—A Future-Directed View," not only discusses the basic control process, but points out that the best control system is one that prevents deviations from occurring. Although the term "feedforward control" is not widely used, the idea certainly is congruent with MBO.

In the second article, "The Position and Function of Budgets in an MBO System," Dale D. McConkey discusses the relationship between MBO and budgeting. Clearly, objectives must be congruent with budgets. Yet, unfortunately, they are all too often not integrated, causing many dysfunctional consequences.

In the third article in this section, "Split Roles in Performance Appraisal," Herbert H. Meyer and his associates describe their experiences and findings at the General Electric Company. These authors point up the problems of traditional performance appraisals in which the superior plays two conflicting roles: a judge and a counselor. Furthermore, a once-a-year comprehensive performance appraisal is of questionable value. Instead, frequent reviews and coaching are recommended.

The fourth article, "MBO: Appraisal with Transactional Analysis" by Heinz Weihrich, focuses on the delicate interaction between superior and subordinate in the appraisal session. To improve appraisal, Transactional Analysis (TA) is suggested. Indeed, Adult-Adult transactions between superior and subordinate, as well as the adoption of the "I'm OK—You're OK" life position, will benefit all participants in the appraisal discussion.

The last article, by Harold Koontz, focuses on "Making Managerial Appraisal Effective." Actually, the approach recommended by Koontz has two main components. One pertains to appraisal against objectives, which, of course, is a key aspect of MBO. The other component of the approach focuses on appraising managers as managers. Specifically, managerial activities are grouped into the managerial functions of planning, organizing, directing/leading, and controlling. Managers are then evaluated on how well they carry out these managerial activities. Consequently, this approach helps to pinpoint deficiencies in managing. This, in turn, can become the basis of management development, a topic further discussed by Henry L. Tosi, Jr., in the next section.

Harold Koontz
Robert W. Bradspies

# 1

# Managing Through Feedforward Control— A Future-Directed View

Managers have long been frustrated by making the occasional discovery —*too late*—that actual accomplishments are missing desired goals. Anyone responsible for an enterprise or any department of it has suffered the discomfiture of realizing that typical control reports merely inform him what has already happened and that most control analyses are really post-mortems. It does, indeed, do little good to find out late in December that inventory levels were too high at the end of November because of something that happened weeks or months before. Nor is it helpful to learn that a program is behind schedule or incurring excessive costs because of past events.

Most current control systems rely on some form of feedback. Unfortunately, a feedback loop must sense some error or deviation from desired performance before it can initiate a correction. This is, of course, after the fact. Moreover, since correction takes some time to become effective, the deviation tends to persist. The costs incurred, in many cases, increase directly with the duration of the error.

For example, the costs of holding excessive inventory are proportional to the time the excess inventory is held. The time slippage in a program may continue until correction is applied, and the costs of making up for the time lost usually seem to rise at an increasing rate. It is not surprising, therefore, that most managers consider the problem of control to be one of early recognition of deviations so that correction can be applied promptly. Although many managers have solved the problem to some extent through careful planning, simulative techniques, and network systems of control (PERT/CPM), truly effective control has rarely been achieved.

To achieve more effective control, it is necessary to reduce the magnitude of the error. To avoid the problems inherent in the response time of a feedback system, deviations should be anticipated. The only way to do this, short of using a crystal ball, is to monitor the critical inputs to a

Reprinted by permission of the publisher, *Business Horizons*, June 1972, pp. 25-36.

program. If we watch changes in inputs, we can determine whether these would eventually cause failure to achieve desired goals. Time will then be available to take corrective action.

At first glance, it may seem that such a method would be difficult to use in practice. Fortunately, there is now available an approach to effective managerial control through adapting the principles of feedforward control. This form of control is increasingly being used in systems engineering.

## The Process of Control

Although planning and control are closely related, most managers see planning as the establishment of objectives or goals and the selection of rational means of reaching them, and regard control as the measurement of activities accompanied by action to correct deviations from planned events. It may thus be perceived that the function of managerial control is to make sure that plans succeed.

It is obvious that any system of controls requires plans, and the more complete, integrated, and clear they are, the better control can be. This simple truth arises from the fact that there is no way one can know whether he is going where he wants to go—the task of control—unless he first knows where he wants to go—the task of planning.

Control also requires an organization structure that is complete, integrated, and clear. The purpose of control is to detect and correct deviations in events; this must necessarily be done through people responsible for them. It does little good for a manager to be aware of variances but not know where in the organization structure the responsibility for them lies.

Given these prerequisites, any type of control and any control technique fundamentally involves the same basic process. *First,* standards must exist. While an entire plan can be used as the standard of control, the inability to watch everything usually forces a manager to select relatively few critical points that will reasonably measure how planned accomplishments are proceeding. *Second,* the logic of control requires measurement of performance against standards. *Third,* the process calls for taking action to correct deviations from plans.

### Shortcomings and Needs

Control is really not this simple in practice, however, especially in management. Its basic features should be regarded as a cybernetic system as outlined in Figure 15. These steps represent the kind of feedback system that is involved in the simple room thermostat or the myriad of other control devices that one finds in mechanical and electrical control systems. But it dramatizes what every manager knows so well and many

**Figure 15**
Management Control as a Cybernetic System.

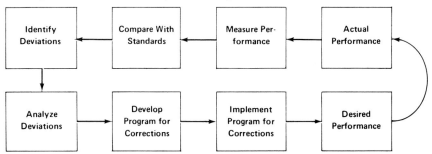

feedback engineers do not consider when they attempt to apply their thinking to management problems.

Simple feedback is not enough. Even the much-heralded ability of electronic data processing specialists to furnish information in real time, that is, as events are happening, is seldom good enough for management control. The fastest possible information may measure actual performance, may often be able to compare this measurement against standards, and may even be able to identify deviations. But analysis of deviations and the development and implementation of programs for correction normally takes weeks or months, if the correction can be made at all. Moreover, during this time lag, variances often continue to grow.

An inventory above desired levels may take months to analyze and correct. A cost overrun on a project may not even be correctable. A delay in an aspect of engineering or production, if recoverable at all, may be remedied only by an expensive crash program. Feedback is not much more than a post-mortem, and no one has found a way to change the past.

---

. . . there is no way one can know whether he is going where he wants to go—the task of control—unless he first knows where he wants to go—the task of planning.

---

### Need for Future-directed Control

Intelligent and alert managers have recognized that the only problems they can solve are those they see, and the only way they can exercise control effectively is to see the problems coming in time to do something about them. In 1956, the senior author of this article identified future-directed control as one of the major principles of managerial control: "Since the past cannot be changed, effective control should be aimed at preventing present and future deviations from plans."[1] At this time it was emphasized that control, like planning, must be forward-directed and that it is fallacious to regard planning as looking ahead and control as looking back.

The simple principle of future-directed control is largely disregarded in practice, mainly because managers have been so dependent on accounting and statistical data instead of forecasts of future events. They have been too preoccupied with decimal accuracy, which can only be attained —if at all—from history. In the absence of any means to look forward, reference to history, on the assumption that what is past is prologue, is admittedly better than not looking at all. But no manager attempting to do an adequate job of control should be satisfied with using historical records, adequate as they are for tax collection and reporting on stewardship of assets to stockholders.

As a matter of fact, Norbert Wiener, the father of cybernetics, recognized the deficiencies of common feedback. He pointed out that, where there are lags in a system, corrections (the "compensator") must predict, or anticipate, errors. Thus, what he referred to as "anticipatory feedback" is often needed, particularly in human and animal systems. However, judging by the slowness in developing future-directed controls or anticipatory feedback in management control systems, there is little evidence that this variation of feedback has had the impact on thinking and practice that might have been expected.

**Techniques of Future-directed Control**

Relatively few techniques of future-directed control have been devised. Perhaps the most widely used is the continual development and revision of various kinds of forecasts, utilizing current expectancies to forecast probable results, comparing these with performance desired, and then developing programs to avoid undesired forecast events. Many managers, for example, after realistically working out their sales forecasts may be disappointed with the anticipated results; they then may review their programs of product development or marketing to see where changes can be made.

Cash forecasts are also a widely employed kind of future-directed control. Because banks do not normally honor checks without funds in an account, companies seldom can risk waiting until late November to find out whether they had adequate bank balances for checks written in October; instead, they engage in future-directed control by assuring that cash balances will be adequate to absorb charges.

One of the best approaches to future-directed control in use today is the formalized technique of network planning, which is exemplified by PERT networks. In PERT/TIME the discrete events required to accomplish a given program result are depicted in network form (since few programs ever are linear in the sense that one portion of it is sequentially followed by another), and the time required to finish each event is contained in the network. As will be recalled, when this is done, the planner can determine which series of events will have the least slack time.

The simple PERT network shown in Figure 16 will illustrate this long-used technique and how the most critical path—the one with the least slack—can be identified. A major advantage of this tool is that, through careful planning and measurement of progress in each event, any time slippage becomes evident long before the program is finished. The time available to finish the remaining events is one of the inputs to those events; if it is less than the minimum desired time, steps can be taken to accelerate any event along the critical path that lends itself to speed-up at minimum cost.

**Figure 16**
Simple PERT Network.*

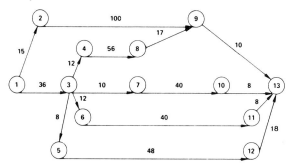

If, for example, there is no slack time on the critical path of events "1-3-4-8-9-13" (in other words, if delivery has been promised in 131 days), the manager knows that if event "3" is ten days late the entire project will be late unless something is done now. Although PERT has tended to become so complex in practice that its use for actual managerial control has declined, it is basically the best single device of future-directed control that has yet been put into practice.

## Feedforward in Engineering

As early as 1928, U.S. Patent No. 1,686, 792 was issued to H. S. Black on a "Translating System," which incorporated the principle of feedforward control in engineering systems. However, the application of feedforward in electrical and process systems did not come into common use until a few years ago.[2]

---

*Circled numbers are measurable or verifiable events, and numbers on arrows are estimates of days required to complete an event.

In its essence, engineering feedforward control aims at meeting the problem of delay in feedback systems by monitoring inputs and predicting their effects on outcome variables. In doing so, action is taken, either automatically or by manipulation, to bring the system output into consonance with a desired standard before measurement of the output discloses deviation from standard. Thus, while feedback control relies on detecting errors in controlled variables as system outputs, feedforward is based on detecting and measuring system disturbances, and correcting for these before the system output change occurs. The basic concept of a feedforward and feedback system is outlined in Figure 17.

**Figure 17**
Comparison of Feedback and Feedforward Control Systems.*

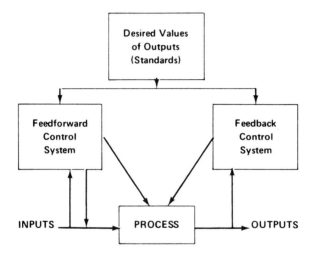

Feedforward has had wide application in the chemical and petroleum processing industries. It has been found particularly valuable where constant temperatures of material flow, exact mixtures, and various forms of chemical reactions require the precision that ordinary feedback, with its normal cycling, cannot achieve.

Perhaps the simplest form of feedforward control is contained in a system to maintain a fixed temperature of hot water leaving a heat exchanger where cool water inputs are heated by steam inputs. A thermostat on the water outlet would hardly be adequate, particularly with intermittent and variable uses of hot water; sudden changes in water

---

*In a feedback system, correction of outputs are fed back into the process. In a feedforward system, undesired variations of inputs are fed into the input stream for correction or into the process before outputs occur.

output would probably cause bursts of cold water and steam inputs with resultant cycling of the water temperature.

To solve this problem, a systems design would provide a controller that would adjust the opening of the steam valve slightly. As the hot water usage starts to increase, the steam will be on its way into the tank before the water temperature drops below standard. A second feedforward loop might monitor the steam temperature and increase the rate of steam usage if its temperature should fall, in order to maintain the same heat input. By typing mathematical calculations into a computer that translates information to the input control valves, the oscillations characteristic of simple feedback systems can be reduced or entirely avoided.

However, even the most enthusiastic proponents of feedforward control admit that, if input variables are not known or unmeasurable, the system will not work. Therefore, for the best control, the use of feedback for output variables is also suggested.

---

"But a little analysis and ingenuity could result in much wider use of effective controls and even the future-directed controls now in existence could be greatly improved."

---

## Feedforward in Human Systems

The feedforward applications one finds in everyday life are far simpler than engineering applications. A motorist who wishes to maintain a certain speed does not usually wait until he notes that his speedometer has fallen below this speed as he goes up a hill. Instead, knowing that the incline represents a disturbing variable in the system of which he is a part, the driver is likely to start correcting for the expected decrease in speed by accelerating in advance.

Similarly, the average person does not wait until a rainstorm actually feeds back to him the need for an umbrella before he carries one. Nor would a successful hunter aim his gun directly at a flying bird; he would "lead" it to correct for the delay in his own system, his reactions, the gun, and the shot velocity.

It, is, therefore, surprising that more thorough and conscious feedforward techniques have not been developed in management, particularly since the delay factors in ordinary feedback correction are so long. As mentioned previously in this article, this has been done by such means as forecasting end results and PERT/CPM networks. But a little analysis and ingenuity could result in much wider use of effective controls and even the future-directed controls now in existence could be greatly improved.

A number of illustrations of how the principles of feedforward might be used in management may be given. Many require development of mathematical models of the system so as to provide managers information of forthcoming trouble in time for correction, but space does not permit the display of such models here. The approach of feedforward can be shown by several simple schematic models. For this purpose, the cases of control of cash, inventories, and new product development will be presented.

### Feedforward in Cash Planning

Since cash forecasting lies at the base of cash planning and control, this widely used technique of control is one of the best for revealing the application of feedforward to management. The basic inputs and construction of a cash control system may be seen in Figure 18. As can be noted, a number of input variables account for a desired future cash level. This model, representing a fairly simplified prototype of reality, shows that if any of the input variables differ from those premised when the cash plan was made, the desired cash level for the future will be affected.

As can be seen, many of these variables can have either a negative or positive effect on cash flow and the desired cash level at a given time in the future. It is readily apparent that normal feedback techniques are not adequate, and constant monitoring of the various input variables, with a feedforward of their influence on cash, is necessary for careful cash control. Of course, one way to avoid the problem of shortages is to have available a ready bank line of credit. But what is likely to happen in this case is that the enterprise will keep unnecessarily high balances of cash, with resultant avoidable interest costs or loss in investment income.

It is also clear from cursory examination of this feedforward system that a mathematical model programmed to a computer can readily trace the influences of changes of input variables on cash flow and availability. Neither this nor careful monitoring of input variables should be very difficult to do in practice.

### Feedforward in Inventory Control

One of the most difficult problems in business is the proper control of inventories. Many enterprises incur large and often unexpected cost increases, as well as sizable demands for cash because of inadequate control of inventories. Moreover, as experience continually teaches us, an inventory discovered to be out of control on the high side is extremely difficult to get under control except, of course, through that most costly of all solutions—writing off excess stocks.

Also, the costs of carrying inventory, due to expenses from handling and storage, interest, property taxes, and possible obsolescence, are high-

**Figure 18**

Input Variables for a Cash Plan.

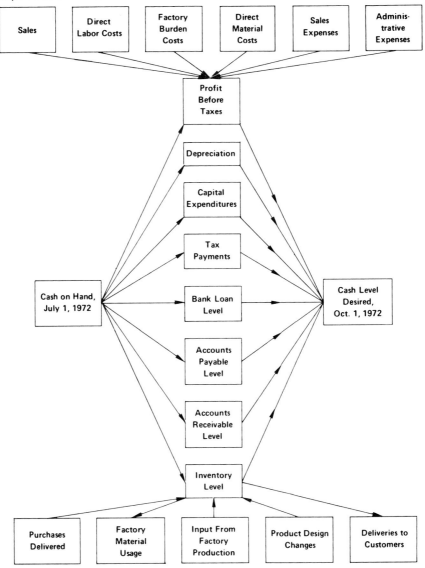

er than generally assumed; 25 percent of inventory value per year is often regarded as a resonable estimate. Nor should it be overlooked that inventory shortages often have high costs because of missed sales or lost customers.

In recent years, operations researchers have presented a vast array of mathematical inventory models and refinements. There can be no question that they have contributed greatly to effective planning and control of inventories, and many can be used as the basis for effective feedforward in inventory control. The difficulty with many models is that they tend to concentrate unduly on such matters as economic order quantities and safety stock levels. These may be appropriate for a mass production operation, but may not take into account the many other input variables, such as obsolescence or property taxes, that make effective inventory control so difficult and important.

Any company will do well to develop its own inventory model, using, of course, the many standard algorithms and techniques available, but taking into account as many as possible of the variables that may influence actual inventory accumulation.

The schematic diagram shown in Figure 19 reveals the complexity of inventory control. Once a desired inventory level is established in a way that minimizes costs in the light of demands for adequate inventory, the total (whether expressed in dollars or days of sales) tends to be used as a standard. Actual results are compared to it through feedback with little or no monitoring of the input variables on which the desired level was determined.

The attempt is normally made to maintain the inventory within desired limits by using only reorder point, economic order quantity, and maximum inventory level. In the simplest manual system, when a withdrawal is noted on a stock record, the balance is compared with the reorder quantity. When the balance on hand falls below this level a purchase order is issued. All of this may take place without considering the predictive changes of the original inputs.

The effect of such action may be to allow inventory to go out of control and raise costs. For example, if the rate of sales increased for a particular item, a company could find itself reordering too frequently or even running out of stock, thus increasing costs unnecessarily. Conversely, if sales decrease, a company could find that it was wasting cash by holding excess inventory. If sales declined further and a company continued reordering, it could find itself with a large obsolete stock.

If, instead, a company regularly monitored input variables, inventory levels could be adjusted by feedforward control by following the original decision paths and adjusting inventory purchases. In a company that used a manual inventory control system, for example, a simple monitoring system could be devised. It need only consider significant changes in input.

However, it must be admitted that a more sophisticated computer-controlled inventory system would be able to adjust more accurately for the effects of smaller changes in input variables and thereby reduce overall operating costs by keeping inventory under control.

In reviewing the various input variables, it can easily be seen that different departments within the company would have to be responsible for feeding information (probably into a central inventory planning and

**Figure 19**
Effect of Input Variables on Determining Desired Inventory Level.

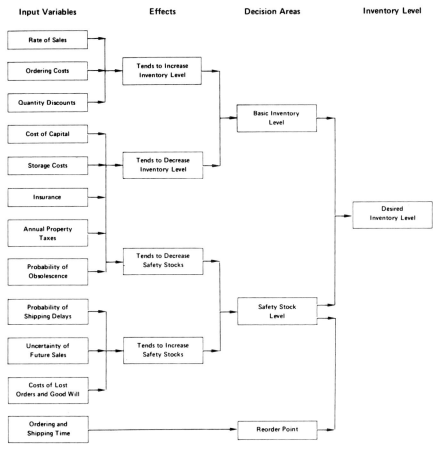

control unit) on the variables within its field of knowledge. For example, ordering costs, economic order quantity, and quantity discounts are usually best known by the purchasing department; shipping time and unscheduled delays in shipping are data that could be regularly expected from the traffic department.

Given a recognition of the types of input variables and a system for regularly collecting information on them, it should be easy to anticipate what is likely to happen in inventory. In feeding forward this information, it should be practicable to develop a kind of inventory control that is truly future directed.

### Feedforward in New Product Development

The typical new product development program is, in the first instance, a system of interlocking contributory programs, as shown in Figure 20. It can be readily seen that this is similar to a PERT planning and control

**Figure 20**
Feedforward Through a System of Interlocking Contributory
Programs of a New Product Program.

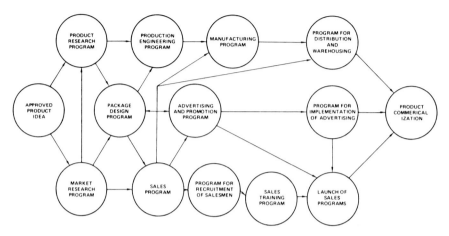

network. If times and costs are estimated for each program event in the network, the accomplishment of each subsidiary program becomes an input variable by which it is possible to feedforward the probable delays and costs of the completion of the program.

Moreover, each of the major programs in this network can be further broken down into a system of input variables so that completion of the total program can be forecast. Action can be taken in time to make necessary corrections and keep it under control. For example, within the product research program, there will normally be a number of subsidiary programs or events. These may include establishment of design definition and specifications; preliminary design of the product; development of a breadboard model; and testing the model.

Each of the other programs can be broken down into a number of subsidiary events or programs. These, in turn, constitute input variables to the individual programs necessary for the completion of a total product development program; their monitoring can feedforward both time and cost factors against the standards desired for the total program.

In addition, analysis can disclose a number of other possible, and usually unplanned, input variables that may affect a desired end result. There are likely to be many of these, including such influences as delay in obtaining needed parts; failure of some part in a test; illness or departure of a key engineer; interference of a higher priority program; or change in a customer's desired specification. While not all of these can be carefully estimated in advance, and some may even be unforeseen, feedforward control can recognize the impact of such disturbances and provide for action in time to avoid program failure.

### Change of Goals

In feedforward control systems in engineering, the systems are almost inevitably designed to correct input variables so that a given standard or goal may be achieved. In its application to managerial problems, the same approach can be used, but it should not be overlooked that the system may lead to changes in goals.

By placing emphasis on input variables, both those foreseen as a part of the program and those unforeseen, feedforward applications can furnish a means of regularly reviewing program goals themselves. A material change in interest rates, for example, may make a review of inventory goals desirable. Or a new development in product technology or market tastes may require a reevaluation of a product program. Managers must always keep in mind that goals and programs may become obsolete.

## Feedforward Control Guidelines

Although many other examples of application of feedforward to management control might be given, it is hoped that the transfer of engineering principles to management situations will be clear enough to help open the way toward the systematic application of feedforward in many areas. This can be done more easily than it may first appear. But in doing so several guidelines should be kept in mind.

1. *Thorough planning and analysis is required.* As in all instances of management control, thorough and careful planning is a primary prerequisite. But, especially in applying feedforward, this planning must be as thorough as feasible. Input variables should not only be identified but seen in their relationship and impact on desired end results.
2. *Careful discrimination must be applied in selecting input variables.* Since not all variables that *may* have some effect on output can be identified and monitored in typical management systems, it is essential that only the more critical variables be selected for watching. This is, of course, one of the key requirements of the managerial art—to identify those elements that make a material difference in the operation of a plan.
3. *The feedforward system must be kept dynamic.* There is always the danger that input variables will be identified in the analysis stage and only these will be monitored. The alert manager will, of course, watch for new influences, either within or outside the control system, which might seriously effect a desired output. New technology, unexpected changes in loan rates and availability, changes in customer tastes, and even unanticipated changes in social or political pressures are examples of input variables that may not have been foreseen.

4. *A model of the control system should be developed.* Clearly, if a feed-forward system is to be utilized, the area in which such control is desired must be defined, with the various significant input variables identified and their effects on desired goals analyzed.

   This model may be a simple schematic drawing. It is far better, of course, to use an appropriate mathematical model that can be programmed in a computer. This way, the manager can take into account a larger number of input variables, more accurately calculate their impact on program goals, and be able more quickly and accurately to take corrective action.

5. *Data on input variables must be regularly collected.* Feedforward control is, of course, not possible without regular collection of pertinent data concerning the input variables so that the impact of this information can be carefully weighed. It is in this area that fast information availability is highly desirable and real-time information could have much meaning for control.

6. *Data on input variables must be regularly assessed.* No purpose can be served if input data are not regularly and carefully assessed to ascertain their influence on future program results. Barring unforeseen and unprogrammed variables, a computerized system can deliver this assessment quickly. However, for many feedforward systems the experienced eye and judgment of a top analyst may be good enough to point toward future deviations from planned results.

7. *Feedforward control requires action.* Few, if any, techniques or systems of management control are self-activating. All the system can do is to surface information that indicates future troubles, hopefully in time for something to be done to avoid them. This, of course requires action. But if the system can be designed with enough lead time for a manager to take action, that is all that can be expected. And astute managers ask for nothing more than to be able to see their problems in time to do something about them.

There can be no doubt that feedforward is largely an attitude toward the analysis and solution of problems. It is the recognition that feedback information is just not adequate for management control and that a shift must be made away from emphasis on quickly available data on final results to quickly available data on those input variables that lead to final results. It is a means of seeing problems as they develop and not looking back—always too late—to see why a planning target was missed.

1. Harold Koontz, "A Preliminary Statement of Principles of Planning and Control," *Academy of Management Journal,* I(April, 1958), pp. 45-61.
2. See, for example, L. F. Lind and J. C. C. Nelson, "Feed Forward: Concept in Control System Design," *Control & Instrumentation* (April, 1970), pp. 39-40;

F. G. Shinskey, *Process Control Systems* (New York: McGraw-Hill Book Company, 1967), Chapter 8; F. G. Shinskey, "Feedforward Control of pH," *Instrumentation Technology* (June, 1968), pp. 69ff.; J. A. Miller, P. W. Murrill, and C. L. Smith, "How to Apply Feedforward Control," *Hydrocarbon Processing* (July, 1969), pp. 165-72.

A review of engineering literature discloses a few references to feedforward control early in the 1960's, but the real volume of writing has occurred since 1967.

# 2

# The Position and Function of Budgets in an MBO System

Of all the questions raised by the dramatic growth of Management by Objectives few are more indicative of disorganized confusion than those relating to the position and role of budgets in an MBO system. The following are but a few of the situations faced by the author in recent months:

*Company A* — The president indicated that the company had been operating with MBO for two years and now believed it was time to implement a budget system.

*Comment:* Budgets are an integral part of an MBO system and the company could not have been practicing MBO without them.

*Company B* — This company followed the practice of approving budgets during February of each year and then having its managers write their objectives during the ensuing six months.

*Comment:* The budget is on the wrong end of the planning objective setting process. Budgets should conclude, not begin, the process. There is little basis on which to approve the budgets unless the objectives and plans have been formulated.

*Organization C* — Every two years the head of a Canadian government department is required to submit and defend the budget for his operations at a "budget justification" meeting. He inquired as to whether or not it would be a good idea to also have his objectives and plans prepared and available for the same meeting.

*Comment:* Objectives and plans are the only way the budget can be "justified." Without the objectives and plans, the budget cannot be tested for realism.

*Company D* — The senior management team was thoroughly convinced it was operating under an MBO system simply because all operations were covered by operating expense and capital budgets.

*Comment:* Budgets are only one part of an MBO system. By themselves they're usually a sterile exercise in compiling numbers — an exercise in futility.

Reprinted with permission from *The Business Quarterly*, School of Business Administration, The University of Western Ontario/London, Canada, Spring, 1974, Vol. 39/No. 1, pp. 45-50.

*Organization E* — The head of this social agency had issued instructions to his managers that the budget should cover only the objectives of each manager. If a subject was not covered by an objective it should not be included in the budget.

*Comment:* Budgets cover more than just objectives because the latter are usually limited to priority matters. Routine matters are not covered by objectives but the cost of the routine is reflected in the budget.

*Organization F* — In the early days of an MBO installation, it was found that this organization had three different budgets intended to serve three different purposes — financial planning, motivation and control.

*Comment:* One budget, properly designed and constructed, should serve all three purposes.

All of the above reveal a rather alarming amount of misconception and confusion regarding the role of budgets. Also, they indicate the failure of many organizations to update the traditional approach to budgeting to make it compatible with an MBO system. The resulting void has a major impact on the effectiveness of the MBO efforts.

Budgets have a key role to play, but only when this role is thoroughly understood and budgets are placed in their proper position. Otherwise, they operate to the detriment of MBO.

## Traditional Budgeting Is Obsolete

The impact of twenty years of widespread practice of Management by Objectives has brought about dramatic changes in the traditional practice of management. Many parts of the management process have been rendered obsolete.[1] The latter includes the traditional view of budgeting and its relationship to planning.

Commonly, budgets have been looked upon as "a plan or estimate of future income and expenses." They were heavily oriented to control.

An excellent example of the traditional approach to planning and budgeting is illustrated by the following case involving a university chancellor:

The date is July 20, 1973, and one of the chancellors of a large university is conducting his annual planning session for the 1974 year.

He announces that the total budget for 1974 for all units under his direction will be $10 million allocated individually as follows:

| | |
|---|---|
| Director of Housing ..................................................... | $ 2 million |
| Director of Program Development .............................. | 1 million |
| Director of Communications Center ........................... | 3 million |
| Director of Residence Halls ...................................... | 1 million |
| Director of Testing Program ..................................... | 2 million |
| Chancellor's Office .................................................... | 1 million |
| TOTAL | $10 million |

The 1974 budgetary figure represents a reduction of 10% from 1973 levels in accordance with a mandate from Governor I. B. Good to increase the productivity of all state activities by a comparable amount.

The chancellor provides the following ground rules to his department heads for their guidance when preparing their plans for 1974:

A.  Emphasis will be on increased productivity.
B.  There will be no lessening of quality standards.
C.  Budgetary allocations will be adhered to strictly, both in total and by individual units.
D.  Final budgets are due on September 1, 1973.

The chancellor concludes the meeting with a pep talk about the satisfaction derived from doing a job well under trying circumstances.

Each of the Directors submitted his budget and the final budget was assembled on September 1. It reflected the following:

### Recommended Budget

| | |
|---|---|
| Director of Housing ..................................................... | $ 2 million |
| Director of Program Development .............................. | 1 million |
| Director of Communications Center ........................... | 3 million |
| Director of Residence Halls ...................................... | 1 million |
| Director of Testing Program ..................................... | 2 million |
| Chancellor's Office .................................................... | 1 million |
| TOTAL | $10 million |

The chancellor commended his staff for their planning expertise.

As with most traditionalists, this chancellor has made several telling mistakes—all of which will decrease his effectiveness as well as that of his organization. First, his approach precluded any but a cursory participation on the part of his managers. They parroted back to him what they assumed were predetermined figures and what their boss wanted to hear. Second, he deliberately refused to establish any competition among his managers for the available capital. Those who had been guilty of operating inefficiently in the past were given the same consideration as those who had been breaking their backs and operating in a highly effective manner. Thus, emphasis was placed on spending the money made available—not on optimizing results. Third, the chancellor has positioned the budget on the wrong end of his so-called planning process. He's assigned a cost allowance to each manager without first giving any consideration to priorities and what SHOULD be done during the year. Fourth, in the chancellor's approach, controlling took priority over motivating managers to greater accomplishment.

## Updating Budget's Purpose

The purpose and role of budgets must undergo considerable updating if budgets are to perform their required role—and it is a most important one—within an MBO system.

Budgets must be primarily viewed as "the planned allocation of resources to the manager's objectives." This is more than a change in definition! It involves an entirely new way of looking at budgets and their role.

Also, it requires viewing the very role of management in a new light. The true role of a manager can be viewed as "optimizing the return on the resources entrusted to him." It is the total optimization of all of a company's resources (capital, people, plant and equipment) by all of its managers which, in the last analysis, determines the success of the organization. Resources available to an individual manager are always limited in a healthy organization. A company which doesn't establish competition for its resources is a sick company as is a company which has more resources than it knows what to do with. Therefore, an effective planning and budgeting approach should always promote competition among its managers for the available resources. Except in those rare instances where exigencies of the moment may dictate a different priority, the available (and always limited) resources should be awarded to the manager who can justify a return of twelve per cent on the resources in contrast to another manager whose objective will return only eight per cent.

The revised definition and approach to budgeting means that:

A. The formulation of objectives and plans precedes the preparation of the budget.
B. Objectives are based on a priority of needs of the organization.
C. Each manager is given the opportunity to compete for available resources by demonstrating what he will do with the resources if they are awarded to him.

Thus, from an MBO viewpoint, budgets in their simplest form are the quantification in dollars and cents of what the objectives and plans of all managers viewed collectively mean in profit and/or loss for the target period.

Now let's return to the university chancellor and examine the manner in which he could have used the MBO approach to optimize his results.

His first remedial step would be to begin his process earlier in the year, say in January or February of 1973 when preparing plans for 1974. This earlier start will permit additional dialogue between him and his directors and among the directors themselves on major points which they must coordinate with each other.

Next he would not begin his briefings by assigning each of the directors a budget allocation. Instead, he would provide his directors with the ground rules within which they would do their planning. These ground rules might include the following:

A. Emphasis will be on increased return on the resources used.
B. Each director will submit specific objectives covering the major results he plans to achieve.
C. All objectives must be supported by concrete plans for achievement.
D. All plans and objectives must be justified to the maximum extent possible.
E. One overall organization objective is to lower total expenditures by the maximum extent possible consistent with contribution.
F. First draft of objectives and plans is due by March 15, 1973.
G. Final allocation of resources will be based on the relative merits of each director's objectives and the priorities of the overall organization.

In this revised approach, the chancellor has given each of his directors an opportunity to compete for the available resources. In effect he has said, "Tell me what you should be doing during 1974, justify it, and then we'll determine how much of the resources you will be awarded." Now, he's practicing a motivational approach to planning.

## The Updated Version in Practice

The rightful position of budgets can be seen by viewing the format of a typical profit plan for an organization operating under MBO. Figure 21 is a simplified version of the profit plan constructed under a motivational approach. The budget flows from objectives, not vice versa.

This format clearly indicates the budget in its proper position. This positioning promotes what is commonly referred to as the motivational approach to profit planning. The manager begins his planning with practically unlimited opportunity to optimize his results. He knows that his results are limited only by his ability to justify the contribution he can make. He doesn't begin his planning with a budgetary constraint. Figure 22 illustrates the position of the budget in a "fiscal" approach to planning. The objectives flow from the budget.

**Figure 21**
Position of the Budget in a Profit Plan (Prepared under the
"motivational" approach).

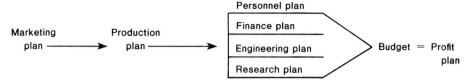

The manager in charge of each of the six major functions prepares his operating plan, containing his objectives and plans to achieve them. The operating plans are coordinated with all managers on a need to know basis. Then a budget is prepared. The budget thus flows from the objectives and plans.

**Figure 22**
Position of the Budget in a Profit Plan (Prepared under the
"fiscal" approach).

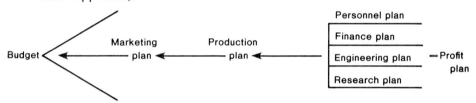

The budget is enunciated first and then objectives and plans are written to support the budget. Objectives and plans thus flow from the budget. This is an outgrowth of the "fiscal" approach to planning, i.e., revenue was projected, then costs were projected, and the difference constituted the objective.

## The Planning Sequence

The relationship of budgeting to planning and the role budgets should play can be illustrated by following the step-by-step sequence of the preparation of a profit plan for a particular year. The calendar year 1974 will be used in this illustration:

### Step 1

The top management of the organization issues what is commonly referred to as "the call for the profit plan" for 1974. Typically, this call is issued by the chief executive officer to each of the officers reporting to him.

This call will contain the following information to be used as guidance for lower levels of management as they prepare their "operating plans" (objectives and plans to achieve them):

A. The overall objectives of the organization for 1974.
B. An analysis of the outside environment as it may impact on the company's operations in 1974, e.g., the competitive picture, the economy in general, the industry picture, et cetera.
C. The priorities of the company during 1974.
D. The major assumptions on which the 1974 overall corporate objectives have been based.
E. The ground rules to be followed by lower level managers when preparing their operating plans.
F. A timetable for preparing the operating plans.

The manager should already be in possession of an approved long-range plan—commonly covering five years—for his department. This, of course, provides him with considerable guidance as he prepares his 1974 plans and objectives.

## Step 2

Each of the officers and department heads completes the necessary analysis and coordination with other managers and then submits his operating plan covering all of his operations for 1974. In essence, his operating plan will include:

A. The objectives recommended for the target period.
B. The plans by which each of the objectives will be achieved. (Sometimes referred to as "programming the objectives.")
C. "Ball Park" numbers as to what the objectives and plans mean in terms of revenues, expenses, and rates of return, plus capital required.

In effect, each of these managers is preparing an estimated budget covering his planned operations. It is emphasized that the manager prepares this budget *after* determining what he plans to accomplish. He does not begin his planning with a set of budget figures handed to him from above.

## Step 3

This step comprises the analysis and consolidation of the operating plans of all of the officers into a total profit plan for the organization. (See Figure 21).

A. The operating plans of all of the officers and their departments will be subjected to a penetrating financial analysis and a consolidated budget will be prepared for the total company.

B. The president and his staff[2] will review the total profit plan for consistency with company objectives, ground rules, and priorities.

C. The president may discuss with each of his officers the officer's operating plan and suggest revisions or complete changes.

D. A consolidated budget is prepared reflecting the changes resulting from C, above. Resources are allocated to the objectives based upon how well each manager competed for the available resources and the priorities which have been set for the target period.

E. The consolidated budget is compared to the overall objectives of the corporation for the target period.

F. If the consolidated budget is consistent with the corporate objectives, the operating plans are approved.

G. If the consolidated budget is not consistent with the corporate objectives, one of two approaches will be followed:

   (1) The operating plans will be returned to the officers for additional analysis and efforts to try to bring them up to the corporate objectives, or,

   (2) The operating plans—if considered valid—are accepted and the corporate objectives are adjusted accordingly.

Additional comment is in order with respect to G, above. The hallmarks of an achievement-oriented manager are twofold; (1) a willingness to take the necessary time and effort to arrive at well formulated objectives and plans in the first place and, (2) to be completely unwilling to adjust the objectives downward unless there is absolutely no alternative action which he can take to prevent the downward adjustment.

Thus, in G above, when all of the individual operating plans do not add up to the overall corporate objectives, the first recourse should not be to lower the overall objectives. First, complete emphasis should be devoted to leaving the objectives at their present levels and then pursuing all possible alternatives for overcoming the void.

## Step 4

Figure 21 indicates that preparation of the budget is the concluding part of the profit plan. And, this is an accurate portrayal when the profit plan is viewed for a particular target period, say one year.

However, in a very real sense, there is never a "conclusion" to the planning process—it is a continuous and ongoing part of the job of all managers. Once the profit plan has been approved it is not filed away to be removed from the files and read sometime in the future. It must be looked upon as a viable, living document which the manager uses as the major guide for his day-to-day actions. Actual performance against the plan will be evaluated as the year unfolds. Certain revisions will be necessary during the year to keep the plan realistic. The experience gained with the plan during one year will serve as the basis for much of what is included in the profit plans for subsequent years.

Thus, the planning process should be considered as a continuous circle or loop in which:

A. Objectives, plans, and budgets are prepared for a particular target period.
B. The objectives, plans, and budgets are approved and the manager begins operating under his plan.
C. Results vs. plan are evaluated continuously during the target period and at the conclusion of it.
D. The entire process is repeated beginning with the preparation of objectives, plans, and budgets for the next target period.


## Conclusion

Budgets have a key role to play in the MBO system but they are not an end in themselves. Once properly viewed and constructed, they provide a valuable vehicle for controlling or monitoring; however; their primary thrust should not be for control purposes.

The primary thrust of budgeting must be to motivate managers to optimize their results. Control is a secondary, later consideration and should come about as a by-product—not as the main product.

The transition from "control" to "motivational" budgeting necessitates a change not only in the positioning of the budget but, also, a rather radical change in the position and orientation of the budget director. Traditionally, he has been a member of the controller's staff and as such has had a financial statement orientation of looking backwards at what has already happened. He must start considering himself as a member of the management team looking ahead. A backward orientation implies control. A forward orientation permits the motivational approach.

This transition is not easily made. It requires a radical departure from decades of training and practice which emphasized the function of the budget director as one who looked at corporate life through a rear view mirror where he often saw little but controls, reports, and variances. Unfortunately, even today, only a few schools of business approach budgeting from an MBO, motivational approach.

The motivational approach to budgeting requires that:

A. Competition for resources be emphasized.
B. Results not be predetermined by beginning the planning process with budgetary allocations.

C.  Each manager be permitted and encouraged to demonstrate the contribution which he is capable of making, before resources are awarded.
D.  Budgets should flow from objectives. Objectives should not flow from budgets.

Management by Objectives, properly implemented and directed, is a potent means for motivating managers to greater performance. MBO is an achievement-oriented approach. The role of budgets must be one which capitalizes on the motivational qualities which are inherent in the system.

1.  For an in-depth treatment of this impact see Dale D. McConkey, "MBO—Twenty Years Later, Where Do We Stand?" *Business Horizons*, Volume 14, August 1973.
2.  The president's staff in this case may include the financial officer, the top planning manager, and other staff specialists. In some cases it may include a budget committee.

# 3

# Split Roles
# in Performance Appraisal

Herbert H. Meyer
Emanuel Kay
John R.P. French, Jr.

- *What is the purpose of the appraisal interview?*
- *How much effect does it have on job performance?*
- *Why is it in conflict with salary action?*
- *How else can workers be motivated to improve?*

In management circles, performance appraisal is a highly interesting and provocative topic. And in business literature, too, knowledgeable people write emphatically, pro and con, on the performance appraisal question.[1] In fact, one might almost say that everybody talks and writes about it, but nobody has done any real scientific testing of it.

At the General Electric Company we felt it was important that a truly scientific study be done to test the effectiveness of our traditional performance appraisal program. Why? Simply because our own experience with performance appraisal programs had been both positive and negative. For example:

• Surveys generally show that most people think the idea of performance appraisal is good. They feel that a man should know where he stands and, therefore, the manager should discuss an appraisal of his performance with him periodically.

• In actual practice, however, it is the extremely rare operating manager who will employ such a program on his own initiative. Personnel specialists report that most managers carry out performance appraisal interviews only when strong control procedures are established to ensure that they do so. This is surprising because the managers have been told repeatedly that the system is intended to help them obtain improved performance from their subordinates.

We also found from interviews with employees who have had a good deal of experience with traditional performance appraisal programs that few indeed can cite examples of constructive action taken—or significant improvement achieved—which stem from suggestions received in a performance appraisal interview with their boss.

## Traditional Program

Faced with such contradictory evidence, we undertook a study several years ago to determine the effectiveness of our comprehensive performance appraisal process. Special attention was focused on the interview between the subordinate and his manager, because this is the discussion which is supposed to motivate the man to improve his performance. And we found out some very interesting things—among them the following:

- Criticism has a negative effect on achievement of goals.
- Praise has little effect one way or the other.
- Performance improves most when specific goals are established.
- Defensiveness resulting from critical appraisal produces inferior performance.
- Coaching should be a day-to-day, not a once-a-year, activity.
- Mutual goal setting, not criticism, improves performance.
- Interviews designed primarily to improve a man's performance should not at the same time weigh his salary or promotion in the balance.
- Participation by the employee in the goal-setting procedure helps produce favorable results.

As you can see, the results of this original study indicated that a detailed and comprehensive annual appraisal of a subordinate's performance by his manager is decidedly of questionable value. Furthermore, as is certainly the case when the major objective of such a discussion is to motivate the subordinate to improve his performance, the traditional appraisal interview does not do the job.

In the first part of this article, we will offer readers more than this bird's-eye view of our research into performance appraisal. (We will not, however, burden managers with details of methodology.) We will also describe the one-year follow-up experiment General Electric conducted to validate the conclusions derived from our original study. Here the traditional annual performance appraisal method was tested against a new method we developed, which we called Work Planning and Review (WP&R). As you will see, this approach produced, under actual plant conditions, results which were decidedly superior to those afforded by the traditional performance appraisal method. Finally, we will offer evidence to support our contention that some form of WP&R might well be incorporated into other industrial personnel programs to achieve improvement in work performance.

## Appraising Appraisal

In order to assure a fair test of the effectiveness of the traditional performance appraisal method, which had been widely used throughout General Electric, we conducted an intensive study of the process at a large GE plant where the performance appraisal program was judged to be good; that is, in this plant—

. . . appraisals had been based on job responsibilities, rather than on personal characteristics of the individuals involved;

. . . an intensive training program had been carried out for managers in the use of the traditional appraisal method and techniques for conducting appraisal interviews;

. . . the program had been given strong backing by the plant manager and had been policed diligently by the personnel staff so that over 90% of the exempt employees had been appraised and interviewed annually.

This comprehensive annual performance appraisal program, as is typical, was designed to serve two major purposes. The first was to justify recommended salary action. The second, which was motivational in character, was intended to present an opportunity for the manager to review a subordinate's performance and promote discussion on needed improvements. For the latter purpose, the manager was required to draw up a specific program of plans and goals for the subordinate which would help him to improve his job performance and to qualify, hopefully, for future promotion.

## Interview Modifications

Preliminary interviews with key managers and subordinates revealed the salary action issue had so dominated the annual comprehensive performance appraisal interview that neither party had been in the right frame of mind to discuss plans for improved performance. To straighten this out, we asked managers to split the traditional appraisal interview into two sessions—discussing appraisal of performance and salary action in one interview and performance improvement plans in another to be held about two weeks later. This split provided us with a better opportunity to conduct our experiment on the effects of participation in goal planning.

To enable us to test the effects of participation, we instructed half the managers to use a *high participation* approach and the other half to use a *low participation technique*. Thus:

• Each of the "high" managers was instructed to ask his appraisee to prepare a set of goals for achieving improved job performance and to submit them for the manager's review and approval. The manager also was encouraged to permit the subordinate to exert as much influence as possible on the formulation of the final list of job goals agreed on in the performance improvement discussion.

• The "low" managers operated in much the same way they had in our traditional appraisal program. They formulated a set of goals for the subordinate, and these goals were then reviewed in the performance improvement session. The manager was instructed to conduct this interview in such a way that his influence in the forming of the final list of job goals would be greater than the subordinate's.

### Conducting the Research

There were 92 appraisees in the experimental group, representing a cross section of the exempt salaried employees in the plant. This group included engineers; engineering support technicians; foremen; and specialists in manufacturing, customer service, marketing, finance, and purchasing functions. None of the exempt men who participated as appraisees in the experiment had other exempt persons reporting to them; thus they did not serve in conflicting manager-subordinate roles.

The entire group was interviewed and asked to complete questionnaires (a) before and after the salary action interview, and (b) after the delayed second discussion with their managers about performance improvement. These interviews and questionnaires were designed to achieve three objectives:

1. Assess changes in the attitudes of individuals toward their managers and toward the appraisal system after each of the discussions.
2. Get an estimate from the appraisee of the degree to which he usually participated in decisions that affected him. (This was done in order to determine whether or not previous lack of participation affected his response to participation in the experiment.)
3. Obtain a self-appraisal from each subordinate before and after he met with his manager. (This was done in order to determine how discrepancies in these self-appraisals might affect his reaction to the appraisal interview.)

Moreover, each salary action and performance improvement discussion was observed by outsiders trained to record essentially what transpired. (Managers preferred to use neither tape recorders nor unseen observers, feeling that observers unaffiliated with the company—in this case, graduate students in applied psychological disciplines—afforded the best way of obtaining a reasonably close approximation of the normal discussions.) In the appraisal for salary action interviews, for example, the observers recorded the amount of criticism and praise employed by the manager, as well as the reactions of the appraisee to the manager's comments. In the performance improvement discussions, the observers recorded the participation of the subordinate, as well as the amount of influence he seemed to exert in establishing his future success goals.

### Criticism and Defensiveness

In general, the managers completed the performance appraisal forms in a thorough and conscientious manner. Their appraisals were discussed with subordinates in interviews ranging from approximately 30 to 90 minutes in length. On the average, managers covered 32 specific performance items which, when broken down, showed positive (praise) appraisals on 19 items, and negative (criticism) on 13. Typically, praise was more often related to *general* performance characteristics, while criticism was usually focused on *specific* performance items.

The average subordinate reacted defensively to seven of the manager's criticisms during the appraisal interview (that is, he reacted defensively about 54% of the time when criticized). Denial of shortcomings cited by the manager, blaming others, and various other forms of excuses were recorded by the observers as defensive reactions.

Constructive responses to criticism were *rarely* observed. In fact, the average was less than one per interview. Not too surprising, along with this, was the finding that the more criticism a man received in the performance appraisal discussion, the more defensively he reacted. Men who received an above-average number of criticisms showed more than five times as much defensive behavior as those who received a below-average number of criticisms. Subordinates who received a below-average number of criticisms, for example, reacted defensively only about one time out of three. But those who received an above-average number reacted defensively almost two times out of three.

One explanation for this defensiveness is that it seems to stem from the overrating each man tended to give to his own performance. The average employee's self-estimate of performance *before* appraisal placed him at the 77 percentile. (Only 2 of the 92 participants estimated their performance to be below the average point on the scale.) But when the same men were asked *after* their performance appraisal discussions how they thought their bosses had rated them, the average figure given was at the 65 percentile. The great majority (75 out of 92) saw their manager's evaluation as being less favorable than their self-estimates. Obviously, to these men, the performance appraisal discussion with the manager was a deflating experience. Thus, it was not surprising that the subordinates reacted defensively in their interviews.

### Criticism and Goal Achievement

Even more important is the fact that men who received an above-average number of criticisms in their performance appraisal discussions generally showed *less* goal achievement 10 to 12 weeks later than those who had received fewer criticisms. At first, we thought that this difference might be accounted for by the fact that the subordinates who received more criticisms were probably poorer performers in general. But there was little factual evidence found to support this suspicion.

It was true that those who received an above-average number of criticisms in their appraisal discussions did receive slightly lower summary ratings on over-all performance from their managers. But they did not receive proportionally lower salary increases. And the salary increases granted were *supposed* to reflect differences in job performance, according to the salary plan traditionally used in this plant. This argument, admittedly, is something less than perfect.

But it does appear clear that frequent criticism constitutes so strong a threat to self-esteem that it disrupts rather than improves subsequent performance. We expected such a disruptive threat to operate more strongly on those individuals who were already low on self-esteem, just as we expected a man who had confidence in his ability to do his job to react more constructively to criticism. Our group experiment proved these expectations to be correct.

Still further evidence that criticism has a negative effect on performance was found when we investigated areas which had been given special emphasis by the manager in his criticism. Following the appraisal discussion with the manager, each employee was asked to indicate which one aspect of his performance had been most criticized by the manager. Then, when we conducted our follow-up investigation 10 to 12 weeks later, it revealed that improvement in the most-criticized aspects of performance cited was considerably *less* than improvement realized in other areas!

### Participation Effects

As our original research study had indicated, the effects of a high participation level were also favorable in our group experiment. In general, here is what we found:

• Subordinates who received a high participation level in the performance interview reacted more favorably than did those who received a low participation level. The "highs" also, in most cases, achieved a greater percentage of their improvement goals than did their "low" counterparts. For the former, the high participation level was associated with greater mutual understanding between them and their managers, greater acceptance of job goals, a more favorable attitude toward the appraisal system, and a feeling of greater self-realization on the job.

• But employees who had traditionally been accustomed to low participation in their daily relationship with the manager did not necessarily perform better under the high participation treatment. In fact, those men who had received a high level of criticism in their appraisal interviews actually performed better when their managers set goals for them than they did when they set their own goals, as permitted under the high participation treatment.

In general, our experiment showed that the men who usually worked under high participation levels performed best on goals they set for themselves. Those who indicated that they usually worked under low levels performed best on goals that the managers set for them. Evidently, the man who usually does not participate in work-planning decisions considers job goals set by the manager to be more important than goals he sets for himself. The man accustomed to a high participation level, on the other hand, may have stronger motivation to achieve goals he sets for himself than to achieve those set by his manager.

## Goal-Setting Importance

While subordinate participation in the goal-setting process had some effect on improved performance, a much more powerful influence was whether goals were set at all. Many times in appraisal discussions, managers mentioned areas of performance where improvement was needed. Quite often these were translated into specific work plans and goals. But this was not always the case. In fact, when we looked at the one performance area which each manager had emphasized in the appraisal interview as most in need of improvement, we found that these items actually were translated into specific work plans and goals for only about 60% of our experiment participants.

When performance was being measured 10 to 12 weeks after the goal-planning sessions, managers were asked to describe what results they hoped for in the way of subordinate on-the-job improvement. They did this for those important performance items that had been mentioned in the interview. Each manager was then asked to estimate on a percentage scale the degree to which his hoped-for changes had actually been observed. The average percent accomplishment estimate for those performance items that *did* get translated into goals was 65; while the percent estimate for those items that *did not* get translated into goals was about 27! Establishing specific plans and goals seemed to ensure that attention would be given to that aspect of job performance.

## Summation of Findings

At the end of this experiment, we were able to draw certain tentative conclusions. These conclusions were the basis of a future research study which we will describe later. In general, we learned that:

• *Comprehensive annual performance appraisals are of questionable value.* Certainly a major objective of the manager in traditional appraisal discussions is motivating the subordinate to improve his performance. But the evidence we gathered indicated clearly that praise tended to have no effect, perhaps because it was regarded as the sandwich which surrounded the raw meat criticism.[2] And criticism itself brought on defensive reactions that were essentially denials of responsibility for a poor performance.

• *Coaching should be a day-to-day, not a once-a-year, activity.* There are two main reasons for this:

1. Employees seem to accept suggestions for improved performance if they are given in a less concentrated form than is the case in comprehensive annual appraisals. As our experiment showed, employees become clearly more prone to reject criticisms as the number of criticisms mount. This indicates that an "overload phenomenon" may be operating. In other words, each individual seems to have a tolerance level for the amount of criticism he can take. And, as this level is approached or passed, it becomes increasingly difficult for him to accept responsibility for the shortcomings pointed out.

2. Some managers reported that the traditional performance appraisal program tended to cause them to save up items where improvement was needed in order to have enough material to conduct a comprehensive discussion of performance in the annual review. This short-circuited one of the primary purposes of the appraisal program—that of giving feedback to the subordinates as to their performance. Studies of the learning process point out that feedback is less effective if much time is allowed to elapse between the performance and the feedback. This fact alone argues for more frequent discussions between the manager and the subordinate.

• *Goal setting, not criticism, should be used to improve performance.* One of the most significant findings in our experiment was the fact that far superior results were observed when the manager and the man *together* set specific goals to be achieved, rather than merely discussed needed improvement. Frequent reviews of progress provide natural opportunities for discussing means of improving performance *as needs occur,* and these reviews are far less threatening than the annual appraisal and salary review discussions.

• *Separate appraisals should be held for different purposes* .Our work demonstrated that it was unrealistic to expect a single performance appraisal program to achieve every conceivable need. It seems foolish to have a manager serving in the self-conflicting role as a counselor (helping a man to improve his performance) when, at the same time, he is presiding as a judge over the same employee's salary action case.

## New WP&R Method

This intensive year-long test of the performance appraisal program indicated clearly that work-planning-and-review discussions between a man and his manager appeared to be a far more effective approach in improving job performance than was the concentrated annual performance appraisal program.

For this reason, after the findings had been announced, many GE managers adopted some form of the new WP&R program to motivate performance improvement in employees, especially those at the professional and administrative levels. Briefly described, the WP&R approach calls for periodic meetings between the manager and his subordinate. During these meetings, progress on past goals is reviewed, solutions are sought for job-related problems, and new goals are established. The intent of the method is to create a situation in which manager and subordinate can discuss job performance and needed improvements in detail without the subordinate becoming defensive.

## Basic Features
This WP&R approach differs from the traditional performance appraisal program in that:

- There are more frequent discussions of performance.
- There are no summary judgments or ratings made.
- Salary action discussions are held separately.
- The emphasis is on mutual goal planning and problem solving.

As far as frequency is concerned, these WP&R discussions are held more often than traditional performance appraisal interviews, but are not scheduled at rigidly fixed intervals. Usually at the conclusion of one work planning session the man and manager set an approximate date for the next review. Frequency depends both on the nature of the job and on the manager's style of operating. Sometimes these WP&R discussions are held as often as once a month, whereas for other jobs and/or individuals, once every six months is more appropriate.

In these WP&R discussions, the manager and his subordinate do not deal in generalities. They consider specific, objectively defined work goals and establish the yardstick for measuring performance. These goals stem, of course, from broader departmental objectives and are defined in relation to the individual's position in the department.

## Comparison Setting
After the findings of our experiment were communicated by means of reports and group meetings in the plant where the research was carried out, about half the key managers decided they would abandon the comprehensive annual performance appraisal method and adopt the new WP&R program instead. The other half were hesitant to make such a major change at the time. They decided, consequently, to continue with the traditional performance appraisal program and to try to make it more effective. This provided a natural setting for us to compare the effectiveness of the two approaches. We decided that the comparison should be made in the light of the objectives usually stated for the comprehensive annual performance program. These objectives were (a) to provide

knowledge of results to employees, (b) to justify reasons for salary action, and (c) to motivate and help employees do a better job.

The study design was simple. Before any changes were made, the exempt employees who would be affected by these programs were surveyed to provide base-line data. The WP&R program was then implemented in about half of the exempt group, with the other half continuing to use a modified version of the traditional performance appraisal program. One year later, the identical survey questionnaire was again administered in order to compare the changes that had occurred.

**Attitudes and Actions**

The results of this research study were quite convincing. The group that continued on the traditional performance appraisal showed no change in *any* of the areas measured. The WP&R group, by contrast, expressed significantly more favorable attitudes on almost all questionnaire items. Specifically, their attitudes changed in a favorable direction over the year that they participated in the new WP&R program with regard to the—

. . . amount of help the manager was giving them in improving performance on the job;

. . . degree to which the manager was receptive to new ideas and suggestions;

. . . ability of the manager to plan;

. . . extent to which the manager made use of their abilities and experience;

. . . degree to which they felt the goals they were shooting for were what they *should* be;

. . . extent to which they received help from the manager in planning for *future* job opportunities;

. . . value of the performance discussions they had with their managers.

In addition to these changes in attitudes, evidence was also found which showed clearly that the members of the WP&R group were much more likely to have taken specific actions to improve performance than were those who continued with the traditional performance appraisal approach.

## Current Observations

Recently we undertook still another intensive study of the WP&R program in order to learn more about the nature of these discussions and how they can be made most effective. While these observations have not been completed, some interesting findings have already come to light— especially in relation to differences between WP&R and traditional performance appraisal discussions.

**Perceived Differences**

For one thing, WP&R interviews are strictly man-to-man in character, rather than having a father-and-son flavor, as did so many of the traditional performance appraisals. This seems to be due to the fact that it is much more natural under the WP&R program for the subordinate to take the initiative when his performance on past goals is being reviewed. Thus, in listening to the subordinate's review of performance, problems, and failings, the manager is automatically cast in the role of *counselor*. This role for the manager, in turn, results naturally in a problem-solving discussion.

In the traditional performance appraisal interview, on the other hand, the manager is automatically cast in the role of *judge*. The subordinate's natural reaction is to assume a defensive posture, and thus all the necessary ingredients for an argument are present.

Since the WP&R approach focuses mainly on immediate, short-term goals, some managers are concerned that longer range, broader plans and goals might be neglected. Our data show that this concern is unfounded. In almost every case, the discussion of specific work plans and goals seems to lead naturally into a consideration of broader, longer range plans. In fact, in a substantial percentage of these sessions, even the career plans of the subordinates are reviewed.

In general the WP&R approach appears to be a better way of defining what is expected of an individual and how he is doing on the job. Whereas the traditional performance appraisal often results in resistance to the manager's attempts to help the subordinate, the WP&R approach brings about acceptance of such attempts.

## Conclusion

Multiple studies conducted by the Behavioral Research Service at GE reveal that the traditional performance appraisal method contains a number of problems:

1. Appraisal interviews attempt to accomplish the two objectives of—
   . . . providing a written justification for salary action;
   . . . motivating the employee to improve his work performance.
2. The two purposes are in conflict with the result that the traditional appraisal system essentially becomes a salary discussion in which the manager justifies the action taken.
3. The appraisal discussion has little influence on future job performance.
4. Appreciable improvement is realized only when specified goals and deadlines are mutually established and agreed on by the subordinate and his manager in an interview split away from the appraisal interview.

This evidence, coupled with other principles relating to employee motivation, gave rise to the new WP&R program, which is proving to be far more effective in improving job performance than the traditional performance appraisal method. Thus, it appears likely that companies which are currently relying on the comprehensive annual performance appraisal process to achieve improvement in work performance might well consider the advisability of switching to some form of work-planning-and-review in their industrial personnel programs.

1. Douglas McGregor, "An Uneasy Look at Performance Appraisal," HBR May-June 1957, p. 89; Harold Mayfield, "In Defense of Performance Appraisal," HBR March-April 1960, p. 81; and Alva F. Kindall and James Gatza, "Positive Program for Performance Appraisal," HBR November-December 1963, p. 153.
2. See Richard E. Farson, "Praise Reappraised," HBR September-October 1963, p. 61.

# 4

# MBO: Appraisal with Transactional Analysis

Management by Objectives (MBO) is considered one of the most effective approaches to management. Indeed, many practicing managers embrace it and integrate it with their job. But, there are also those who point at the shortcomings—especially if MBO is used only as an appraisal tool—citing undesirable side effects of MBO.

The question, then, becomes who is right, those who hail the successes or those who point at the pitfalls? The intent here is to build on the sound aspects of MBO, add an important ingredient—transactional analysis (TA)—and thus overcome its potential pitfalls. The approach is to build on the strengths of MBO and to overcome its weaknesses. By looking at some of the problems more closely, it is apparent that what is wrong is not the MBO concept, but how MBO is practiced. Before focusing on TA, let's briefly review important MBO concepts.

*Management by Objectives.* MBO is a philosophy as well as a process. Its early application was in appraisal. Later, the motivational aspects were recognized. Some companies also include long-range planning in the MBO process. My preference is to see it as a system of managing, in which key management activities in planning, organizing, staffing, directing, and controlling become an integral part of MBO.[1]

Reduced to its essentials, MBO involves the following steps: (1) setting objectives, (2) directing activities toward the achievement of objectives, and (3) measuring performance against these objectives. This discussion will emphasize the third step: the measurement of performance. More specifically, we will be concerned with the relationship of the superior-subordinate in the appraisal process.

*Some Problems Still Persist.* In the historical development of management, MBO was certainly a step in the right direction. In its early application, MBO overcame some of the problems of traditional appraisals that emphasized personality traits. In MBO appraisal, on the other hand, the focus is on results. Performance is evaluated against verifiable objectives, rather than purely subjective judgments by the superior. Moreover, in MBO the attention is on contributions individuals make to the broader organizational aims.

But, in the delicate interaction between a supervisor and an employee, many problems still persist. There are still those supervisors who think that unless *they* set the objectives for employees, no performance will be forthcoming. There are still those who ignore the needs of employees and who are not tapping the individual's motives to contribute to organizational objectives. There are still those who set unrealistic objectives for employees only to punish them when the goals are not achieved, regardless of whether or not the non-achievement was due to external, uncontrollable circumstances. There are still those who would rather see employees fail just to prove their own superiority. And finally, there are still those who think that MBO is a tool to pressure for performance at the expense of human costs. How far is this removed from the MBO philosophy!

MBO, when properly practiced, integrates personal and organization objectives. It elicits commitment of individuals through genuine participation in the decision making process. It provides the basis for self-control whereby the individual determines largely for himself how to achieve the objectives, which were set in a collaborative manner with his supervisor. And finally, MBO provides for genuine freedom, utilizing the potentials and creativity of individuals while contributing to the organization's aims. Where, then, does MBO fail? One of the important areas is the ineffective interaction between an employee and his supervisor. It is suggested here that transactional analysis can become an effective tool to deal with this problem.

## Transactional Analysis and Appraisal

Transactional analysis (TA) was introduced by Eric Berne, and further popularized by Thomas A. Harris' book, *I'm OK—You're OK*. But the real value of TA for managers has not yet been generally recognized. It is clear that many transactions occur between a supervisor and an employee, but there are few that are as crucial as those found in appraisal. This is so because appraisal involves our ego states. Judgments are made, and most of us feel uncomfortable in such situations, be it as a supervisor or as an employee.

*What is TA?* TA is concerned with transactions between people. In a transaction, the presence of another person is acknowledged in some way. The other person then, responds, for example, by saying something, or through gestures, or other means of communication. This explanation of TA perhaps sounds too broad. Therefore, I think one can better understand TA by looking at four kinds of analysis: (1) structural analysis,

(2) transactional analysis, (3) games analysis, and (4) the analysis of life positions.

1. *Structural Analysis.* In structural analysis, the focus is on the individual. Everyone has within himself three ego states. The colloquial terms to describe them are: Parent, Adult, and Child. These terms do not refer to actual parents, adults, or children, but rather they are ego states which comprise our personality. This is why we capitalize them in this discussion, and illustrate them as follows:

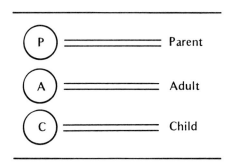

The *Parent ego state* pertains to those brain recordings which are unquestioned events imposed by the external environment during early life. It also refers to attitudes and behavior related to these events. The things we learn early in life influence our behavior as managers. Does this sound too abstract? Well, here is an example from a managerial situation. The supervisor, in interaction with an employee, would, in the Parent ego state, comment: "Do as I say," perhaps citing company rules, regulations, and policies, rather than giving a sound explanation for his orders.

The *Adult ego state* refers to rational thinking, information gathering and processing, reality testing, and the like. In the organizational setting, MBO appraisal is—and this is important—based on self-control. The supervisor and the employee jointly set goals. Later, performance is measured against pre-established objectives, but the evaluation is largely done by the employee himself. Deviations are then noted and their causes are analyzed. Problems are solved in an objective manner with the Adult ego state guiding the interactions.

The *Child ego state* is not related to age. Rather it pertains to internal events recorded in the brain, also during early life. It refers more to feeling aspects, such as fear, anxiety, searching for approval; but it also includes the creative aspects of a person. In an ineffective appraisal, for example, the employee may blame others for his non-achievement of pre-established goals. Or, he simply may take a carefree attitude, taking his managerial job casually, not caring about performance at all. On the positive side, the Child ego state may also be helpful, facilitating the creative search for alternatives to solve a particular problem.

The described ego states, the Parent, Adult, and Child, are present in all of us. In appraisal, as noted, one may find that one or the other dominates in the interactions between the superior and the subordinate. Recognizing the ego state that influences our behavior will make us more effective during appraisals either as supervisors or as employees.

2. *Transactional Analysis.* A transaction, as used here, involves the interaction of ego states of people. In our discussion, it will be the superior and subordinate during the appraisal process. The interaction can be illustrated as follows:

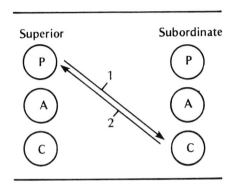

This, of course, is very pertinent to appraisal. Typically, we find interactions as shown in the diagram. The supervisor evaluates the performance of an employee, possibly with a pointing index finger. (Note that we communicate not only through the spoken language; our gestures and facial expressions are sometimes more important than what we say.) In response, the employee replies, perhaps, with a "Yes, sir." Is this MBO, based on self-control? Certainly not.

---

Recognizing the ego state that influences our behavior will help to make us more effective during appraisals either as employees or as supervisors.

---

A more constructive transaction would be on the Adult-Adult ego state level. Here the inequality of power relations does not stand in the way of genuine Adult interactions. Both the supervisor and the employee engage in appraisal—i.e., primarily self-appraisal—of performance. Both are involved in evaluating past performance. But the appraising is mostly done by the employee. The supervisor and the employee then analyze deviation from standards, searching for the causes. Both engage in problem

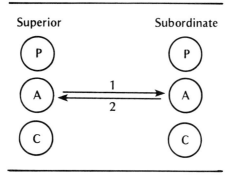

solving. Both develop strategies to prevent problems from recurring, and both set realistic, yet challenging, objectives for the future. Yes, both learn from the past. But the past cannot be changed—the future can. Consequently the thrust of the appraisal is positive—it is on the future. It is there where the opportunities for improved performance lie.

The two illustrations above were complementary, that is, the interactions indicated by lines in a diagram were parallel. As pointed out, traditionally we find a Parent-Child interaction in appraisal. Note that this kind of interaction can continue for a long time without an interruption. Of course, this is not a very effective way. However, a real breakdown in communication occurs when the transactions are non-complementary, as illustrated by the crossed lines in the following diagram:

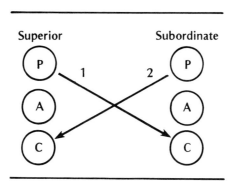

The supervisor, evaluating the performance of the employee, could get a response something like this, "Who do you think you are, judging my performance!" In such a case, the appraisal setting has become a battleground rather than the occasion for focusing on the development of the individual.

Besides these three illustrations, different transactions can transpire. These may originate in either Parent, Adult, or Child. Similarly, the responses can be Parent, Adult, or Child. Perhaps now that we have the basic tools for the analysis of transactions we can recognize our predominant modes of interaction with others. This would be the first step in modifying our behavior, an important desirable outcome of appraisal.

3. *Analysis of Games.* A game has been defined by Berne as follows: Descriptively it is a recurring set of transactions, often repetitious, superficially plausible, with a concealed motivation; or, more coloquially, a series of moves with a snare, or "gimmick." It is clear that games, as used here, are basically dishonest, self-defeating, and destructive. Their underlying theme is "Mine is better than yours," a game played by children, but also played in different versions by employees in organizations. Unfortunately, appraisal is often the occasion for organizational games. Berne has a whole classification of games and, I am sure, new ones will be identified. Recognizing the games—especially our own—is useful, but to call the games of others is rather risky. One should not be surprised to get an angry response. So, the first step in developing honest interactions would be to identify our own games and stop playing them, because if they are not stopped they will be repeated.

MBO appraisal involves not only looking at past performance, but it also includes planning for the future and setting of new goals, especially improvement and creative ones. There, then, are some examples of games played during the typical appraisal. There may be a supervisor who responds to the suggested creative objectives of an employee with "Yes, but . . . ." The reasons given after the "but" may vary from being impractical, not pertinent, or outright silly. This game, it is clear, completely destroys any initiative in the employee.

There is the other boss who sets goals for employees (note that this is not congruent with MBO philosophy which emphasizes participation in setting objectives) so unrealistically high that individuals may get frustrated and never reach the objectives. Consequently, when appraisal time comes, the boss can argue that the non-achievement of objectives does not justify a raise in salary.

Employees play their games, too. For example, one may set objectives purposely at an unrealistically low level just to prove to a superior what an outstanding person he is when performance is measured against these low standards. In all, it is evident that games organizational people play during the appraisal process are rather destructive.

4. *Life Positions.* Every one of us has learned to play roles which are acted out through most of our lives. Rather early in life we adopt psychological positions, positions related to ourselves and others. We will discuss four of them and see how they relate to appraisal.

a. *I'm not OK—You're OK.* This is a position adopted early in life. A person with such an outlook feels inferior because he compares himself to others he considers OK. Of course, in any comparison one will fall short in some respects. As we know, in performance appraisal this is not uncommon. Often the employee, operating from the Child ego state and a not-OK-position, views the supervisor as the all-knowing Parent figure. While this is common in the organizational setting, it is clear that this does not release the potential of the subordinate, nor is it a healthy position for growth.

b. *I'm not OK—You're not OK.* This is a rather hopeless position. The subordinate may, for example, display a regressive behavior, and the appraisal process with the superior (who is also considered not OK) is an effort resulting in futility. The individual may show extreme withdrawal and an effective interaction between the supervisor and the employee is hardly possible.

c. *I'm OK—You're not OK.* This is a position in which the employee, for example, may feel persecuted. Thus, he may blame others, without justification, for the failure of not achieving the pre-established objectives. Hatred or anger may be harbored—often beneath the surface—against the superior, fellow workers, or the organization in general. It is a position wherein one feels he is right and everyone else is wrong. This, it is clear, is an extremely difficult situation for a supervisor.

d. *I'm OK—You're OK.* This is, of course, basically the healthy position. The employee evaluates his performance against pre-established, verifiable objectives. He knows and acknowledges whether or not he achieved them. He solicits the help of his superior (whom he considers OK) to develop plans for the future which are designed to build on strengths and to overcome weaknesses. He is not blind to his shortcoming, but views them as a challenge. He is confident in his abilities and feels good about his accomplishments. Moreover, he trusts his superior, who is not out to "get him," and collaborates with him in his own personal development which, in turn, contributes to organizational objectives.

## Conclusion

Management by Objectives is one of the most successful approaches to management. When applied to appraisal, it still has weaknesses. To overcome them, transactional analysis is recommended. The understanding of the four aspects of TA will make the delicate interactions between the supervisor and the employee during the appraisal process more productive.

1. Recognizing our predominant ego state—Parent, Adult, or Child—is the first step to better self-knowledge. Based on an understanding of ourselves, the most appropriate behavior can be selected.

2. In transactional analysis we become aware of our interactions between our ego states and those of others. The predominant Parent-Child interaction between supervisor and employee can be supplemented, if not replaced, by productive Adult-Adult behavior whereby the superior and subordinate—in a collaborative manner—set objectives, develop action plans, and evaluate performance against standards. If deviations occur, both engage in positive problem solving behavior with the aim to learn from the past and determine the future.

3. Organizational games are, to say the least, dysfunctional. At worst, they are outright dangerous. Games must be recognized for what they are. They prevent honest interactions between supervisor and employees with the result that the individuals themselves, as well as the organization, suffer. Knowledge of the games we play, on the other hand, leads to the desire to stop them.

4. Our life position—pertaining to the OK or not OK of ourselves and others—will determine whether or not appraisal against verifiable objectives will be effective. A healthy "I'm OK—You're OK" position is the basis for effective appraisal, which then becomes a collaborative process between the superior and subordinate. Both evaluate past performance in a constructive manner. Both learn from the past, but they determine the future by planning ahead and setting new goals.

In summary, the complex and delicate process of appraisal against verifiable objectives is greatly facilitated by the use of transactional analysis. It provides insights about our ego states and our interactions with others. It is a positive and constructive approach that is beneficial for the individual and the organization.

1. Heinz Weihrich. "A Study of the Integration of Management by Objectives with Key Managerial Activities and the Relationship to Selected Effectiveness Measures." Unpublished doctoral dissertation, University of California, Los Angeles, 1973.

# 5
# Making Managerial Appraisal Effective

The development of valid appraisals of managers over the past quarter century has been slow, in spite of the giant strides of the management revolution. Yet few would deny that appraisal is the key to management development and that, at least in the long run, the quality and vigor of managing make the difference in the success or failure of any organized enterprise. Without meaning to downgrade the importance of entrepreneurial genius and the profit-making potential of such non-managerial talents as marketing, production or engineering, no company can expect to enjoy prosperous growth for long without strong management. There are many companies that have been poorly managed, but have made high profits through special talents in marketing, production, or engineering. However, there is evidence that genius in these functional operating areas does not usually bring *long run* success unless the company, as a total system, is well managed. Moreover, it is well known that such non-business operations as government agencies and universities often fail in achieving their goals efficiently because of managerial shortcomings.

Perhaps the most exciting development in managing generally and in managerial appraisal in particular has been the growing use of management by objectives in the past decade. However, even this sensible and promising approach to management is often poorly conceived and implemented. Despite the excitement generated by it, by far the majority of business, government, and other organizations still evaluates managers on the basis of outmoded and discredited trait or work-quality appraisals. And even where management by objectives is done well—as in a very small percentage of organized enterprises—appraisal of performance does not necesarily measure how well a man is doing *as a manager.*

## What Should Be Measured?

Managerial appraisal should measure performance as a manager in meeting goals for which a *manager,* in whatever position he occupies, is responsible. Obvious as this is, examination of a large number of appraisal systems used by business, government, and other organizations discloses a lack of understanding of this truism, or at least an unwillingness or inability to translate understanding into practice.

Appraisal should measure both *performance* in accomplishing goals and plans and *performance* as a *manager*. No one would want a person in a managerial role who appeared to do everything right as a manager but who could not turn in a good record of profit-making, marketing, engineering, or whatever his area of responsibility might be. Nor should one be satisfied to have a performer in a managerial position who cannot operate effectively as a manager. Performers are sometimes "flashes in the pan" and many have succeeded through no resources of their own.

**Performance in achieving goals.** In assessing this aspect of the manager's job, the newer systems of appraising performance against preselected verifiable goals represent the best means that have yet been devised. The criteria of this aspect of performance are a manager's goals (including the intelligence with which he selects them), the programs he devises to accomplish them, and his success in achieving them. Many who have operated under this system of appraisal have claimed that these are adequate standards and that, in the course of evaluation, elements of luck or other factors beyond the manager's control can be considered in arriving at an appraisal. To some extent this may be true. But there are too many cases of the sparkling performer being promoted despite these factors and the performing failure being inaccurately blamed.

**Performance as a manager.** I would urge that performance in selecting and achieving goals be supplemented by an appraisal of a manager as a *manager*. One must grant that a manager at any level undertakes non-managerial duties and these cannot be overlooked. The primary purpose for which a manager is usually hired and against which he should be measured, however, is his performance as a manager and not his work as an engineer, accountant, or salesman. Therefore, one of the major bases on which he should on which he should be appraised is how well he understands and practices the managerial functions of planning, organizing, staffing, directing, leading, and controlling. For standards in this area we must turn to the fundamentals of management.

## Requirements for an Effective Managerial Appraisal System

The following are requirements for an effective program of managerial appraisal:

1. *The program should measure the right things.*—As pointed out above, the effective program must weigh both performance in accomplishing managerial goals and performance as a manager. It is also entirely possible that the evaluator might wish to measure a manager's exper-

tise in non-managerial skills and knowledge. But a manager who does well on the two standards of goal performance and managerial performance can draw upon expertise in non-managerial areas.

2. *The program should be operational.*—The most effective appraisal program will not be an exercise separate from the operations of the individual manager. It should be operational in the sense that it evaluates what a manager does in his job and not, as has been the case with traditional appraisal programs, what raters *think* of the man and his work habits.

3. *The program should be objective.*—Any appraisal program gains as it becomes more objective: both appraisers and the appraised prefer objectivity. Verifiability, the key to objectivity, is present if, at the end of the period, it can be said with certainty that something has or has not been accomplished. The better programs of management by objectives accomplished this largely by making goals verifiable either in quantitative terms ( for example, dollars of sales or profit or percentage of scrap reduction) or in qualitative terms ( for example, a marketing program having certain characteristics to be completed by a certain date). But even in these programs, as well as in the management appraisal program below, complete objectivity has not yet been achieved.

4. *The program should be acceptable.*—Any management technique or program that people do not understand and accept is likely to be ineffective. If forced to, people will give lip service and fill out forms. However, if they understand and believe in a program and see it as a means of helping them accomplish their own personal desires through contributing to group goals, they will use it and feel a sense of commitment to it.

5. *The program should be constructive.*—An effective managerial appraisal program should be constructive by helping individuals to improve their abilities and work. An effective appraisal program will not only determine how well an individual meets position requirements, an important requisite, but it should also point to his errors, weaknesses, or failures, and by giving him an understanding why these occurred, teach him or open his eyes to his training or learning needs.

## Deficiencies of Traditional Appraisal Systems

Despite the fact that any knowledgeable manager knows his defects, for many years, and even commonly today, managers have been evaluated against the standards of personal traits and work-oriented characteristics. A typical system might list ten to fifteen personal characteristics such as leadership, ability to get along with people, industry, judgment, initiative, and others. It might also include such work-oriented characteristics as job knowledge, ability to complete assignments, production or cost results, or seeing that instructions and plans are carried out. Given these standards, the rater is then asked to evaluate his subordinates on the basis of one of five or six ratings ranging from unacceptable to outstanding.

The practical problems of these programs are well known. Ratings are highly subjective. Serious fair-minded managers are reluctant to affect a person's life or career on such subjective standards. Any subordinate who receives less than a top rating is likely to feel that he has been unfairly dealt with. The basic assumption of these appraisal systems, that there is a connection between performance and traits or work qualities, is also highly questionable.

The results of such deficiencies are predictable. Most managers dislike making such appraisals and see it as a paperwork exercise that must be done because someone has ordered it done. Raters understandably tend not to be very discriminating. It is hardly surprising that a study of ratings of Naval officers a few years ago found that of all officers of the U.S. Navy rated over a period of time, 98.5 percent were "outstanding" or "excellent" and only 1 percent were "average"!

Many attempts have been made to strengthen these rating systems. Traits have been carefully defined. For example, in one form, "judgment" was defined as "how capable is he of differentiating the significant from the less significant in arriving at sound conclusions?" Other systems encourage open-ended comments by the rater whereby he is asked to supply evidence on performance he feels is pertinent for appraisal. However, the results have been disappointing in terms of light cast and discrimination shown. Attempts have been made to improve the rating process by forcing the rater to rank his subordinates, forced choice questionnaires, and requiring listing of critical incidents. Even having ratings made by peers, subordinates, superior's superiors and groups have not been very successful, since the standards themselves are essentially nebulous.

## Appraising Against Objectives: The First Meaningful Approach

The most promising tool of managerial appraisal yet practiced is the system of evaluating managerial performance against the setting and accomplishing of verifiable goals. Once a program of managing by objectives is operating effectively, appraisal is a fairly easy step. What is involved in seeing how competently a manager sets his objectives, their relationship and contribution to objectives of the enterprise and its parts, and how well performance against them is achieved.

To a very great extent, advantages of appraising cannot be separated from the benefits of managing by objectives. Clearly, to appraise performance against objectives is to asume that objectives have been established and that the person being appraised has been working toward their attainment. The most important advantage of such a system is that it can result in much improved managing. Actionable objectives cannot be established without planning—and results-oriented planning is the only kind that makes sense. Managers are forced to think of planning for *results,* rather than merely planning *activities* or *work.* It also requires a manager to think of the way he will accomplish given results, the organization and personnel he will need to do it, and the resources and interdepartmental assistance he will require.

A major strength of a system of managing by objectives is the almost certain clarification of organizational positions and structure. It dramatizes the fact that delegation should be done in accordance with results expected and goal assignments should, if possible, be consistent with a position that carries clear responsibility for their accomplishment.

Coordination of planning and budgeting is assisted. As many companies have found out, in addition to a need to understand superiors' and subordinates' objectives, managers should know the goals and achievements of those in other departments who affect their own goal accomplishment. The production manager, for example, would be foolish not to have his objectives coordinated with those of marketing or research and development.

One of the great advantages of a system of managing by objectives is that it elicits commitment for performance. No longer is a man just doing work, following instructions, and waiting for guidance or decisions—he now has a clearly defined purpose. Furthermore, he has had a part in actually setting his objectives, has had an opportunity to put his ideas into the making of plans, now understands his area of authority and has hopefully been able to get a number of decisions from his superior at the time goals are agreed upon to assure that he can accomplish his goals. When managing by objectives has been done well, a man becomes master of his own fate and feels a real sense of commitment to his goals.

One of the frustrating problems of effective control is selecting those critical points in any situation that a manager must watch if he is to be assured that his actions are conforming to plans. In cases of effective management by objectives, this problem is often solved. Now the manager knows what he should watch and has standards against which to measure his progress. Indeed, there has probably been no development in management that has contributed so much to improving the quality of control and pin-pointing information needs.

Thus, appraisal is an operational "fallout," as is shown in Table 1, from a system of managing. It need not be a world of forms and reports separate from managing. Information on what a man has done against what he agreed was a reasonable target is readily available. Moreover,

**Table 1**
The System of Managing and Appraising by Objectives[1]

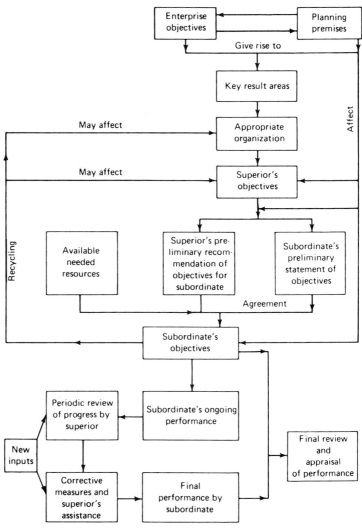

it is available in an atmosphere of the superior working with and helping his subordinate, not sitting in remote judgment of him.

## The Problems of Appraising Against Objectives

In spite of its being promising and sensible, appraising against objectives is not the easy answer to evaluating managers. Even the best operating program has limitations—there are great difficulties and weaknesses in practice. Since it only measures end-result performance, it overlooks how effective a manager is as a manager.

**Deficiencies in the system.** Even with considerable analysis, study, and supervision, goals with the right degree of "stretch" or "pull" are difficult to set year in and year out. Characteristic of all planning is the uncertainty inevitable in anything intended to operate in the future. More work and study is needed to establish verifiable and actionable objectives, rather than to develop many typical plans which only lay out work to be done. Objectives must not be too easily attainable. Experience has shown that, at least in the earliest days of a program, most people set goals too high. Later, when goal achievement becomes a standard of appraisal and sometimes a determinant of compensation or promotion, there is a natural tendency for subordinates to understate goals to assure that they will exceed them. Goal appropriateness can only be determined by an experienced superior, although this good judgment can be developed in the manager only with time and trial and can become highly objective in instances where goals of other managers in similar positions are available for comparison.

In almost all systems of management by objectives—particularly where goals are used for appraisal—goals are usually short-term, seldom longer than a year and often quarterly or less. There is a danger that emphasizing short-term planning and results may be at the expense of the longer term. The need to get short-term performance, say one or two years, may undermine long-range plans. This can be particularly dangerous if managers rotate to other positions. Meeting this danger requires that short-term goals be carefully and specifically geared to long-term plans and objectives and that the appraiser never lose sight of this need. For companies that have longer-range plans and objectives, this should not be difficult.

Critics of programs of managing by objectives feel that there may be an overemphasis on a few major objectives and that the other aspects of a job are neglected. This is a weakness in the system as well as practice. No workable system of managing by objectives can cover every detail of a man's job. Moreover, managing by objectives is a tool of managing and not the entire task.

One of the great weaknesses in appraising performance against verifiable objectives is that it is entirely possible for a man to meet or miss his goals through no action of his own. On occasion, new products have been extremely successful in a market and have made the marketing effort look exceptional, even though the quality of the program and its implementation were poor. Conversely, there are many corporate financial planners who have missed their cash procurement goals when unexpected tightness developed in a money market. Although most raters often take external and unexpected factors into account, it is extremely difficult to do. Can we be sure that performance success was not due to luck or factors beyond a man's control? The outstanding performer is always a "fair-haired boy," as long as he performs; the nonperformer cannot escape having a cloud cast over him. Even in a well-managed company with a record of thorough managerial appraisals and bonuses based on these appraisals, an individual rose rapidly to the corporation's presidency following a period of success based almost entirely on changes in consumer tastes which were beyond his control.

**Weaknesses in practice.** Analysis of programs of managing and appraising by objectives has also disclosed many difficulties and weaknesses in practice. Learning the system is difficult. For one thing, those who have been accustomed to planning find it difficult to shift to developing actionable objectives. Because of the difficulties in learning the system, it is urgent that people who are expected to operate under it understand the nature and philosophy of the program—what it is, how it works, why it is being done, how appraisal will work, and, above all, how everyone will benefit. Like most other worthwhile programs it cannot be installed by edict and distributing forms and instructions with an order to participate.

A major reason why managing by objectives, as well as planning and budgeting, does not work is the lack of adequate guidelines. People must have some planning premises and some understanding of company policies and the directions of other plans and objectives to do their planning effectively. No one can plan in a vacuum. How will the planner fill the vacuum—with supportive data or with impressions and guesses?

Goals must represent a coordinated, interconnected network. A man may achieve his own objectives at the expense of the company. A production manager, for example, may be so zealous in accomplishing cost reduction goals through scheduling long runs of a product that he defeats inventory level objectives or the sales manager's objective of having full lines of product available at all times. A company is a system. If goals are not interconnected and mutually supportive, paths are pursued that seem good for an individual but are detrimental to the company as a whole. What is needed, as one company has described it, is a "matrix of mutually supportive goals."

A sure cause of failure is for the principal to set arbitrary goals and hand them to his subordinates. There is no question that the superior must approve and have the last say on his subordinates' goals—but there is also no question that completely setting goals for subordinates is self-defeating. No one can feel a sense of commitment to objectives that are thrust on him. He may even feel a sense of resistance which may not be expressed openly but will take the form of excuses or beating the boss at his own game. Furthermore, arbitrary goal setting deprives the superior of the knowledge and experience that those who report to him almost always have.

It is clear that, if goals are to be meaningful and are to be used as a standard of appraisal, they must be verifiable in either a quantitative or qualitative way. Because goals expressed in numbers are the most verifiable, there is too often insistence on quantities and numbers. We should not forget that not every worthwhile end-result can be expressed quantitatively. Lower and middle management programs have been known to fail because of the expression of their goals in numbers. The management by objectives program in such a situation becomes a "numbers game" and the more intelligent subordinates beat their bosses at it.

Particularly where quantitative goals are used, there has been a natural tendency to set up company-wide targets for somewhat similar positions and use these as a standard of appraisal. But this can be dangerous. National standards in an unusual operation, even when applied to similar managerial roles, would not be applicable to managers operating in dissimilar markets and environments. In one company where such standards were used, the result was frustration, resistance, no real sense of commitment, filling in forms, and playing the numbers game.

There are still other deficiencies in practice. As in budgeting, some companies are inflexible and do not change objectives during a period of time, normally a year. It is true that if objectives can be changed easily and often they cease to be meaningful. However, if goals are materially obsolete, there is no sense in keeping them.

In many programs, progress toward goal accomplishment is not adequately monitored. Particularly where goals can only be achieved in a period of a year or more or where a company is accustomed to setting goals annually, there is a danger that a principal, for fear of interfering with his deputy, may sit back and fail to keep track of progress during the period. While not taking over the task from his subordinate, or interfering with his operation, the superior should, of course, have information to watch progress, should counsel with his subordinate, and give him assistance in solving problems and removing obstructions to his performance. Managing and appraising by objectives cannot become abdication of responsibility.

Perhaps the major problem in practice arises from seeing management by objectives only as an appraisal program instead of a way of managing. Even though search for a better appraisal method did give managing by objectives its strongest impetus, it is likewise true that the system is not likely to work if only used as a device for appraisal. Management by objectives must be a way of managing, a way of planning, as well as the key to organizing, staffing, directing, and controlling—it is then a part of managing, a summary of what has been done, and not a difficult separate operation.

## Supplementing Appraisal by Objectives: Appraising Managers as Managers

As encouraging as appraisal of managerial performance against verifiable objectives is, it still leaves much to be desired. No one interested in long-term enterprise success would want managers who could not accomplish goals, nor would they want performers in a managerial role who could not manage.

A few companies have recognized the importance of evaluating the quality of managing. Some have asked for appraisal in such broad areas as planning, organizing, coordinating, leading, motivating, and controlling. Others have broken down these areas into broad subcategories such as, in the case of organizing, job assignments, clarity of responsibilities and authorities, and delegation effectiveness. Even fewer companies have gone farther. The St. Regis Paper Company has aided managers in their appraisals by preparing and distributing a booklet called *Guidelines for Managing*, which is really a brief summary of basic principles of management. However, the standards thus far used for appraising managers, as managers have been too broad and too susceptible to general and subjective judgment.

The program suggested here is a somewhat experimental step toward appraising managers as managers.[2] However, it has been tested by presentation to a number of executives in both business and government, and, above all, it has been tested by experience. In one company with three domestic divisions and five wholly owned subsidiaries overseas, it has been used as a major method of appraising middle- and top-lovel managers for five years. Coupled with a program of appraising managerial performance against verifiable objectives, it has not only been the means of evaluating managers but also the basis for bonuses paid to them.

**The program.** The program involves taking each function of a manager in accordance with standard managerial analyses (planning, organizing, staffing, directing, and controlling) and setting up checkpoint questions under each to reflect basic principles of management. As imperfect as the basic principles of management may be and as much judgments as may be required for their use in practice, they do give the evaluator bench marks to determine whether persons understand and are following the basics of management. Even though application of principles to an individual manager's operations requires a degree of subjective judgment, this is far more meaningful than the general questions often used as standards of appraisal. They at least focus attention on what may be expected of a manager *as a manager*.

While the total list of seventy-three questions is too extensive to be repeated here, some samples are given. In planning, for example, a manager may be rated by such check questions as the following:

*Does he set for his departmental unit both short-term and long-term goals in verifiable terms that are related in a positive way to those of his superior and his company?*

*Does he understand the role of company policies in his decision-making and assure that his subordinates do likewise?*

*Does he check his plans periodically to see if they are consistent with current expectations?*

*In choosing from among alternatives, does he recognize and give primary attention to those factors which are limiting or critical to the solution of a problem?*

In the area of organizing, such questions as the following are asked:

*Does he delegate authority to his subordinates on the basis of results expected of them?*

*When he has delegated authority to his subordinates, does he refrain from making decisions in that area?*

*Does he regularly teach his subordinates or otherwise make sure they understand, the nature and operation of line and staff relationships?*

*Does he distinguish in his operations between lines of authority and lines of information?*

In the area of controlling, such questions as the following are asked:

*How effectively does he tailor his control techniques and standards to reflect his plans?*

*Does he develop controls that point up exceptions at critical points?*

*Does he keep abreast of, and utilize, newer techniques of planning and control?*

*Does he help his subordinates develop control techniques and information that will show them how well they are doing in order to implement "control by self-control"?*

Other questions are asked in these areas as well as in the areas of directing (leadership) and staffing. Furthermore, in order to solve the problem of semantics and understanding of terms and techniques so prevalent among managers, those who have used this system are strongly urged to use a standard book on management with page references for each question. Without repeating each of the seventy-three check-point questions, along with the explanations required for effective use of the program, the subject matter areas may be seen in Table 2. It should be pointed out that any summary does not clearly reflect emphasis on an area since experience has shown that certain critical questions may shed as much light as a number of questions in certain areas.

In developing this system, it was hoped to make ratings highly objective by designing the checkpoints and questions to be "go-no-go": the manager being rated either did or did not follow the basics involved. However, this was not found to be practicable and degrees of "how well"

**Table 2**

| Basic Subject Areas | | No. of Questions |
|---|---|---|
| **Planning** | | |
| Goal Setting | | 3 |
| Furnishing and utilizing planning guidelines | | 4 |
| Quality of decision making | | 7 |
| | Total | 14 |
| **Organizing** | | |
| Appropriate structure | | 3 |
| Delegation | | 6 |
| Line, staff, functional authority, and service departments | | 4 |
| Committee and group meetings | | 2 |
| Organizational planning and operations | | 4 |
| | Total | 19 |
| **Staffing** | | |
| Exercise of staffing responsibility | | 1 |
| Training and development | | 5 |
| Appraisal | | 3 |
| Selection and promotion | | 2 |
| Compensation | | 1 |
| | Total | 12 |
| **Directing and Leading** | | |
| Motivation | | 2 |
| Communication | | 3 |
| Participation | | 4 |
| Leadership skills and practices | | 3 |
| | Total | 12 |
| **Controlling** | | |
| Tailoring controls | | 4 |
| Control information | | 4 |
| Control action | | 3 |
| Effective budgeting | | 2 |
| Utilizing newer techniques | | 3 |
| | Total | 16 |
| | Total checklist questions | 73 |

had to be inserted on each question, with rankings from 0 (inadequate) to 5 (superior).

In order to give the numerical ratings for each question some rigor, each is defined. "Superior," for example, is defined as "a standard of performance which could not be improved upon under any circumstances and conditions known to the rater." Other attempts to reduce subjectivity and lack of discrimination in rating include (1) the requirement in the final annual appraisal that a narrative with incident examples be given to support ratings; (2) review of ratings by the superior's superior; and (3) making the evaluation of raters dependent in part on the discrimination and care shown in their evaluations. A degree of objectivity is also introduced by the number and specific nature of the checkpoint questions. Also, it was found that encouraging self-rating and comparison with the superior's rating served to elicit discrimination. Moreover, as is often the case, persons rating themselves tended to be more severe on themselves than their superior was.

**Advantages of the program.** Clinical experience with the program has shown certain advantages. By focusing on the essentials of management, this method of evaluation gives operational meaning to what managing really is. One upper level manager, who was in fact a good manager, declared after discussing his first ratings with his superior that, despite having read many books on management and having attended many seminars, this was the first time he really understood what managing is. By use of a standard reference text for interpretation of concepts and terms, much of the semantic and communication difficulties, so commonly encountered are removed. Such things as "verifiable objectives," "staff," and "delegation" take on consistent meaning. Likewise, management techniques and their proper application become uniformly understood.

The program has also proved to be a tool for management development by calling to a manager's attention certain basics that he may have long disregarded or had not understood. In addition, the approach has been found useful in pinpointing areas where weaknesses exist and toward which development efforts should be aimed. Furthermore, as intended, the program acted as a supplement and a check on appraising managers with respect to their effectiveness in setting and achieving goals. If a manager had an outstanding performance in goal accomplishment but was found to be deficient as a manager, those in charge were encouraged to look for the reason. Normally, one would expect a truly effective manager to be also successful in meeting goals.

**Weaknesses in the program.** There are some shortcomings in the program. The program applies only to managerial aspects of a given position and not to such technical abilities as marketing and engineering that might also be important. These, however, should be reflected in the goals selected and achieved. There is also the problem of the apparent complexity of the total of seventy-three checkpoints; to rate on all of these does take time, but it was believed that the time was well spent.

Perhaps the major defect of the program is the unavoidable element of subjectivity remaining. However, it still has a fairly high degree of objectivity and is certainly far more objective than the practice of having managers appraised in broader areas of the managerial functions as has been common in the few cases where serious attempts have been made to evaluate managers as managers. At least the checkpoints are specific and go to the essentials of managing.

## Moving Toward More Effective Appraisals

After many years of frustration from utilizing trait and work-oriented qualities as standards of managerial appraisal, there is at last some hope that our more alert and intelligently managed organizations are moving toward more meaningful evaluation of those to whom we trust the responsibilities of managing. Certainly, appraisal based on selection and achievement of verifiable objectives is a tremendous step in the right direction. It is such a breakthrough, however, only if it is applied with care and intelligence. It concentrates, as it should, on what a manager *does* rather than on what someone subjectively thinks of him. When coupled as a standard of evaluation with appraisal of a manager as a manager, there is hope that we can, at long last, begin to approach the area of evaluating managers logically and effectively.

But devices and approaches will not solve the problem. There is ever the danger that top managers will adopt techniques and forms without accompanying them with an understanding of the philosophy in back of them, without the tools and assistance subordinates need, and without the hard work, time, commitment, and leadership necessary to make them work. No management technique is self-actuating and many have failed through executive malnutrition, particularly from the top.

In the area of managerial appraisal, the results should be worth the effort required. Few would deny the strategic importance of the quality of managing in every level and in every kind of enterprise. It is probably true that managerial appraisal has been the weakest link of the entire chain of the management process. While the proposals suggested here may not completely solve this problem, they are believed to be important steps in the right direction.

## Suggestions for Further Reading

R. B. Finkle and W. S. Jones, *Assessing Corporate Talent* (New York: John Wiley and Sons, Inc., 1970).

C. H. Granger, "How to Set Company Objectives," *Management Review* (July, 1970), pp. 2-8.

R. A. Howell, "A Fresh Look at Management by Objectives," *Business Horizons* (Fall, 1967), pp. 51-58.

J. W. Humble, *Improving Business Results* (London: McGraw-Hill Publishing Company, Ltd., 1970).

J. W. Humble, *Management by Objectives in Action* (London: McGraw-Hill, 1970).

A. F. Kindell and J. Gatza, "Positive Program for Performance Appraisal," *Harvard Business Review* (Nov.-Dec., 1963), pp. 153-60.

H. Koontz, *Appraising Managers as Managers* (New York: McGraw-Hill Book Company, 1971).

H. Levinson, "Management by Whose Objectives?" *Harvard Business Review* (July-Aug., 1970), pp. 125-34.

D. McGregor, "An Uneasy Look at Performance Appraisal," *Harvard Business Review* (May-June, 1957), pp. 89-94.

G. S. Odiorne, *Management by Objectives* (New York: Pitman Publishing Corporation, 1965).

A. Patton, "How to Appraise Executive Performance," *Harvard Business Review* (Jan.-Feb., 1960), pp. 63-70.

A. P. Raia, "A Second Look at Goals and Controls," *California Management Review* (Summer, 1966), pp. 49-58.

E. C. Schleh, *Management For Results* (New York: McGraw-Hill Book Company, 1961).

H. L. Tosi and S. J. Carroll, "Managerial Reaction to Management by Objectives," *Academy of Management Journal* (Summer, 1968), pp. 70-78.

H. L. Tosi, J. R. Rizzo, and S. J. Carroll, "Setting Goals in Management by Objectives," *California Management Review* (Summer, 1970), pp. 70-78.

T. L. Whisler and S. F. Harper (eds.), *Performance Appraisal: Research and Practice* (New York: Holt, Rinehart and Winston, Inc., 1962).

W. S. Wikstrom, *Managing By- and With- Objectives* (New York: National Industrial Conference Board, Inc., 1968).

1. Harold Koontz, *Appraising Managers as Managers* (New York: McGraw-Hill Book Company, 1971).
2. *Ibid.*, chapters 5-6.

# Section 6 Selected MBO Subsystems

**Objectives**
1. To recognize the importance of integration of selected managerial subsystems into a comprehensive MBO system.
2. To understand how the selection of managers, human resource development, and compensation contribute to effective MBO.

**Figure 23**

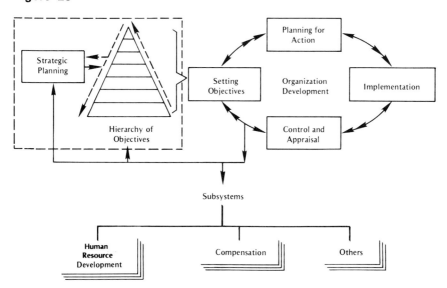

## Selected MBO Subsystems

For MBO to be effective, it has to be an integrated system. A high-performing manager expects to be considered for *selection* to a higher position. Similarly, the function of *management development* is not to keep the trainers busy; instead it aims at making managers more effective. Managerial deficiencies and strengths should be identified through performance appraisal against objectives, and manager development then needs to be designed to overcome the weakness of individual managers and to develop their strengths.

Also, a *compensation* system should reward good performance. The measurement of performance should be fair and objective, and one way to evaluate performance is the measurement against verifiable objectives. In practice, however, linking compensation and evaluation may have undesirable side effects, as discussed in this section.

In the first reading, "Selection by Objectives—A New Approach to Managerial Selection," George S. Odiorne and Edwin L. Miller show the limitations of traditional selection methods. They then review four approaches to selection. Finally, these authors suggest a fifth approach that synthesizes the useful features of the others, but adds an important aspect by focusing on job objectives for making selection decisions.

The second article, "Management Development and Management by Objectives—An Interrelationship" by Henry L. Tosi, shows that the management development efforts of an organization must be related to MBO. In fact, learning and development are essential for understanding what MBO really is.

The third reading, by Stephen J. Carroll and Henry L. Tosi, deals with one of the more controversial aspects of MBO, namely compensation. Although the various research findings are neither conclusive nor in complete agreement, these authors suggest that the MBO program should be related in some way to the reward system. This does not mean, however, that salary decisions should be made at the same time that performance is reviewed. In fact, the salary issue may create an emotional atmosphere that may not be conducive to a rational discussion of performance and finding the causes for possible deviations from performance standards. Consequently, the salary decision may be communicated to subordinates at a later session. For some positions, other factors, such as external market considerations and the scarcity of particular skills, may also have to be considered in the determination of salary levels and ranges. In conclusion, wage administration is a complex task. The MBO approach helps in developing a fair reward system, but it is not a cure-all. Other factors must also be taken into account.

# 1

George S. Odiorne
Edwin L. Miller

# Selection by Objectives—
# A New Approach
# to Managerial Selection

The foreman of a gang of lumberjacks was being solicited for a job by a rather spindly looking little man. The giant gang-boss scoffed: "Why, this work would kill you. Just to show you what I mean, why don't you take this ax and go chop down that giant fir?"

Despite the grins of the regular crew, the little man approached the tree and with a quick flurry of blows had the giant conifer on the ground. The grins turned to whistles of awe, and the foreman's voice took on a tone of respect.

"Holy Mackeral, fella, that's great! Where did you learn to chop down trees like that?"

"I worked on the Sahara forest job."

"Forest? I thought the Sahara was a desert."

"*Now* it is."

This tale might be an illustration of how selection by objectives would look in the lumbering business. No personality tests, no aptitude tests, little concern about degrees held. Just a good record of having achieved good results in the past and on-the-spot demonstration of some of the key behavior which might be required on the job ahead.

The entire matter of employment methods is under serious fire from a number of quarters, and perhaps a new approach to the selection of persons for employment, or for promotion—which is really internal selection—is indicated.

## What's Wrong with Present Selection Methods

The major shortcomings of present day selection methods seem to fall into these major categories:

• *Techniques are mainly for low level workers.* Since Hugo Munsterberg and others about sixty years ago seriously undertook the study of employment testing, the major emphasis has been upon the selection of workers.[1] The problems of early identification of high talent manpower, and the techniques for hiring and promoting managers, engineers and staff persons are different and at this stage very problematical.[2]

Reprinted by permission of the publisher, *Human Resource Management* (formerly Management of Personnel Quarterly), Fall, 1966, pp. 2-10.

• *Psychological testing has come under serious fire.* From within the profession and from outside, numerous attacks have been leveled at psychological tests.[3] They comprise an invasion of privacy, some hold. They have logical improprieties, say others. They breed conformity, say still others. Whatever the merits of these charges, the effect nonetheless has been to cast a cloud over their use in selection. A small fringe of charlatans promising psychological miracles in a manner akin to the snake oil peddlers of old have not done much to clarify the issues.

• *The civil rights laws have shaken many long-accepted practices.* The civil rights law of 1964 has shaken traditional employment practices seriously.[4] Not only are racial guidelines to hiring barred, but women are protected from discrimination in hiring and promotion because of sex.

• *The mad rush is to college graduates.* Despite a rapidly rising curve of enrollments in the colleges, the rush at the exit door of the institutions of higher learning is greater.[5] Surely one of the most bizarre and absurd fads ever to sweep industry, the clamor to collect degree holders for every white collar position shows no sign of abatement. There is apparently little inkling of manpower planning to identify which job requires a degree and which one doesn't.

While all of these shortcomings could be expanded at length, and the list itself lengthened, they comprise typical evidence of the illness that presently besets the hiring and promotion process.

This article outlines a *new approach* to the selection process. It makes a quick tour of the four major methods now being used in selection, then turns to a more detailed explanation of a new—or fifth—approach to selection. The purpose isn't to deny the value of the four, but to place them in a new perspective and improve the effectiveness with which they are used.

The paper is based on experiments done in industrial and governmental organizations in applying the system of management by objectives to the selection process. The method described here thus becomes *Selection by Objectives.*

The article presumes that the first step in management is to establish objectives and to obtain commitments in advance to seek them.[6] It also presumes that the person who has achieved objectives consistently in the past is more likely to achieve them in new situations. It is further proposed that these selection criteria have primacy over testing, hunch, behavioral inventories, or background. Thus, the major purpose of selection procedures should be to uncover evidences of achievements against objectives in the past.

Personnel staffing decisions are gambles in much the same way that a decision to bet on a particular horse is a gamble. Both decisions are based on predictions of performance among alternative choices. Predictions of the future are estimates or expectations based upon observations of past and present achievements and the known or assumed relationship between these observations and future wants.[7] For the horseplayer, prediction of the outcome of a race might be based in part on such variables as ancestry of the horse, performance in previous outings, current times, and physical condition of the horse and the jockey. For the manager involved in personnel staffing decisions, the prediction of a candidate's performance will be based upon observations of variables believed to be associated with or determinative of the desired level of future performance. In either case, the horseplayer or the manager is seeking to identify the winner. Needless to say, there are many poor choices and many disappointed people.

Employment managers and supervisors have always concerned themselves with trying to identify the best man for the job. Typically the supervisor makes his decision based upon his ability to size-up a man. In far too many instances, this method has led to failure and unsatisfactory performance. Errors in personnel staffing decisions can be costly mistakes. For the individual poorly placed, his inability to perform his work competently, and the consequent prospect of reprimand or dismissal can lead to his frustration and possible personal bodily harm. For the company, mistakes in personnel staffing decisions frequently lead to increased expense to the business in terms of recruiting, selection, training, and production. Although major stages in the development of a scientific approach to selection are well-known, the objectives-results approach—tried experimentally by the authors (and on a tentative and sometimes unconscious basis in many places)—has not to their knowledge been consciously described. Such a description of the Fifth Approach is the purpose of this article.

## The Four Approaches to Selection Now in Use

The systems of selection used to date have fallen into four major categories, described here in summary form. These selection techniques are based upon the major presumptions of the person applying them.

1.  The personal preference method. This is still the most commonly-used method, even when disguised by the apparatus of science; the hunch of the manager, his biases, or his likes and dislikes determine the selection of employees.
2.  The occupational characteristics approach. Earliest of the scientifically based methods, this method applied aptitude measurements to applicants, and allowed one to attempt to predict success on the job.
3.  The behavioral approach. Another scientific approach to selection of employees was that of identifying behavior patterns out of the past, and predicting that such behavior (as demonstrated in tests or

verified through resume and reference checks) would continue into the future. With these results matched against job requirements, success could be predicted.

4. The background approach. The fourth method is evidenced most strongly in the career pattern studies of Warner and Abbeglen, and evidenced by the search for college graduates in campus recruiting. It presumes that successful managers and professionals can best be selected by studying the careers of the already successful, and hiring those who best seem to duplicate them.

### The Fifth Approach

What is suggested here is that a new approach is now possible, synthesizing the useful features of the others plus an important new addition, a new point of origin for selection. Because it proposes to supplant the others, and in fact has proven more successful where applied, a brief review of each of the former four methods is in order.

### The Personal Preference Method

The proprietary right of an owner to make the decisions about who shall be hired and who shall not be hired to work in his business grows out of the property rights of ownership. If the small merchant or manufacturer decides to hire only members of his own lodge, church, or family, there are few constraints upon his doing so. Title VII of the Civil Rights Act of 1964, if applicable to him, theoretically limits his exercise of this right in public interest. Clearly he cannot flout the law openly, but his preferences may lead him to the creation of standards which make the law ineffective while serving his preferential biases. The administration of the law in future years may corner him in these subterfuges, although at present the strong voluntary compliance aspects of the law can leave him relatively untouched. Since many of his biases are unconscious—and hotly denied if pointed out—they are difficult to eradicate from outside the firm. Kahn's studies of the employment of Jews,[8] and the open challenging of tests in the Motorola decision on the basis of their "culture biased" aspects illustrate the tacit application of how bias might be used or alleged.

These personal preferences originate in the emotions and sentiments of the employer and extend from hiring alumni to Zulus simply because the employer feels the way he does about the people he wants around.

### The Internal Characteristics Approach

Since psychologists are usually the only professionals qualified to devise and validate tests of psychological characteristics it is not surprising that testing of various kinds has all of the strengths and limitations of psychology itself as a science. In recent years, this approach has come under fire for a variety of reasons. Writers of a moralist type have written with great fervor about the invasion of privacy which attends testing. By selecting questions out of the body of extensive test batteries, congressional committees and critical writers have generated righteous wrath. "Did you ever want to kill your father," for example, reads poorly when it becomes a headline in a Washington newspaper. Martin Gross, Vance Packard, and others have attacked the indignities which occur when psychologists pry.[9] Other criticisms have come from within the profession itself. Logical improprieties in testing are often discussed in professional journals. Still other critics have been behavioral scientists who have queried the scientific propriety of some testing methods.[10] As a result, it is now forbidden in government agencies to use personality tests upon job applicants, and this ban has recently been extended to government contractors by letter sent to all such contractors. Not totally banned, the list of limits placed upon their use has been sufficiently complicated that the actual effect will be a falling off of this kind of testing.

*Two families of tests*
The purpose here isn't to outline the varieties of tests and their advantages and disadvantages; the aim is to outline only the objectives of tests which comprise the "inward characteristics" approach to selection. Achievement tests would not fall into this approach, since they measure demonstrable behavior being observed, but two others do: aptitude and personality tests.

*Aptitude tests*
Because of the magnitude of the wastes and losses in selection there has arisen a more and more insistent demand to reduce errors in staffing decisions. It is this necessity that has given rise to aptitude prediction by means of testing. At the present, various kinds of psychological tests are the chief means for making aptitude prognosis.

Testing in all applied sciences is performed on the basis of samples, and human aptitude testing is not essentially different from the application of tests in other sciences. The thing sampled in aptitude tests is, in most cases, human behavior. Specifically, a psychological test is the measurement of some phase of a carefully chosen sample of an individual's behavior from which extrapolations and inferences are made. Measuring differences among people through the use of psychological tests has made a signal advance to understanding and predicting human behavior.

In its simplest terms, aptitude testing rests on a correlational relationship between a normally distributed predictor variable (which may or may not be related to the skills and abilities required on the job) on the one hand, and another normally distributed measure of satisfactory performance on the other hand.[11] The simple matching task is to eliminate, on the basis of the relatively inexpensive predictor variable, those individuals with little likelihood of success on the job—obviously an easy task in theory but beset by complexities in practice.

The conception of specialized aptitudes and the desirability of having tests of behavior which will indicate in advance latent capacity has its roots in ancient history. Over twenty-three hundred years ago, Plato proposed a series of tests for the guardians of his ideal republic. His proposal was realized in the United States Army mental tests of World War I.

The use of tests to measure aptitudes didn't receive much interest until the late nineteenth century when a number of psychologists became interested in mental testing and the psychology of individual differences.[12] The tests of the early aptitude psychologists were largely individual tests. This approach changed with the advent of World War I. Based on the pioneering work of A. S. Otis, a set of tests which not only could be administered to a large number of subjects at the same time but could be scored by semimechanical means appeared on the scene.[13] Nearly two million army recruits were tested, and aptitude testing on a group basis was born.

Following rapidly upon the heels of the spectacular accomplishment of psychological testing in the army, industry picked up the cue that tests could be effectively used in employment and personnel work. The individual worker came to be considered a conglomerate of traits that could be measured by tests. It did not matter whether these traits were regarded as innate or acquired. What mattered from the employer's viewpoint was that tests could be utilized in the selection and job placement of workers. The result of this hasty and ill-advised exploitation of an approach really useful in its own field was temporary failure and disillusionment. Quite naturally, a distinct reaction against aptitude testing set in.

The road back from almost complete denial of aptitude testing in industry has been paved with both successes and failures. Today, aptitude testing is finding ever-increasing use in American industry. Aptitude testing has proven to be helpful in staffing decisions involving clerical personnel, salesmen, and certain other industrial occupations; however, in that area where effective prediction is most desperately needed—in managerial selection—aptitude testing has met with only limited success.[14]

One of the most telling criticisms of aptitude testing is that made by Hull in 1928.[15] He suggested that something in the neighborhood of .50 might be a practical limit for validities of tests. Nothing in the history of selection testing has radically revised this figure after almost 40 years.

Nevertheless the quest goes on—to develop tests which can efficiently estimate or forecast aptitudes and success on the job from test scores.

*Personality tests*
Success on the job is not solely determined by ability; it is also attributable in part to the personality and interest of the worker. Aptitude tests are not tests of motivation and interest; consequently, something else is needed to measure these dimensions of the worker. Not only is the supervisor interested in finding out whether the worker *can do* the job, he is also interested in determining whether he *will do* the job. It is to this question that personality and interest inventories in the industrial setting are addressed.

The instruments used to assess the "will do" side in prediction come in all shapes and sizes. Some of these devices are simple inventories, others are based on specific personality or motivational theories. Some seek to measure those aspects of the personality called temperament traits. Still others are projective in design and are intended for "global assessments" of personality.[16]

These instruments are impressive in their diversity and approach. However, notwithstanding their multiplicity of technique and design, the history of personality and interest measurements in industrial selection has been something less than spectacular. Much of the variety in approaches to the measurement of personality stems from the desire to overcome the deficiencies in existing tests and the fact that the relationship between the predictor variable and the criteria are infinitely complex and dynamic.

Many of the tests presently used in assessment, particularly in the selection of managers, are general personality tests which have not been validated for managerial performance but rather for the identification of particular personality traits. The relevance of these traits or characteristics to successful performance on the job frequently comes about because of some intuitive judgment as to the type of man one would like to have. Relatively few attempts have been made to forecast accurately the demands placed on the applicant once he is in the organization. Thus, it seems that we may be playing Russian Roulette with the future of the enterprise by attempting to select managers through screening devices which in effect merely assure us that all those admitted to managerial ranks are alike. Fortunately, this is not the problem for the organization today as it might be in the future. At present, the validities of personality tests are low enough so that the consistent use of any of the personality tests will allow enough people to slip by that the organization will be protected against poor judgment about the qualities it thinks it is selecting.

What is needed by management with regard to its personnel staffing is apparently a heterogeneous supply of human resources from which individuals can be selected to fill a variety of specific but unpredictable needs. Thus the problem with personality tests is much more than that of overcoming distortion due to faking, presenting an idealized concept of oneself rather than a realistic self-appraisal, and a lack of self-insight. The basic issue is ability to predict the future with an extremely high level of probability. This clairvoyance will be a long time in coming.[17]

### The Behavioral or Skills Approach

A third approach to selection has been through tests which are less concerned with inner qualities, or inferences about such qualities. Behavior—activity which can be seen or measured—has been the subject of measurement and observation in this cluster of selection devices. In its simplest form, it was the test applied to the itinerant craftsman who wandered from town to town in the early part of the century. The boss of the machine shop would simply give him a piece of metal and a drawing and tell him to "make this." If he made the piece to precise specifications, did it quickly, with few errors, he was hired. The achievement test of typing skill was to place the applicant in front of a typewriter and have her type. Her work was timed, checked for errors, and if she performed well she was hired.

The use of such tests—which aren't any more psychological than the height and weight of the applicant are psychological—are still used, and are extremely useful screening devices. There has been an attempt to extend such testing to selection of managerial applicants, or candidates for sales, professional, or technical positions. Perhaps the most comprehensive plan for this approach is that of Robert N. McMurry, whose pattern interview program,[18] coupled with tests and full dress exploration of behavior histories, is widely used by many firms.

Actually a combination of personality, aptitude, and behavior history approaches, McMurry's system hypothesizes that the prediction of what a man will do in future assignments is already written in the record of his past behavior. Determinism is the underlying assumption here. If a man has been a job hopper in the past (has held five jobs in the past five years) he will probably be a job hopper in the future. The goal of the pattern interview then is to probe intensively into the resume, filling in each gap to uncover "patterns" of behavior. It is presumed that these patterns will persist into the future.

The McMurry system, which has been widely adopted and copied by firms and by a corps of consultants who have developed similar plans, delves into attitudes by eliciting verbal reactions to the conditions of past employment. An applicant who states that most of his past employers have been incompetent, unpleasant, or otherwise deficient may be predicted to adopt similar verbal responses about the new employer after the initial period of adjustment is over. Further, one may predict such things as leadership, creativity, and maturity by asking questions which get at past behavior from which reasonable inferences can be made. Table 1 shows how such questions might be devised in this behavioral approach to managerial selection.

**Table 1**
Using Verbal Responses to Obtain Predictors of Future Attitudes or Capacities

| Trait | Question Which Will Highlight the Trait |
|---|---|
| Creativity | Has the applicant ever created anything? |
| Leadership | Has he ever led anything? |
| Loyalty | Does he speak well for former employers, school, parents, and associates? |
| Maturity | Has he been dependent upon others? Has he destroyed things which were his responsibility? Has his behavior been excessively oriented toward pleasurable activities? |

The assumptions in this line of questioning are that people's behavior doesn't change, or that it may be costly to change it. Such being true, the time to find the undesirable behavior patterns in applicants is when they are still applicants. One might even hire persons with less than desirable behavior patterns, knowing what the defects are and allowing for them.

Clearly more scientific than some of the more esoteric methods of personality and aptitude testing, McMurry's system nonetheless shares the limitation that it is deterministic, and is more apt to achieve conformity in hiring than any other outcome.

The distinctive feature of this approach is that it presumes that a *pattern of behavior* is the key ingredient in hiring. Reference checks, intensive attention to past behavior, and the reports of past observers about the behavior of individuals, are coupled with the hardest possible probing into every aspect of the applicant's past results in order to create an extensive dossier which gives the interviewer the equivalent of many years of personal acquaintanceship with the applicant. The interview which is vital in this approach, may be non-directive when it will manipulate the individual into revealing things he might not otherwise divulge.

Telephone checks of former employers are larded with probing questions to strip aside the amenities which former employers customarily drape over people they've fired.

The method's most important shortcoming, although it comes closer than many other approaches, is that it deals mainly with behavior and not with the effects of that behavior in results.

### The Background Approach to Selection

One of the fastest rising in popularity, the background approach has resulted in a dramatic rise in campus recruiting in recent years. In fact, much of the pressure upon the campus recruiting process has grown out of an unstated and sometimes unconscious assumption that a college degree is needed for most managerial and staff positions. There are some interesting assumptions here.

1. It is assumed that the person who has a degree learned something in college. It is further assumed that this learning is something which he will carry to his first and subsequent positions. It is further assumed that the learning will convert into behavior on the job, and the behavior in turn will produce results that could not be produced by the non-college graduate.

2. Much of the drive to garner diploma-holders was caused by studies which show that 75% of the present crop of chief executives of the largest firms are college graduates. The studies of Warner, Abegglen and others, it is held, comprise predictors of the promotability of college graduates.[19] To some extent, this has become describable by the favorite cliché of the psychologists—"a self-fulfilling prophecy." Companies which presume that only college graduates can do managerial work enact policies which permit only college graduates to become managers. As a result, over time their ranks become filled with college graduate managers. As example, one utility company for many years recruited at colleges, limiting interviews to those in the upper brackets of their class in grades. Later they found that only high mark students succeeded.[20]

Where are the soft spots?

• There are many studies which show that the most successful automobile dealers, real estate men, and successful small business operators are not college men.[21]

• The two largest firms in the country in sales and profit have diametrically opposed policies with respect to the promotion of college men into managerial positions. In AT&T the college man enjoys a distinct edge. In General Motors, where results are primary guides to internal selection, a vast majority of managers are not college graduates, including at this writing the president. GM *has* an extensive college recruiting program, however its asumptions are different from some of its corporate counterparts. GM assumes when it hires a college graduate that he will demonstrate what he has learned once he is on the job, and that this learning will be verified by the results he achieves rather than by the degree he acquired before joining the firm. (Ford, number two in manufacturing industries, shares GM's pattern of selecting managers.)

• The background approach has the limitations of all the single-cause approaches to selection. It examines a single variable (academic degree) and generalizes this as a predictor. In fact, some combinations of degrees are automatic guarantees of rapid rise in the large corporation. The man with a BS degree from Massachusetts Institute of Technology and an MBA from Harvard, for example, may never have to really work again. His rise to the general management post is assured. Admittedly, he has already, as a youth, gone through several screens that many fail to survive, but his subsequent progress will not be measured by his results-achieved until he reaches a crucial position in the firm. Who would dare to give him a bad appraisal? He might remember it when he gets to the top. His salary progress will be swift in order that the jump need not be too great when he arrives at the top.

The suggestion here isn't that background is not useful information, but rather that as a single predictor it has the limitations of all single-cause explanations for multiple-cause outcomes. Meanwhile, this approach to selection gains momentum. The average cost of recruiting an MBA at Michigan in 1966 was $2100. This doesn't include any of the cost of education, merely the cost of moving the inexperienced graduate from classroom to his first office. After he arrived he received an average monthly pay of $750, with a range running up to $2000 for certain rare types in the upper reaches of academic grade achievement.[22] What this is doing to salary administration inside these firms staggers the imagination. The average monthly salary in 1966 was some 30% above that offered three years ago.

## The Fifth Approach

An objectives-results approach doesn't presume to displace all of the presently-used methods. It merely subsumes them to other criteria and shapes the plan for selection in somewhat different terms.

It starts with statements of job objectives for the job being filled, rather than with job descriptions which have been oriented toward skills, experience, and man-requirements. The method turns secondly to a measurement of the candidates' results on past jobs.

The approach breaks these objectives down into three major categories of objectives, and uses the selection process to uncover predictors in the individual's history which would point up probabilities of his operating at each of the three levels. The presumption in this selection of managers is that routine duties are a *must* requirement and that movement into the higher levels is demonstrated by problem solving results and, most especially, by innovative or change-making abilities. (A special and somewhat temporary kind of objective will be learning-objectives, in which the candidate must complete a learning or training program in order to bring himself up to the minimum (regular) requirements of the position for which he is applying.)

These duties comprise an ascending scale of excellence in management achievement, and the tools of selection should be designed to identify these objectives in the job and to uncover, in the candidate's results on past jobs, predictors of these kinds of results for the future.

**Figure 24**

innovation or change-making objectives

problem solving objectives

regular, ordinary, or routine objectives

**Defining the Objectives**

This fifth approach to selection starts with a clarification of the objectives of regular or routine duties, of the problems to be solved, and of the innovations sought. The first step in the fifth approach calls for a change in the job requisitioning procedures. For a typical position in which a job applicant might be considered, the employment manager or recruiter—or the manager himself if he is to do his own hiring—constructs a roster of job objectives, broken into the major categories. A sample description of the objectives for a general foreman (manufacturing) is shown in Table 2. From this guide it is seen that this position has more regular duties than it has problem-solving or innovative duties. These could be broken out as selection criteria. Other positions might emphasize the requirements of problem solving.

Table 3 shows the objectives for a systems engineer. This list of objectives, constructed by a group of 100 managers in systems engineering laboratories, could inspire an entirely different approach to selection from the traditional method. Here is an example of a different approach to selection, based on this set of objectives. Acme System Company is recruiting people for engineering posts to fulfill a long-run contract. It also hopes that out of this group will emerge some managers for the future. Some tangible effects might alter the selection procedure:

1. Despite the common nature of many of the activities, this work will be primarily innovative or problem solving. All job information sought in interview should aim at reaching a conclusion about such results achieved by the candidate in the past.
2. Certain kinds of objectives cannot be expected from new hires directly from college. In the objectives shown in Table 3, those which could be expected of the beginner are handled apart from those which would be required of the experienced professional who might be expected to start in immediately and achieve most of his objectives.
3. The inquiry about the candidate should aim at uncovering how his past results in each of these areas indicate probable achievements of similar results in the future. Such questions as the following might be used.

| Objective | Line of questioning |
|---|---|
| To apply laws and principles of systems engineering to specific problems in a project. | • Courses taken? <br> • Grades? <br> • Do they apply here? <br> • Special research done? <br> • List of past projects? <br> • Key issues in technical field? <br> • Does he see any interdisciplinary approaches? <br> • Is he mathematically sound? |
| To interpret objectives for technical projects. | • What projects has he designed experiments for? <br> • How has he decided on working plans and approaches? |

It is apparent that the one conducting the interview and making umpire-like judgments as to the past achievements in terms of results must be conversant with the objective of the man's job. The specifics of the question aren't of major concern here, but rather that the interviewed be seeking evidence of results in both kind and amount. The short illustration presented above demonstrates that the end product of selection by objectives comes from a different look at the work the man is expected to do when he is hired.

## When Objectives Are Set for the First Time

Before a company can select by objectives, it must establish what the objectives for the position being filled actually are. The statements of the systems engineer's functions had to be constructed for this study

**Table 2**

Sample Job Objectives for General Foreman—Manufacturing

| Objectives | Indicative Past Achievements |
|---|---|
| 1. To aid in selection of foremen for production | Has he ever picked a foreman, or does he have some firm ideas on what a foreman's functions should be? |
| 2. Train foremen on the plant floor | Does he know the foreman's major objectives and functions? Has he ever broken in a new one? How many? Have any of them been subsequently released? Promoted? |
| 3. Production quantity | What departments has he led? What were the output requirements? Did the department meet them? Exceed them? What occurred during his tenure in terms of levels of output? What did he do which might have affected output? |
| 4. Quality | What was the reject rate when he started? What direction did it go? How did he get along with the inspectors? quality manager? What techniques for improvement did he use? |
| 5. Cost control | What cost results did he achieve? How did his prime costs vary? His indirect labor? Indirect materials? Direct materials? Direct labor? Did he use any cost reduction methods such as work simplification? What were the effects? Has he submitted any improvement ideas in costs? |
| 6. Employee relations | What was the turnover rate when he assumed charge? Did it change? Grievance rates? Absenteeism? Any special methods used or introduced? Were any attitude surveys done in his area, and with what effect? |

since they did not exist in the firm at the time of the study. The statements of responsibilities were hammered out in small conference groups with the managers of these engineers. Only those statements which over 90% of the managers felt were of above average significance for the jobs of the systems engineers in that lab were included. Others were specifically reflected by the majority. (Community and civic activities, training technicians, and delegation to technicians were rated as of little or no significance.) While one may deplore the standards set by the managers in some areas, it must be realized that this is the climate into which the new engineers are going to be hired.

The same step can be taken elsewhere, partially by asking the present incumbents what they think their objectives are but more importantly, by asking the manager of the position to clarify the objectives for that position. It is he who will administer salaries, appraise for the annual performance report, coach, and recommend promotions.

**Table 3**
List of Typical Functions and Results for a Systems Engineer

| Function | Result Criteria |
|---|---|
| 1. Interprets organiza- tion objectives when laying out project | Upon receiving tasks, projects, or assignments must develop working plans and approaches to achieve them which requires interpretation of sponsor's objectives. |
| 2. Checking progress for compliance | Must check with superior or customer to de- termine whether direction and rate of progress are satisfactory. Has few if any complaints that he is checking back too often (being too depen- dent) or too infrequently, thus getting off the track too far. |
| 3. Making stop-or-pro- ceed decisions | Makes decisions on work whether to proceed a course of study or action or drop that course and try another. Generally gets concurrence of customer or superior. Should run into occasional blank wall if he is really experimenting. |
| 4. System engineering skill | Applies laws and principles of systems to the solution of specific problems in the project. Has well stocked memory for principles, has access to many more, and learns new ones quickly. Manipulates memories into new and original mixes. |
| 5. Visual display of concepts | Devises, plans and executes visual displays (drawings, sketches, working models, bread- boards, etc.) of the underlying concepts. |
| 6. Communicating ideas | Clarifies ideas, converts them into the lan- guage of the receiver, transmits them effec- tively, gets feedback to assure understanding: includes report writing and technical manuals. |
| 7. Adherence to policy | Stays customarily within accepted and pro- mulgated guides to technical action in that firm, the industry, the lab unless overriding reasons dictate otherwise. |

Others rated highly important included Self-Development activity, and introduction of new ideas.

## Predicting Success on the Basis of Results

Once job objectives are in hand, all selection methods should focus on uncovering result-getting activity in the history of the applicant. If the accustomed way of thinking about hiring suggests "Why, we're doing that right now," please read on. Most application forms or proposed resumé forms do not demand specific statements of results achieved. Take the case of the government agency which was stymied by its selection prob- lem because it found so many people at the higher levels had resumés including such information as the following:

1956-59
Director of Underground Utilization of Overhead Manpower, Department
of Midair Coordination and Development. GS-15
   "Had full responsibility for coordination and implementation of all
liaison missions of this service base. Reported directly to the deputy chief
of staff-Coordination. Base operated with 6000 military and civilian personnel, and annual budget $32 million.

Such nonsense implies that the applicant is the sole leader of 6000 men,
spending thirty million dollars yearly, and it surrounds him with an aura
of responsibility. The agency required that resumés be written to include
answers to the question:

   What did you actually achieve during that period: give year by year
   summaries. Who could we talk with to verify these achievements? How
   many of them were attributable to your efforts, how many were jointly performed with others?

The replies were matched with some intensive looks at the vacant positions to see what the objectives and criteria were for the persons being
hired. The result was a drastic change in the way selections were made,
and while it is still early to be certain, preliminary reports indicate a
sharpening of performance in the newly-placed persons.

   Another example occurred in a firm which was seeking a college grad
trainee for a marketing management position. One of the prime candidates was labelled as having "leadership" because he was president of
the student council in college. At the urging of the writers, the firm
probed a little deeper along these lines:

   During your year as president what did the council do? What condition
   was the treasury in when you took over? When you left? Did you finish
   any projects which would make a lasting effect on student life? Who could
   we talk to that would know best what the achievements of the council were
   under your leadership?

This intensive line of questioning elicited from the young man himself
the fact that the year had been marked with constant trouble growing
out of his inability to handle the officers and get programs going. He
had been selected "on my good looks, I guess, and the coeds make up a
big part of the vote." The very king-pin criterion of the selection decision proved to be the weakest link.

   Job applicants have increasingly recognized the values of listing accomplishments on their resumés rather than claiming attributes or positions which emit golden glows. Some personnel men have shied away
from the use of such information, because "Most people will dress it up,
and you can't really tell whether the interviewee was responsible, or just
went along for the ride."

   The same cautious skepticism is needed in evaluating accomplishments and results as is needed in statements of responsibilities, personal-

ity, or background. How can one overcome the tendency of applicants to paint an over-rosy picture?

1. Ask specifically how much of the achievements listed are genuinely attributable to their own efforts and how much were shared with others. For example the following question has produced some candid responses in interviews observed and reported:

"Your record shows some fine achievements in this past job. Now many of us do things jointly with others. What *percentage* of this achievement would you say is directly attributable to you or your subordinates?"

"Now, you note that these achievements are partially shared with Mr. A, the controller. You estimate that . . . . % of this is rightly attributable to you and your organization. Do you think that Mr. A would agree with your estimate of that percentage?"

The only reason, generally, a candid and honestly-held estimate may be withheld is that the applicant doesn't know, is deluding himself, or is lying. Verification procedures, reference checks and telephone reference chats substantiate the information. Rather than checking such matters as initiative, drive, personality, and the like, the interviewer restates the achievements the applicant has claimed and simply asks the informant, "Would you agree that the achievements he has stated for his performance in your company are accurate? If not, how did they differ?"

## Private Good and Public Weal—A Conclusion

Hiring and promotion policy and practice badly need an overhaul. The perpetuation of our firms, and the observance of public interest through equitable selection are at stake. We have learned from all of our past experiences. Selection by objectives won't guarantee success, but may help us improve our averages. It may also stem the onrushing trend toward hiring overqualified people and ease the job opportunities for the present unemployables. It is a method of rewarding excellence rather than conformity or social class of origin.

1. Hugo Munsterberg, *Psychology of Industrial Efficiency*, Boston, Houghton Mifflin, 1913.
2. Mr. Joseph Dooher and Elizabeth Marting, *Selection of Management Personnel*. Vol. 1, New York, American Management Association, 1957.
   Thomas A. Mahoney, Thomas H. Jerdee, and Allen N. Nash, *The Identification of Management Potential*, Dubuque, Wm. C. Brown Co., 1961.
3. William H. Whyte, Jr. *The Organization Man*, New York, Simon and Schuster, 1956.
4. Howard C. Lockwood, "Critical Problems in Achieving Equal Employment Opportunity," *Personnel Psychology*, XIX, Spring, 1966, pp. 3-10.
   A. G. Bayroff, "Test Technology and Equal Employment Opportunity," *Personnel Psychology*, XIX, Spring, 1966, pp. 35-39.
5. John S. Fielden, "The Right Young People for Business," *Harvard Business Review*, XLIV, March-April, 1966, pp. 76-83.

6. George S. Odiorne, *Management by Objectives,* New York, Pitman Publishing Corp., 1965.
   Edward C. Schleh, *Management by Results,* New York, McGraw-Hill Book Co., 1961.
7. Marvin D. Dunnette and Wayne K. Kirchner, *Psychology Applied to Industry,* New York, Appleton-Century-Crofts, 1965.
8. Robert Kahn *et al., Discrimination Without Prejudice,* Institute for Social Research, Survey Research Center, University of Michigan, 1964.
9. Vance Packard, *The Pyramid Climbers,* New York, McGraw-Hill Book Co., 1962, pp. 279-85.
   Martin Gross, *The Brain Watchers,* New York, Random House, 1962.
10. Harry Levinson, "The Psychologist in Industry" *Harvard Business Review,* XXXVII, September-October, 1959, pp. 93-99.
11. Mason Haire, "Psychological Problems Relevant to Business and Industry," *Psychological Bulletin,* LVI, May, 1959, pp. 174-75.
12. Anne Anastasi, *Psychological Testing,* New York, MacMillan Co., 1954, pp. 8-18.
13. Clark Hull, *Aptitude Testing,* New York, World Book Co., 1928, pp. 16-19.
14. Robert M. Guion, *Personnel Testing,* New York, McGraw-Hill Book Co., 1965, pp. 469-71.
15. Hull, *op cit.*
16. Five widely used inventories are:
    1. California Psychological Inventory
    2. Gordon Personal Profile
    3. Guilford-Zimmerman Temperament Survey
    4. Minnesota Multiphasic Personality Inventory
    5. Thurstone Temperament Schedule
17. As Guion has commented concerning personality measurement: "the available measures have generally been developed for clinical and counseling purposes rather than for selection, they are too subjective, and the evidence of their value is too weak."
18. Robert N. McMurry, "Validating the Patterned Interview" *Personnel,* XXIII, January, 1947, pp. 263-72.
19. W. Lloyd Warner and James C. Abegglen, *Occupational Mobility in American Business and Industry,* Minneapolis, University of Minnesota Press, 1955, pp. 95-97.
20. Frederick R. Kappel, "From the World of College to the World of Work" *Bell Telephone Magazine,* Spring, 1962.
21. Warner and Abegglen, *loc. cit.*
22. Arthur S. Hahn, *Salary Summary of Job Offers and Acceptances to Date Spring, 1966,* Graduate School of Business Administration, Ann Arbor, University of Michigan, June 1966.

# 2

# Management Development and Management by Objectives— An Interrelationship

Every manager is concerned with methods to improve the performance of his subordinates. Two techniques, by no means new to the vocabulary of the executive, have been used by many firms in their efforts to increase the skills and abilities of lower and middle level managers. *Management development programs* have been popular in industry, especially since the end of World War II. Most firms have provided some type of development activity for their managers, including participation in college programs or in-house training lectures. The sophistication of training and development programs runs the gamut from reading interesting pamphlets to the psychic probes of sensitivity training or decision making in the complex environment created in simulations of firms and industries. *Management by objectives* has been advanced by such writers as McGregor (1957) and Drucker (1954). This technique also has been utilized by companies with the ultimate objective of bringing about better managerial performance.

In many cases, where management development programs have been initiated, the results have been somewhat less than satisfactory. The literature on the subject is replete with examples of programs that have failed to accomplish desired results. Programs denoted as management by objectives have not even been subjected to the same experimental scrutiny as developmental programs. Because of lack of experimentation, one can only hypothesize benefits by examining other related concepts which have been examined empirically. (This will be done later in this article.) The purpose of this article is to suggest that these two improvement systems are interrelated and, in fact, have many features in common. The basic premise is: management development does not necessarily encompass or include a management by objectives program, but management by objectives is a form of management development. As such, the implementation or use of "management by objectives" should include, in addition to an analysis and awareness of the objectives, consideration of the characteristics and limitations of management development.

Reprinted by permission of the publisher, *Human Resource Management* (formerly Management of Personnel Quarterly), Vol. 4, No. 2, Summer, 1965, pp. 21-27.

Management development may be defined as "any attempt to *improve managerial effectiveness* through a planned and deliberate process" (House, 1963). The basic premise of management by objectives is suggested by Drucker (1954). "Each manager should develop and set the objectives of his unit himself." Thus, each manager should *participate* in the setting of objectives for his unit, and these objectives should be consistent with the overall objectives of the organization. This technique, Drucker implies, should *improve managerial performance.* It is apparent that both management development and management by objectives have the same goal: improving managerial performance.

## Management Development: Input Variables and Output

Recent research in management development sets forth guides for the implementation of a management by objectives program.[*] A brief review of this research should provide a sound basis for consideration of management by objectives. Let us begin by examining some of the more important concepts that affect the results of management development efforts. Certain *input* factors condition the changes that may be expected as a result of development programs:

1.  Participant characteristics—these characteristics are primarily learning ability, attitudes, personality traits and behavior patterns of the trainees.
2.  Development efforts—these deal with the technique used to induce change to occur.
3.  Leadership climate—this refers to the interpersonal relationships between the trainee and his boss. This factor is especially concerned with the way a superior views the value of the content of the training program and the extent to which he is willing to participate himself, or allow the subordinate (the trainee) to utilize the techniques learned in training.
4.  Organizational climate—this refers to the prevailing "organization attitude" as expressed by the top management philosophy policies and organization structure which control formal rewards and sanctions to organization members.
5.  Organization culture—deals with the expectations of members usually expressed as norms and values and informal activities.

[*]For a more detailed discussion of this research, see Robert J. House's forthcoming book from Bureau of Industrial Relations, University of Michigan, scheduled for publication in the winter of 1965. The author is indebted to Dr. House for permission to use this material for this article. The section of the article is a summary of House's work.

Basically, the following kinds of changes (or *output*) might occur as a result of developmental efforts. These changes may be classified as "objectives" of training efforts:

1. Knowledge changes—the objective is concerned with merely increasing the knowledge level of the participant.
2. Attitude change—development programs might be designed to change the attitude of the trainees. Perhaps the concept of human relations is being taught in the program; practice in human relations requires a "positive attitude" on the part of the trainee.
3. Ability change—basically concerned with improving the methods and skills required on the job and in job related tasks.
4. Job performance changes—attempts to carry ability changes and improvements into the job situation.
5. End operational results—probably the ultimate results desired from training programs of any nature.

The input factors obviously affect the outcome of the management development efforts. Different types of factors, as well as different degrees, will condition the success or failure of a program. It is not our purpose to recount here in detail the ramifications of the complete approach to management development. In general, it suggests that sequential development occurs. This simply means that knowledge changes generally precede attitude changes, attitude changes generally precede abilities changes, and so on.

Examination of the "input variables" leads one to the following conclusions with respect to management development activities. First, management development is capable of improving the skills of those who have undeveloped abilities but have not yet cultivated them. An individual cannot become a president by taking part in management development unless he has the intelligence and motivation to improve his present skills. Second, development efforts must be keyed to the objectives desired by the organization. Therefore, different techniques must be used for improving performance on the job than from those utilized to merely increase one's knowledge of human relations or other areas. Last, the input factors of: (a) leadership climate, (b) organization climate, and (c) organization culture, must be consistent with the content of the program to bring about a participant change. When a manager is exposed to human relations training, for example, and returns to a situation where his supervisor is not human relations-oriented, the manager trainee may:

1. Try to make his boss aware of the benefits of human relations.
2. Change jobs.
3. Hope for a change in supervisory attitude and restrictions.
4. Forget about human relations and do things the way the boss wants.

## Management Development and MBO

Exactly where does management by objectives fit into this framework? To accomplish changes in job performance, the following requirements are necessary:

a. The trainee must be able to practice his training or use his new skill on the job.
b. The superior must engage in performance appraisal of the subordinate's actions consistent with the changes desired.
c. The formal structural factors, such as policies and procedures, must be consistent with the desired changes, *and*
d. Informal group rules must be consistent with the desired change.

These same conditions must be satisfied for "management objectives" programs. The first two probably receive most attention when management by objectives is being considered. In bringing about desired changes, the *superior* is an extremely important factor. Management by objectives especially requires a condition where the superior allows and encourages his subordinates to engage in the goal-setting process. The attitude of the superior toward this participative activity and his willingness to allow participation will obviously condition the extent to which the subordinate actually does engage in the goal-setting process. Later, research will be cited which indicates that even where a firm has made a commitment to the management by objectives concept, goal-setting participation decreases as the level of management decreases.

The *subordinate* must be capable of analyzing and developing reasonable goals for the subunit of the organization he supervises. This suggests he must have a knowledge of:

1. The organization's objectives
2. How to develop objectives for his department
3. How the department's objectives fit in with the objectives of the units at higher organizational levels.

The *performance evaluation* or review is an attempt to feedback information to the subordinate dealing with the extent to which he has met the objectives determined by him in conjunction with his superior. The coaching and periodic review in "management by objectives" must be based on:

1. previously agreed upon standards and goals;
2. and knowledge and skills possessed by the subordinate; where the subordinate does not possess these, he must be trained, or if the goal is important, he must be replaced.

The *philosophy of the top management* must allow for the development of satisfactory organization reinforcements. The executive leadership of the firm or unit must make a *commitment* to the program. Policies must be established and procedures developed which support the program and facilitate participation of all managerial levels. Goal areas and limitations must be so stated that executives at each level are able to determine the degree of freedom within which they can operate and how subordinate goals fit in with overall objectives of organizational unit of which they are a part. Managers of subordinate units must be willing to recognize that some mistakes will be made in the operation of the program. The executive levels of the firm must be willing to live with the program and support it. Promotion and compensation systems of the firm must be reinforcing agents for the program, i.e., rewards should be based on the degree of goal achievement.

Additionally, and most importantly, the top levels of management must allow and encourage their immediate subordinates to set goals. It is only in this manner that the program can filter down to lower organizational levels. It must be made clear that the program *must* be utilized at lower management levels to be effective. Perhaps this might be accomplished by establishing as one objective for all managers an increase in the number of subordinates actually participating in goal setting.

Thus, attempts to change the behavior of individuals also require a change in the formal organization components. Most management development programs as well as "management by objectives" seek changed, i.e., improved, performance behavior. This change in behavior generally occurs when two conditions prevail. First, the persons involved must have the required knowledge, skills, and attitudes consistent with the kind of behavior desired. Secondly, the subordinate must receive the proper backing from his superior as well as the organization.

## Implementation Considerations

Management by objectives may be difficult to implement for several reasons. Managers may feel:

1. The determination of objectives takes an unreasonable amount of time.
2. They do not have subordinate personnel capable of utilizing the system.
3. They are ignorant of the technique and the way it works.
4. By allowing participation of subordinates in the setting of objectives, they will lose control of their organization.

The philosophy of top management and its desire to initiate a program of management by objectives must be harmonious with existing or planned forms of organizational practices and procedures. These procedures must provide at least the format which the lower levels follow in using the system in their work. In this phase of development, the following questions must be resolved:

1. What kind of appraisal system or systems should be utilized? Should an interview between the boss and the subordinates be the primary vehicle? In general, what kind of appraisal forms should be used and how? Should the evaluation of each manager be held privately or in group conferences?
2. How often should personnel be appraised? Should there be an annual or semiannual review period? Or perhaps, should it be more often?
3. How should the results of the appraisal be communicated to higher levels of management? What information should be provided to the subordinate? Should he only be made aware of his success or failure?
4. What provisions will be made by the firm for individual assistance? Will any programs be sponsored to provide needed skills found lacking in the appraisal process? How will the individual shortcomings of each manager be handled? Should the supervisor act as a coach when shortcomings are found?
5. How much flexibility will be built into the program? Once major goal areas have been determined by top management, what freedom of action will the lower and middle manager have for emphasizing different goals or setting goals in different areas?

The answers to these questions should then be formalized in a policy and procedures manual as a guide for the "management of objectives" program. The next step is the communication of this information to other managers in the firm. This communication program should be designed to provide information to lower level managers, develop favorable attitudes toward the use of management by objectives, and finally have the program implemented.

One way of gaining acceptance by management is to force the use of the program. As the manager uses it, and finds that operational results improve, he may conclude that:

1. While there is an initial investment of time, future time economies are realized in contacts with subordinates since they are now more aware of the goals and methods for achieving them.
2. Improved performance of his unit might change his perception of the capacities and capabilities of his subordinates.
3. He now knows what the program is and how it works.
4. His control is facilitated since his performance criteria are better developed.

If he also finds that his peer group, i.e., other managers at the same level, is using the program successfully and has favorable attitudes toward it, pressures toward conformity may reinforce his other experiences resulting in favorable attitudes and acceptance. This approach takes time and is largely left to chance. It relies on the ability of the executive to see the relationship between improved performance and the utilization of the new system. If the resulting performance is unsatisfactory, then the previous attitudes pertaining to the ineffectiveness of management by objectives will be reinforced. Subsequent attempts to introduce the program may meet with more difficulty.

The organization should attempt to develop an integrated learning and acceptance program prior to the implementation of management by objectives. This will enhance the probability of acceptance by managers. This program should consist of two phases. First, managers should be exposed to management by objectives in a "learning phase." This part is an introduction to the concepts and an explanation why and how the firm desires the system to be used. Secondly, there should be a consideration of changing and reinforcing attitudes of the managers about management by objectives.

## The Learning Phase

Knowledge of management by objectives should precede its use by managers. Managers at all levels must know:

1. What "management by objectives" is.
2. What are the objectives of the firm.
3. How to develop subunit objectives consistent with firm objectives.
   (For a case in point, see McIntyre, 1963)

Managers must be aware of the impending organizational change. They must know how it will effect them; otherwise, they may resist any changes simply because of insufficient knowledge about the program.

The general topic areas of the learning phase must include at least the following:

1. *The management philosophy and management by objectives.* The lower level managers must know the foundations on which the program lies. Only when the philosophy of management and management by objectives are consistent can the program be expected to work. If top management levels do not, in fact believe and practice management by objectives, there is little reason to believe that such a program can have any meaningful results at lower levels.
2. *Clear definition of objectives.* The firm must define as clearly as possible what it is trying to achieve. Unless the objectives can be stated in some verifiable manner, the subordinate will be unable to determine what he can do to contribute to the overall objective.

Perhaps this process of self examination is one of the most valuable contributions from the management by objective process. It requires that management review and assess the objectives of the firm.

Once this is accomplished, the lower managerial levels can determine departmental objectives consistent with overall company objectives. Upon determination of individual unit objectives, then lower level managers within the unit can determine goals consistent with those of the larger unit of which they are a part.

## Acceptance

If the managers have no opportunity to actively participate in the learning phase, favorable attitudes toward management by objectives may not be developed. Other methods than the mere imparting of knowledge as described earlier must be utilized in order to insure that attitudes change. Before a favorable attitude is developed, the managers must feel that there is some benefit to them as a result of using the new technique. The person in charge and instructing in the learning phase must have technical ability in the field, either real or perceived by the trainees. He must, in short, be a "highly credible" source (Hovland, Janis and Kelly, 1953). Perhaps management, in this phase of implementation, could be more effectively replaced by an outside consultant. The content of the training material must present both the positive and the negative effects of management by objectives. Certainly managers will be exposed to both sides in day-to-day operations. The practicing manager will resent being told how to tune his department by an outsider, especially when the outsider shows no appreciation of operating problems.

Obviously, this type of training material is highly "ego involved." It affects the manager himself. It touches on the very way he performs his job. Resistance to change may develop unless the participants have the opportunity to assess the system and make their own judgment regarding its usefulness. The training sessions should include discussions, *guided by the trainer,* of how the program will work and what are the personal benefits to be derived from its use. Positive attitude change may be facilitated, at least in the short run, by reminding the participants of their positions as managers. It is necessary, however, that the management reference group must be a positive one, i.e., one with which participants desire to be associated.

There are certain other conditions, previously mentioned or implied, which would limit the extent to which favorable attitudes can develop. One must remember that the implementation occurs on the job. This calls for an organization environment which is supportive in nature to the kind of attitude desired. If the concepts presented in these two training phases violate existing norms regarding the superior-subordinate relationship, the prevalent attitude will conform more closely to the norm, rather than the concepts presented in the classroom. The manager may rationalize his behavior in such a way as to convince himself that the best system is the one he uses, not the one presented by the trainer or advocated by top management.

The development of a philosophy of top management along the lines previously discussed is important. It is the philosophy *and the resulting decisions and policies* which will affect the attitudes of managers. If for instance, no reward is given for successful achievement of an objective, then lower level managers may assume that objective to be of little importance to higher management. Thus, a whole system of rewards and penalties must be built into the organizational framework. Compensation, promotion, and other organizational rewards must result from successful compliance and operation with the management by objectives concept. Proper implementation on the job occurs only when the manager has the proper reinforcements from the organization.

## The Criteria Problem

A fundamental requirement for an effective management by objectives program is the development of sound criteria for evaluation of personnel. The performance appraisal is critical for the change in behavior desired. It is the core of management by objectives. The use of "hard" criteria is required. Trait and personality characteristics, if used, should only play a negligible part in evaluation. The rating must be based on factors and characteristics which are related to task performance requirements. Kallejian, Brown and Wechsler (1953) have found that where the criteria were not job-related, the interpersonal relationship existing between the rater and the subordinate was more influential in determining a rating than actual performance of the subordinate.

"Hard" criteria, as used here, refer to measurable or identifiable factors or changes. Production levels, market share, sales volume, turnover, and grievance rates are typical examples. Obviously, one must use care in administering these types of criteria. Grievance rates can be reduced by not allowing complaints to advance to or beyond the first stage and giving away the plant "brick by brick." Production costs may be kept to a minimum by delaying necessary preventive maintenance programs. The system, while resting on "hard" criteria, must include some judgmental aspects of the superior's knowledge of how well the subordinate is doing in peripheral, but important areas (Ridgway, 1956). Typically, managers may be concerned with working out goals in areas such as:

1. Safety
2. Tardiness and absenteeism

3. Grievances and grievance rates
4. Turnover
5. Production quotas
6. Scrap and waste
7. Development of subordinates
8. Personal development of the manager.

Performance evaluation and appraisal is a vital part of "management by objectives," and the development of valid criteria is a problem that must be faced. McConkey (1964) suggests that the criteria or objectives must be evaluated by the superior in the following terms:

1. Does the objective represent a sufficient task for the manager during the measuring period?
2. Is the objective a practical and attainable one?
3. Is the objective clearly stated in terms of the task? the measuring period? the method of measuring to be used?
4. Is the objective compatible with the company's plans for the period?

## The Effectiveness of MBO

Evaluation studies of management by objectives are rare. Two of the critical elements of management by objectives programs are performance evaluation and feedback. By examining research in these two areas, one might draw inferences concerning the effectiveness of management by objectives.

*Feedback.* The following results were found when managers or participants in experimental situations received information concerning their performance:

1. Significantly greater results were found when human relations trainees received feedback when compared to groups which received no feedback (Mann 1957).
2. Feedback was effective in improving interpersonal relations between boss and subordinate (Tarnapol 1957).
3. Information was translated more accurately and with more confidence (Leavitt & Mueller 1951).
4. Experimental groups receiving feedback were more efficient than those receiving none in problem solving situations (Smith and Knight, 1959).
5. Groups receiving knowledge of results made more accurate decisions on subsequent problems (Pryer and Bass, 1959).

*Performance Evaluation.* This is designed to determine the extent to which an individual is meeting some standards which are apparently job-related. Usually, there is feedback to the person concerning how well he has done with respect to the standard. In general, studies attempting to determine the effect of performance appraisal have shown:

1. That formally appraised managers are more likely to regard their superiors as exercising the right kind of supervision. These managers also regard their superiors as being more frank in telling the subordinate what they think of the subordinate's performance (Mahler 1957).
2. Positive actions were taken by subordinates when: (a) the appraiser had a supportive attitude and behavior, and (b) the appraisee had an intermediate level of risk preference (Meyer & Walker, 1961 a and b).
3. When the appraisee expected a more favorable rating, the appraisal had a negative effect on his attitude (Kay, et. al., 1962).

## A Study on Goal Setting

A recent study to determine the effects of a program similar to "Management by Objectives," has been reported by Raia (1964). A large firm implemented "goal setting and self-control." A year later, productivity had increased, managers were more aware of the firm's goals, and goals were set in more areas than had been the previous experience. Prior to the implementation of the program, productivity was decreasing at the rate of 4% per month. After the program was instituted, the trend reversed and was increasing at 3% per month.

Care should be taken in the interpretation of these results. The operating results may be only temporary, and the long-term effects on the organization must be examined. In addition, the study did not measure other variables in the organization that might have caused such a change.* Perhaps the most interesting finding was the extent of participation in the program at the lower managerial levels of the organization. "A formalized system of progress reviews is virtually non-existent at these levels." The table on the following page shows the participation levels of various organization echelons. This study suggests that goal setting is primarily used by higher level management groups. If management by objectives is effective, why is it reserved only for the higher levels of management?

---

*These factors were not overlooked, however. It was noted that: "For a number of reasons, decision making had been highly centralized in the firm . . . The advent of the computer . . . made it more feasible to delegate more authority to the lower levels of management. Coupled to a somewhat better supply of capital and managers, these factors set the stage for a managerial philosophy of growth—the growth of individuals as well as that of the company."

| Levels of Management | Number of Respondents | Met with Boss | Percent |
|---|---|---|---|
| Plant manager | 15 | 15 | 100 |
| Supervisors | 48 | 18 | 37.5 |
| Foremen | 42 | 8 | 19.0 |
| Total | 105 | 41 | 36.2 |

## Conclusion

There are many similarities between management development and management by objectives. The variables that must be present to bring about a change in behavior for developmental programs are the same variables required for "management by objectives." This suggests that the firm considering implementing this philosophy and technique be extremely careful in the consideration of the learning and development process that must precede "management by objectives." The organization members must know what is going on. They must know what "management by objectives" is. They must have the ability to implement the program.

Management by objectives is certainly not the panacea for all organizational ills. It is based on the assumption that participation is a valuable and effective method for improving group performance. Some of the previously cited research supports this contention. However, a cautionary note should be added.

1. The development of performance criteria is a difficult process. The criteria must be verifiable and relevant.
2. Feedback must be relatively frequent so that lower-level managers know how they stand. The feedback of information on performance must be related to the functional requirements of the job. Where this condition is not met, unsought consequences may occur.
3. Only when both the superior and subordinate *know* the score at the beginning, i.e., they are fully aware of what the program is, how it operates, how it can benefit them, and how to use the system themselves, can corrective action by the managers be expected.

Drucker, Peter. *The Practice of Management.* New York: Harper & Bros., 1954.

House, Robert J. "Management Development Is a Game." *Harvard Business Review*, July-August 1963.

Hovland, Carl, Irving Janis and Harold Kelley. *Communications and Persuasion.* New Haven: Yale University Press, 1953.

Kay, E., J. R. P. French and H. H. Meyer. *A Study of Threat and Participation in an Industrial Performance Appraisal Program*, General Electric Company, 1962.

Kallejian, Verne, Paula Brown and Irving Wechsler. "The Impact of Interpersonal Relations on Ratings of Performance," in Thomas Whisler and Shirley Harper, *Performance Appraisal and Practice.* New York: Holt, Rinehart & Winston, 1962.

Leavitt, H. F. and Mueller, R. A. H. "Some Effects of Feedback on Communication," *Human Relations,* 4, 1951.

Mahler, W. R. "Bringing About Change in Individual Performance," *Improving Managerial Performance.* General Management Series No. 186, The American Management Association, 1957.

Mann, F. C. "Studying and Creating Change: A Means to Understanding Social Organization," *Industrial Relations Research Association,* 7, 1957.

McConkey, Dale. "Judging Managerial Performance," *Business Horizons,* Fall, 1964.

McGregor, Douglas. "An Uneasy Look at Performance Appraisal," *Harvard Business Review,* May, June 1957.

McIntyre, John. "Management by Results," *Management of Personnel Quarterly,* Summer 1963.

Meyer, H. and Walker, W. A. "A Study of Factors Relating to the Effectiveness of a Performance Program," *Personnel Psychology,* 1961.

Meyer, H. and Walker, W. "Need for Achievement and Risk Preferences as They Relate to Attitudes Toward Reward Systems and Performance Appraisal," *Journal of Applied Psychology,* 45, 4, 1961.

Pryer, M. W. and Bass, B. "Some Effects of Feedback on Behavior in Groups." *Sociometry,* 22, 1959.

Raia, Anthony P., "Goal Setting and Self Control." Unpublished Paper delivered at Midwest Meetings, Academy of Management, Madison, Wisconsin, April, 1964.

Ridgway, V. F., "Dysfunctional Consequences of Performance Measurement." *Administrative Science Quarterly,* September, 1956. Also in Rubenstein, A. and C. Haberstroh, *Some Theories of Organization.* Homewood, Illinois: Richard D. Irwin, 1960.

Smith, E. E. and Knight, S. S. "Effects of Feedback in Insight and Problem Solving Efficiency in Training Groups." *Journal of Applied Psychology,* 43, 1959.

Tarnapol, L. "Training Supervisors by Feedback." *Personnel Journal,* 36, 3, 1957.

Stephen J. Carroll, Jr.
Henry L. Tosi, Jr.

# 3

# Compensation

As indicated previously, some research studies indicate that individuals who perceive that performance is related to the reward system perform at a higher level. In our study, we found that this held true only when goals were difficult. In addition, we found that criticism from the boss was associated with higher effort expenditures among managers who believed that performance was related to the reward system but that there was no such association among managers who did not believe that performance was related to rewards. We also found that a perception that pay was related to performance level correlated significantly with higher satisfaction with pay, with higher satisfaction with the boss, with higher satisfaction with the job, with a perception that the boss would be very concerned with the subordinate's goal failure, and with a more positive attitude toward the MBO approach as a whole* An unpublished study by a student of one of the authors found a relationship, although small, between perceptions of a relationship between performance and the reward system and actual performance ratings.[†] Carroll and Nash found strong perceptions of a relationship between performance and rewards significantly related to plans to use management training on the job.[1]

In spite of the evidence that the performance level does seem to be higher when managers see a relationship between performance and the reward system, a number of studies show very little relationship between salary and performance ratings, even when the managerial level is held constant.[2] What are the opinions of managers themselves with respect to this issue? Lawler has cited two studies that indicated that managers,

---

*The correlations here among perceiving a relationship between performance and pay and the other factors mentioned were $r = .51$ for satisfaction with pay, $r = .38$ for satisfaction with the boss, $r = .39$ for satisfaction with the job, $r = .28$ with perceived boss concern for goal failure, and $r = .22$ with positive attitude toward the MBO program.

[†]The correlation was $r = .23$ (biserial).

especially the better educated, prefer to have their pay based on performance or merit.[3] Thus, the research evidence cited has indicated that performance is likely to be higher when managers see a relationship between performance and the reward system and that managers believe that rewards should be based on merit; yet there appears to be only a slight relationship between rated performance and salaries received.

On the basis of his review of the research on this topic, Lawler concludes that the best pay plan in terms of providing the most motivation to perform at a higher level would be a system of MBO tied to the salary system. He proposes specifically that at the beginning of the year the

> superior and subordinate would jointly decide on three things. First, they would decide on the objectives the subordinate should try to achieve during the ensuing time period. Second, they would decide how the subordinate's progress toward these objectives will be measured. . . . Third, they would decide what level of reward the subordinate would receive if he accomplishes his objectives.[4]

We think that it is probably not possible to specify in advance what rewards a man will receive if he achieves his goals. As we indicated earlier, it is a difficult process to assess goal accomplishment at the end of the year. It is likely for example, that some goals will have been changed to some extent and that there was deficient goal accomplishment on other goals for reasons beyond the subordinate's control. In addition, it is likely that some goals will have been achieved at more than 100 percent and some at less than this figure. The priority or importance of the goals accomplished as well as their difficulty relative to those not accomplished must be considered. Also, as indicated earlier, the means used to accomplish goals must be evaluated. It is obviously of great importance that the organization not reward behavior that is unethical, illegal, or that creates future or other current problems for the organization. A manager might achieve his goals at the expense of creating ill will or future problems for the organization or by contributing to the nonaccomplishment of the goals of others. Another consideration is whether goals were routine or nonroutine goals. If the goals assigned to a manager are routine or normal job duty goals, then by accomplishing his goals the individual is simply carrying out his job.

Thus, compensation decisions based on performance under a MBO program must be made at the end of the period of goal accomplishment rather than before. However, we do agree with Lawler that performance under the MBO program should be related to the reward system and, furthermore, that salary decisions be based on the kinds of goals that were achieved.

Tying the reward system to MBO does not mean that salary decisions must be made and communicated during the final performance review period. Several organizations, including the one that we studied, found that discussing performance improvement and salaries at the very same time did not have good results.[5] The salary issue during such sessions tends to create so much emotional feeling that a rational and objective discussion of performance becomes very difficult if not impossible. Also, during the final performance review period, attention must be directed at determining why goals were or were not accomplished. It is an information-gathering period, and the superior in such a situation simply does not have the necessary information to make such an important decision as a salary decision at that time. Therefore, the salary decision should be made and communicated to the subordinate at a later session after all the facts about a subordinate's performance have been carefully evaluated. The subordinate should be called in and the salary decision should be communicated to him with an explanation of the basis on which it was made. The part of the salary increase that is attributed to goal accomplishment as compared to that which is given for other factors, such as cost-of-living increases or for gaining skills valuable to the organization in the future, should be made clear. Compensation decisions with respect to any supplementary compensation programs, such as stock options, bonus plans, or profit-sharing plans, should also be made and communicated at this time, as, typically, such compensation is supposed to be tied to performance.

MBO may *not* be particularly useful in setting basic compensation levels for particular positions. This requires more information than could be obtained using the objectives approach. External market considerations, such as salaries for similar jobs in other organizations, or the scarcity of individuals with particular skills, must come into play when determining base salary levels and ranges.

Internal wage administration may be facilitated with the objectives approach. MBO can be of assistance in developing salary differentials within a particular job class. By assessing the level of difficulty and contribution of goals for a particular job and comparing them with similar jobs in that class or that type, some determination of the appropriateness of basic compensation differentials can be made.

MBO can also be useful in providing information about changes in job requirements that may necessitate re-evaluation and adjustment of compensation levels for different positions. By observing changes in objectives over time, it may be possible to detect changes in job requirements that would lead to revisions in compensation schedules. A problem here needs to be noted, however. Because of an individual's initiative and aggressiveness, goals may be set that go substantially beyond the current job requirements. If this happens, the appropriate strategy may be to change the position of the individual rather than to redefine the job and make changes in compensation.

1. Carroll, S. J., Jr. and A. N. Nash, "Some Personal and Situational Correlates of Reactions to Management Development Training," *Academy of Management Journal, 13* (1970), pp. 187-196.
2. Lawler, E. E. III, *Pay and Organizational Effectiveness* (New York: McGraw-Hill, 1971).
3. Lawler, 1971, *op. cit.*
4. Lawler, 1971, *op. cit.*
5. Preston, S. J., "J. Stone's Management by Objectives," *Personnel* (London) *1* (1968), pp. 22-25. Meyer, H. H., E. Kay, and J. R. P. French, Jr. "Split Roles in Performance Appraisal," *Harvard Business Review, 43* (1965), pp. 123-139.

# Section 7

## Organizational Experiences with MBO

**Objectives**

1. To survey and understand a wide range of successful MBO applications in organizations.
2. To recognize pitfalls and possible problems in applying MBO, based on the experiences of various organizations.
3. To become ready for diagnosing organizational problems; and to evaluate whether MBO could solve some of those problems.
4. To become aware of the value of managing by objectives.

## Organizational Experiences with MBO

Many organizations in the United States and throughout the industrialized world have implemented MBO programs. Such programs tend to be successful whenever they are tailored to the organization's needs, are well planned, and are well executed. By "successful" we mean that the organizational performance or results improved and that the managers and other employees hold positive attitudes toward the MBO efforts.

But MBO has also failed. Some reasons seem to be (1) a lack of clear definition of what the MBO program was intended to accomplish; (2) unrealistic expectations about MBO as a panacea to solve all problems; (3) an underestimate concerning the time and effort necessary to make MBO work; and (4) the administration of the program, including the paperwork involved. Experienced managers know that it usually takes several years to make MBO viable. Indeed, an MBO program can be seen as a continually evolving and developing process. We view this process in a positive manner, and suggest that organizational changes do not have to be frightening to managers with ability and strong motivation. In fact, we believe that without this dynamic process, an organization tends to stagnate, managers lose interest in their own work, and eventually the organization will face severe difficulties.

In this section we attempt to show the diversity of experiences with MBO and selected cases from very different kinds of organizations.

The first reading by John B. Lasagna discusses the implementation of MBO at the Wells Fargo Bank in California. This approach is flexible and pragmatic, rather than rigid. It focuses on planning and controlling with a minimum of administrative procedure. The extensive use of process consultation could lead one to describe the process as an organization development approach to MBO.

The second article by Walter S. Wikstrom describes Honeywell's approach to MBO, which is interesting for several reasons: (1) MBO is initiated at the top of the organizational hierarchy, but the bottom-up approach of setting objectives is not ignored; (2) emphasis is placed on integrating objectives of various organizational units into a network of mutually supportive goals; and (3) Honeywell cooperates with three other companies in MBO training of managers.

In the third article, "How to Manage the Government for Results: The Rise of MBO," Robert W. Fri describes the application of MBO in government. To be sure, the environment peculiar to government organizations must be taken into account; nevertheless, the public demands results from the government and one way to respond to this legitimate request is through the use of MBO.

The last reading by John M. Ivancevich and his colleagues describes the MBO approach by Tenneco Inc. It is a lengthy article and serves not only to show the experience of Tenneco, but it also is a review of many MBO aspects touched upon throughout the book: (1) the goal setting process, (2) the need for managerial development, (3) the necessity of top management support, (4) the preparation and training for MBO, (5) the integration of MBO with the managerial process, and (6) the implementation of MBO at Tenneco.

What is true for Tenneco may also be valid for other organizations. MBO is not a panacea, nor should it be an addition to the manager's job. Rather, the editors of this book view MBO as a way of managing. If done right, it is a rewarding experience for both managers and organizations.

# Make Your MBO Pragmatic

The intellectually compelling reasons for instituting a management by objectives system—and the potential benefits for managers and organizations—are by now familiar to most businessmen. Installing and sustaining a viable user-oriented MBO process, however, has proved somewhat more complex and elusive than the casual reader of current management literature might suspect.

In actual practice, too much emphasis is placed on implementing a preordained or "set" program—on *what* ought to be done, rather than *how* the process can best meet the changing needs of managers. For MBO to be truly effective, attention must be directed away from the program approach toward a more flexible pragmatic one, otherwise, a company's efforts are likely to be self-defeating for these two reasons:

*First*, the program approach implies a uniform procedure that is imposed on a companywide basis, one that is taught by a training and personnel group with responsibility both for design and for administration. Appropriate forms, instruction manuals, review dates, and checkpoints are implemented to get the program started and to ensure compliance. Consequently the system tends to take precedence over the people who use it. Furthermore, the idea of a boss and subordinate working around mutual objectives is so fundamental that any elaborate effort to educate managers on this subject is tantamount to carrying coals to Newcastle.

*Second*, the program approach is too ambitious to have much practical payoff, especially in large organizations where the complexities of application are the greatest. Allowing for semantic differences, most people list the following areas as legitimate concerns of MBO: planning, control, evaluation, and compensation. In an established organization of any size, it is too much to expect one system to accomplish all four.

In fact, most companies have already implemented evaluation and compensation systems long before they start paying attention to MBO. Such systems usually develop powerful and complex organizational roots and, taken together, represent an "establishment" that may prove difficult to change and not amenable to new approaches. Moreover, MBO should be designed as a developmental process, whereas in actual practice evaluation and compensation are often viewed as administrative functions. In such instances they will, quite likely, dominate the more complex developmental aspects and reduce the MBO process to an appendage of the administrative system. This, in my opinion, is the Achilles' heel of many program approaches to MBO.

At Wells Fargo Bank, we were lucky enough to encounter these problems early in the development of an MBO program. It became obvious that we needed an alternative to the program route when we realized that while we believed MBO to be a *process* (i.e., a way of managing), we had, in fact, been approaching it as a *task* to be implemented, a program to be "done to" people, rather than as something they could "own" and shape to meet their needs.

In this article, I shall show how we developed an MBO process to overcome the problems of a program approach. It emphasizes only the planning and control functions and is designed to be flexible enough to meet individual user needs. After presenting some fundamental assumptions supporting our approach, I shall attempt to walk the reader through this process as it operates in our company.

## The Overall Approach

At Wells Fargo Bank, as in many organizations, an informal MBO-type system was employed by some people, particularly at the very top of the organization. It proved so useful that the senior managers decided to introduce a formal MBO system throughout the bank and assigned the task to the Organization and Management Development section.

Our first thoughts were to design a system to end all systems, one that would do everything for everybody in a way never before done. We even began to design forms that would allow a manager to plan, control, evaluate, and compensate with unprecedented elan.

Fortunately, we moved away from this posture after a series of meetings in which it became clear that to pursue our plans we would have to revise the present evaluation system of the bank along with several long-established subsystems that supported this function. We decided on a pragmatic, flexible, long term (3-5 years) approach, based on serving varying user needs—rather than the assumed collective needs of an entire organization or those of an administrative staff. Briefly, here are the assumptions on which it rests:

• Program approaches attempting to change or improve organizational behavior and processes are somewhat inadequate, if not contradictory, when rational, task-oriented efforts are mounted with the hope that managers will do what trainers urge they should do.

• Clearly separating the planning and control functions from the evaluation and compensation functions will give a new MBO system a better chance of surviving and flourishing in an established organization of any size.

• A rifle approach with a minimum of administrative procedures is superior to a shotgun approach with excessive administrative paraphernalia. We want to make it as easy as possible for managers to plan and control on a day-to-day basis.

•Involving the trainer in the actual process of helping a person write objectives and then having him sit in on the objectives-setting session as a third party is superior to limiting him to the role of pedagogue and administrator.

• Attempts to change managerial behavior en masse usually have disappointing results vis-a-vis the effort expended. This seems especially true in large and established organizations. Therefore, it is best to work with only one "family" group at a time (a boss and his subordinates). Moreover, it is best to move from the top down, systematically evaluating and changing the process to fit the divergent needs of groups at different levels in the organization.

• While a *top-down* implementation is desirable in an organizational sense, the momentum for setting and "owning" objectives should be generated from the *bottom up* in any particular boss-subordinate dialogue.

• A soft-sell posture is better than forcing participation via a program endorsed by top management. Some groups in the organization need little help; other groups might not welcome assistance because it disturbs existing patterns of managing, or simply because they are too busy to take time for another training program. Consequently, it is better to work around these groups, hoping that demonstrated success and peer pressures will result in more commitment to MBO in the future.

### Initiating the Process

We decided that a single workshop in which a boss and his subordinates would meet with several of the Organization and Management Development staff was the best way to introduce the objectives-setting process. But, in keeping with our desire for a flexible approach, we made provisions for additional workshops with altered formats if the participants wanted them. For example, we held as many as four workshops for one group and two for several others. This flexibility allowed us to continually change our approach to fit the needs of a particular user group—and it proved to be one of our best selling points.

Before a workshop session begins, one of our staff contacts a manager to discuss the needs of his organizational group or family. It is made clear that we have no program or "package" to sell and, in fact, his organization may have no use for our services. If he decides to go ahead with us, he is asked to prepare a one- or two-paragraph mission (role) statement that encompasses the next six to twelve months. He is given a copy of Chapter III of George Morrissey's *Management by Objectives and Results*[1] to help crystallize his thinking, and then offered staff services in refining his mission statement. Many managers have welcomed this help, and some have found themselves for the first time thinking about their mission in a disciplined manner.

## The Workshop Session

The format of the workshop on setting objectives is designed to promote as much openness and flexibility as possible. A session, scheduled to run from 60 to 90 minutes, begins with a 15-minute overview outlining the bank's approach. The manager of the group is then asked to pass out a copy of his mission statement to subordinates for their comments. A 15- to 30-minute discussion usually follows concerning the contents and wording of the statement, aided if necessary by questioning from the staff.

These discussions have proved to be a useful and smooth way to accelerate the objectives-planning workshop and to get people thinking about their real needs rather than academic assumptions about MBO. As one participant put it: "This is the first time we have all had a chance to talk about these things together, and I think it's a great idea."

### Establishing Categories

Once the mission statement has been discussed, we give a 5- to 10-minute presentation on how to formulate individual objectives, stressing that good objectives statements should concentrate on *what* and *when,* and not why and how.

There is some excellent literature on this subject, but we limit our input to presenting four basic categories for writing objectives. Some writers, of course, suggest more categories while others suggest that categories get in the way and should not be used at all. We mention this diversity of views, then simply offer the following categories as possibly useful:

1. Innovative.
2. Problem solving.
3. Administrative-ongoing.
4. Personal.

Since there are no administrative forms to start with, we have little trouble in convincing our managers that these are simply guidelines, not definite procedure. In fact, we started out suggesting three categories (innovative, problem-solving, personal), but soon found that many participants had a real need for an administrative or ongoing category.

In some groups, managers and subordinates were concerned about things that were neither innovative nor presented any particular problem, but were simply important responsibilities that had to be done well. This recalls an example in Harry Levinson's article, "Management by Whose Objectives?" that tells of some key people going off on innovative binges while the day-to-day necessities of running the business—and making the profits—are ignored with potentially serious consequences.[2]

Our four categories, while certainly not original, give us a good balance and, at the same time, allow enough flexibility for managers in both line and staff positions. To be sure, economic pressures or organizational goals may cause a manager to place a greater emphasis on one or more of these categories, but this is to be expected. In fact, such flexibility gives the boss an excellent opportunity to see the overall direction of a subordinate's effort and then to appropriately add value from his own perspective.

### Objective Penmanship

After the discussion of categories, we move on to some specific guidelines for writing good objectives. Although "rules" in this area are numerous and varied, we find the following to be most useful.

- Start off with an action verb.
- Identify a single key result for each of the objectives.
- Give the day, month, and year of estimated completion.
- Identify costs, i.e., dollars, time, materials, and equipment.
- State verifiable criteria which signal when the objective has been reached.
- Be sure the objective is controllable by the person setting the objective and, if not totally controllable, at least isolate the part that is.

It is also suggested, somewhat arbitrarily, that a person not write more than ten, and preferably only three to five, critical objectives. In selling this idea, perhaps the most salient point we can make is that if a subordinate presents, say, five key objectives to his boss, it is likely that dialogue will be enhanced and the boss will add objectives if he expects additional results. A few *key* objectives, rather than a laundry list containing many activities, makes it easier for boss and subordinate to start talking about the things that need to be done—they can change or add objectives should the need arise.

Regarding this point, perhaps the best payoff in setting good objectives is that they *can* be easily changed, and the easiest way to ensure this is to have a clear, precise definition of an objective in the first place.

In our experience, the ability to alter plans quickly and easily has been one of the real benefits of the MBO process.

## Winding Up

Before terminating the workshop, we prepare the boss and his subordinates for their respective roles in the upcoming objectives-setting session. We suggest that each subordinate write five to ten objectives using the categories and rules already outlined, and then contact a member of our staff for a one-to-one consultation and review of the first draft. In addition, a staff member is available as a "third-party consultant" during the actual boss-subordinate session.

We also introduce the important distinction between expectations and objectives and ask the boss to list his expectations for each of the managers prior to his meetings with them. It is stressed, however, that the thrust for good objectives should come initially from the subordinate; the boss can modify objectives or add expectations after the objectives are "owned" by the person who is responsible for accomplishing them. In this way, both parties have a controllable stake in the process.[3]

At this point group participation usually ends. However, as previously noted, if any group wants a second formal workshop meeting, we can and do accommodate it. In such cases, one option is to hold the actual one-to-one objectives review during the second workshop by arranging separate tables in the meeting room.

## The Consultation Process

The most rewarding feature of our approach to MBO is the one-to-one review of a subordinate's initial objectives draft. Not only has it proved an enormous help to individual managers, but also it has served as a valuable learning experience for the Organization and Management Development staff. Moreover, the one-to-one review often becomes a crucial testing ground that determines whether a staff member will be invited as a third party at the ensuing boss-subordinate session.

The results are equally beneficial whether one or several staff process consultants work with individual group members, although the sessions move a lot faster in the latter case. When a face-to-face review is not possible, we use telephone, interoffice mail, or interoffice teletype. In one instance, a draft was teletyped to one of the staff who did an editing job and then teletyped the changes back within a few hours.

When a face-to-face meeting is possible, it is best to obtain a rough draft of an individual's objectives statement beforehand. Otherwise, time is wasted in unnecessary explanations and communication is sometimes obstructed.

### Third-Party Sessions

Anyone who has done third-party consultation is aware of the difficulty of describing such experiences for didactic purposes. Perhaps the most instructive comment I can make is that the tone and spirit of an exchange must be assessed quickly and dealt with openly by the third party. For example, we try to make sure that both boss and subordinate understand that the momentum should come from the subordinate.

If the reverse happens, the consultant intervenes as tactfully as possible. Often he will attempt to bring the subordinate into an active role by suggesting that the boss can add more effective value once the subordinate has defined a particular objective. It is important to remember, however, that the spirit, content, and quality of any exchange varies with the individuals involved and the skill and awareness of the third-party consultant.

*Vital feedback.* Toward the close of the three-party objectives-setting session (or sessions) the staff consultant asks that an additional objective be added to the mutually established list—a formal review date sometime in the future with the third party invited to attend. It is stressed, however, that there should be, and probably will be, many interim discussions just between boss and subordinate.

A formal review can be helpful to everyone. If the MBO process is enabling participants to plan and control better, another three-way interchange can reinforce new or improved behavior. It also provides the staff consultant with a convenient "hook back" into the live process so that problems can be identified and corrected in a realistic and timely fashion. An ideal review date seems to fall between two and six months, preferably closer to the former period during the first year or two of an MBO effort. Another rule of thumb is to set the third-party review date to coincide with the earliest target date on the objectives list.

*Minimizing administration.* Before concluding the three-way meeting we ask the subordinate to have his objectives, including the formal review date, typed in triplicate. This one-page statement is the final working draft of a person's key objectives. One copy is given to the boss, one is kept by the owner of the objectives, and the third copy is sent to the Organization and Management Development section.

Our copy serves as a follow-up document triggered by the formal review date. This is the only administrative activity involved, and is absorbed entirely by our staff, eliminating all but a minimum of paper work. One of our secretaries files the objectives statement and keeps track of review dates. Each month the appropriate staff member is notified of upcoming reviews, and he contacts each participant about two weeks in advance.

## Conclusion

At Wells Fargo we have recognized that planning and control are too important to an organization to be tied to an administrative system of evaluation and compensation that only periodically engages a manager's attention. Our approach to MBO assumes that well-stated objectives are only *means* toward better managing and not *ends* in themselves. Given the proper corporate climate, they should be vehicles for easy and open exchange between boss and subordinate concerning results important to both.

If a subordinate is reluctant to commit himself to specific and challenging objectives because he dare not fail to meet them, then MBO is by and large a waste of time. On the other hand, if events indicating some difficulty in meeting a given objective are seen as an opportunity to replan and establish new controls in a timely, mutually supportive fashion, then he will more likely engage in both the spirit and the letter of management by objectives.

Looking back, we see some encouraging things happening. We now know that our effort takes a lot more attention and commitment from both the users and the staff than a traditional program approach. In effect, we sacrificed speed of implementation, uniformity, and initial high visibility for a pragmatic, low-visibility approach to solving one of the most difficult problems facing modern organizations—how do we help people manage by objectives and results rather than by crisis, charisma, fear, abdication, or tradition?

Wells Fargo Bank does not profess to have *the* answer to this question, but we feel we are testing *one* possible answer by taking what amounts to an organizational development approach to MBO. To this end we have moved whatever expertise we can muster out of the conference room and into the day-to-day realities of organizational life. So far, this has proved to be a promising beginning for improved planning and control within our management ranks.

1. Menlo Park, California, Addison-Wesley Publishing Co., 1970.
2. Harry Levinson, "Management by Whose Objectives?" HBR July-August 1970, p. 125.
3. Ibid.

# 2

# Managing by—and with—
# Objectives, the Case
# of Honeywell Inc.

"There are two things that might almost be considered fundamental creeds at Honeywell: decentralized management is needed to make Honeywell work and management by objectives is needed to make decentralization work." These words by an executive at Honeywell Inc. sum up the reasons why the company has become heavily committed to using the concepts of management by objectives.

Less than a decade ago neither decentralization nor management by objectives was prevalent at Honeywell. The company prided itself on its use of an informal management style. Although it had grown from $24 million in sales in 1941 to $470 million in 1961, it preferred to operate like a relatively small company. Management of the company rested personally in the hands of the chairman Harold B. Sweatt, and a small group of close associates. They made most of the important decisions and a great many minor ones.

To critics of their methods they countered that "The darned thing works." Nevertheless, by 1961 the company was growing in complexity and size, and Harold Sweatt had already realized that his personal style of management would no longer be appropriate to Honeywell. When, that year, he decided to end his 49-year tenure by moving up to Honorary Chairman, he deliberately set the stage for a chain of events that would remake the management of the company.

A new chairman, president, and executive vice president were named from within the firm. This new team accelerated the job of building a management style more appropriate to the company size and complexity. They introduced an emphasis upon planning, budgeting, and control. To help coordinate the 13 divisions, they created new positions—five product-group executives. They began to demonstrate that they would *not* short-circuit the management structure to make decisions that had been delegated.

The idea also became prevalent that it was every manager's job to make things happen, rather than merely react to what happened. The company was going to try to create the future it wanted, the top command said.

Reprinted by permission of the publisher, from *The Conference Board Record*. (New York: Conference Board, 1968), pp. 21-26.

Within a few years the president moved up to chairman and a new wave of promotions took place. The new team moved toward a chief-executive-office concept. The group vice presidents began to orient themselves more toward the top, rather than chiefly downward to their divisions. This required that the division managers become more independent and entrepreneurial in their thinking and actions. It became clear, however, that to do this successfully, the division managers needed clear guidance from the top—but guidance that would not be unduly confining.

About this time the company moved to eliminate its central sales unit and placed responsibility for selling in the product divisions. The change in organization increased the need for a mechanism that would permit more effective planning within the divisions without sacrificing integration among the divisions and with the corporation as a whole.

Another series of promotions, a few years ago, brought in the present top management group. Having lived through the confusions of reorganizations and changes in top management personnel—having, in fact, been part of the effort to bring a new management style to Honeywell—they were familiar with the problems that had been encountered. They were imbued with the idea that the divisions had to have freedom to manage themselves within a corporate framework.

They believed the corporation should be interested in a division's results but, within broad policy limits, not with the specific details of how they were obtained. They decided to make management by objectives a corporation-wide philosophy of management. The management-by-objectives philosophy was extended to all "profit centers," with "profit center" defined as any operation that could have a substantial impact on business results.

Operating in this style today, planning to create the future has become a continuous process. Each spring the chairman initiates the process by circulating a memorandum that projects the broad goals of the corporation for the next three years, lines out certain strategic interests, and gives some indications of the results expected from individual divisions. The group executives and division managers then prepare their own long-range plans in considerable detail.

These plans are reviewed by top management very thoroughly but they are not officially approved as operating plans; rather they are agreed to as projections of the divisions' thinking about how they can fit into, and must contribute to, the long-range plans of the corporation. The plans of the divisions, with the comments from the review, form the springboard for the detailed operational planning for the next year that begins about September.

At that time, the division managers and their key lieutenants begin preparation of the plan that they will present to top management for approval prior to the start of the fiscal year on January 1. The plan takes the form of a book, the first chapter of which lines out the general goals for the division in terms of profit, volume, return on assets, and new products. This is followed by chapters for each function in the division, showing in great detail how the goals of these subunits will contribute to and support the division's broad goals. This is the document that is discussed by top management, modified as necessary, and given the official stamp of approval as the operating plan for the fiscal year.

## The Planning Process

During its period of transition to its present management style, Honeywell discovered that the process of setting goals can be "too much from the bottom up." Managers need some idea of the expectations of the men above them if they are to set meaningful objectives. These statements of expectations from above, while fairly firm, are subject to rethinking and negotiation in the planning and goal-setting process. From below can then come more realistic suggestions, ideas, and possible goals. In the interaction of the ideas from below and the expectations from above, sound meaningful objectives are developed.

It is for this reason that the planning process for Honeywell begins with the chairman's spring letter outlining the corporation's general goals and strategies for the next three years.

Most of the Honeywell divisions have carried this further by developing and obtaining approval for a division charter. This document specifies the division's legitimate area of business, the fields which it may exploit without treading on other Honeywell divisions' toes. This helps to line out the fields in which it should seek opportunities to develop new products and new systems. Once corporate approval is obtained, the charter becomes the most general statement of the expectations that the division must meet.

Some Honeywell divisions are experimenting with mathematical simulation to determine how best to fit business opportunities together into a charter that allows room for growth and diversification while still serving its purpose of defining and delimiting a specific area within which to operate.

Honeywell has discovered that managers need to be aware of the goals of other men at their same level just as they need to have suggestions from below and expectations from above. When goals are set in isolation from those of other men at the same level, particularly from those of men in other functions, the objectives are apt to become what one executive calls "polar goals." These are goals that are worthwhile considered by themselves, but which are actually in opposition to one another. The company has found that good managers are particularly prone to set polar goals if they are not in contact with other managers.

For example, a sales manager may establish the goal of increasing sales volume for an especially profitable product, with emphasis on new accounts. That might be a very meaningful goal. The credit manager may establish the goal of reducing the number of outstanding accounts. That, too, might be a meaningful goal. But if the sales manager succeeds in increasing the total number of accounts, the credit manager will have greater difficulty in reducing the number of outstanding accounts. These are polar goals.

A network of mutually supportive goals, rather than a collection of polar goals, is achieved through cross-checking meetings, according to this executive. In these meetings, managers present their tentative goals, check the impact on one another and make adjustments. Then they check the impact of the adjusted goals on the division's performance and the corporation's expectations from that division. Further adjustments are made.

This process has proved difficult and time-consuming. However, the goals, and the accompanying plans for attaining them, gradually move closer to an optimum integrated plan that can reasonably be expected to achieve the required results.

Honeywell attempts to have all supervisors throughout the company set objectives for themselves and the units they supervise. In some divisions they have gone even further: all exempt employees, professionals, as well as managers and supervisors, are expected to set objectives and to use them in managing their responsibilities.

In general, each man sets about ten key goals. If properly formulated, these ten key goals cover the full range of his responsibilities. Originally the practice emphasized ignoring routine work and setting goals only for special projects or needed improvements. But experience showed that this often raised problems of emphasis and priorities: Should a manager concentrate on his regular responsibilities or should he give priority to his special objectives? Now the company stresses development of a group of objectives that covers the full range of the job, including such innovative goals as are needed.

Part of the goal-setting process requires the manager and his boss to agree on a ranking and weighing for the set of objectives. This is considered an extremely important part of the over-all planning. It tends to keep men from ignoring some of their goals while overfulfilling others. The company is trying to teach its men that overfulfillment of a goal is not always desirable.

For instance, a salesman may achieve his volume goal and exceed his profit-on-sales goal by concentrating on a high profit item. He may sell 400% of his quota on that item and sell almost nothing else. He might consider that he has achieved his over-all objectives, even though out of balance with his quotas. The company may well suffer, however. Production for example, may have problems making enough of the item he's pushing to meet his sales; there may well be inventory losses on the items not sold that were produced on the basis of the original sales quotas. Furthermore, the easily-sold item may have a limited future, whereas new ones are essential for future growth and profit. The salesman is cautioned that he cannot consider his objectives achieved if he has made the company lose out. The process of ranking and weighing the various objectives is designed to underscore this element.

Because things do not always turn out as anticipated in the competitive business world, Honeywell believes that objectives and plans may have to be altered in the light of events if they are to serve as realistic tools for managing. The company schedules several reviews of progress toward goals during the year. If there are convincing reasons why an objective should be changed, a change can be made. However, it is not something that is taken lightly for it may well involve a major effort in replanning. Changing one goal of one manager may require changing some of his other goals and the goals of other managers as well. If that were not done, the network of mutually supporting objectives might well get out of balance and the results of the larger unit or the division might be adversely affected.

Of course, the company has another reason for discouraging the changing of goals once they are set. It believes that a manager's job is to achieve his goals, not to change them. If it appears difficult to attain a goal once set, his first job is to try to come up with a new plan for achieving it that takes the unanticipated difficulties into account. The replanning effort is justified only if it appears that there is no way to achieve the objective and that, in fact, it would be a mistake to attempt to do so in the new circumstances.

## Training Men to Manage with Objectives

Managers at Honeywell have been exposed to the idea of managing by objectives since 1961, before the company adopted it as a corporate management system. In that year Honeywell and three other Minneapolis firms entered into a cooperative venture that became known as "The Four Company Senior Management Course."[1]

The first unit of the management course is concerned with the concepts of management by objectives and the theme runs throughout all the units. This emphasis derived largely from the fact that the companies had the assistance of consultants from universities and private practice who have been at the forefront in spreading the idea of management by objectives.

About 300 men from Honeywell have attended the course, including the present top officers. Thus the groundwork for teaching men to manage in this fashion had been laid before the company decided to actively promote the system internally. The company has not, however, let the training effort rest solely with The Four Company Course.

Honeywell's manager of training stresses that different men learn in different ways. To carry the concepts down into the divisions, the company has used many means. It has run workshops, training institutes, and divisional courses on management by objectives. The training department has issued formal written materials and sent individual memos. The manager of training makes countless telephone calls and personal visits, counseling managers on how to set goals, how to develop measures of progress, how to manage using objectives.

All the effort is required, he says, because "management by objectives is not self-teaching." The whole idea seems so clear and obvious. But that impression is deceptive, according to men at Honeywell. Really managing by objectives, they find, requires greater precision of thinking than most managers normally use in planning, and greater clarity about where they are going than most managers normally have developed. When the necessity of building a network of mutually supporting objectives becomes clear to managers, they realize that management by objectives, at least what Honeywell means by the term, is not something that "they have always done."

The manager of training says that it is relatively easy to teach most managers to say: "I will do so and so in X amount by date Y." It is much harder to teach men to set a target for the results instead of the means: "I will create such and such changed conditions by date Y." Yet Honeywell believes that objectives must be stated in terms of results, not in terms of the activities to be used to attain the results.

How to set and apply measurements relative to objectives has also proven difficult to convey. The manager of training declares that most managers have to gain some experience setting objectives and using them on the job before they are ready to grasp the real importance of the measurements and to develop skill in applying them.

When managers first start using these concepts, he says, they often have difficulty using their goals as controls in their work. Subjectively, they sense that the goal they wanted to set is right; what is wrong is the measures in which the goal is expressed. The measurements may be imprecise or they may be inappropriate. They don't work as tools for gauging progress toward an objective and for giving early warning of difficulties in reaching it. Once managers have experienced this problem, they are ready to know how to develop precise, appropriate measures that can serve as valuable tools for control.

Finding appropriate measures is far more difficult than finding precise ones, but far more important too. As Honeywell sees it, the appropriate measure gets to the heart of the result that is to be produced. An inappropriate measure, however tidy and precise, draws a manager's attention away from the true goal. The manager of training says that the truth of that fact has to be experienced before it can be learned.

The company is now switching over to using objectives and measurement of results achieved as the basis for managerial performance appraisal. The managerial-trait basis, formerly used, is being discarded except where a trait clearly is relevant to a manager's ability to produce certain results. (Then the trait becomes a proper subject for goal-setting and for measuring the improvement in results.) There is no standard form or procedure for performance appraisal used throughout Honeywell, in keeping with its decentralized organization. Many forms have been developed to fit the needs of the units using them. Figure 25 is an example of an appraisal form recently developed by the Industrial Division.

Compensation is also being geared closely to the management-by-objectives system, but these procedures also vary among the divisions. In some functions the relationship of results to compensation is quite straightforward—almost a mathematical translation. In other functions the process is less mechanical and more human judgment enters into determining its relationship between compensation and results.

It is recognized that it is possible to subvert this system for salary change purposes, to approve "easy" goals, for instance, so that a man can build the record of "achievement" that will justify salary increases his boss wants to grant for reasons having nothing to do with work. But it is difficult to subvert the system because of the necessity of fitting one individual's goals into a network. Furthermore, the network of goals gets to the heart of the business. To tinker with the system is almost certain to cause problems that will reflect on one's ability as a manager. Honeywell has found little evidence of any tinkering purely for salary change purposes.

## Greater Control with More Freedom

According to one Honeywell executive, the change in management style has resulted in a paradox: greater control throughout the organization with much greater freedom of action for most managers.

He explains that, in the past, a few top executives had almost complete operating control and therefore almost complete freedom of action. They stepped in wherever and whenever they wanted to do so, making whatever decisions they felt necessary. But the other managers had little

**Figure 25**

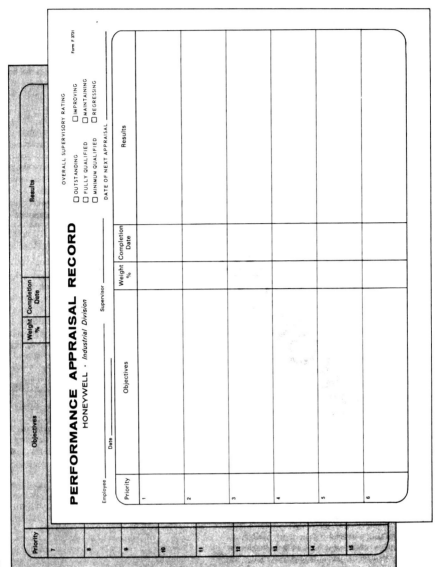

# PERFORMANCE APPRAISAL RECORD
## HONEYWELL · Industrial Division

Form F 3731

Employee _____ Date _____

Supervisor _____

OVERALL SUPERVISORY RATING

☐ OUTSTANDING    ☐ IMPROVING
☐ FULLY QUALIFIED    ☐ MAINTAINING
☐ MINIMUM QUALIFIED    ☐ REGRESSING

DATE OF NEXT APPRAISAL _____

| Priority | Objectives | Weight % | Completion Date | Results |
|---|---|---|---|---|
| 1 | | | | |
| 2 | | | | |
| 3 | | | | |
| 4 | | | | |
| 5 | | | | |
| 6 | | | | |
| 7 | | | | |
| 8 | | | | |
| 9 | | | | |
| 10 | | | | |
| 11 | | | | |
| 12 | | | | |
| 13 | | | | |
| 14 | | | | |
| 15 | | | | |

freedom to manage. They had no guidelines as to what was expected of them and no assurance that any actions they took would not be suddenly countermanded by top authority. For many such managers, managing in Honeywell was unpredictable—almost a game of chance.

Today top management has relinquished some of its former freedom of action. It lines out broad objectives and its short-term expectations of the results that divisions should produce. But it seldom interferes with the specific details of the way a division manages to produce those results. That gives far greater freedom to most of the company's managers. There are policy and standard practice limits on what they can do, but the limits are clearly established. Within these limits, they have authority to act and they have found that no one breathes down their necks while they are acting.

Yet control is in many ways tighter at Honeywell today than ever before. Each manager knows just what is expected of him and how his performance is measured. He has helped to set the objectives and determine the proper measures. Thus each manager can act as part of the corporate control mechanism; each manager can control his own efforts. What top management really controls is the key objectives and goals being sought throughout the firm.

Honeywell executives are convinced that decentralization and management by objectives have been worthwhile. But they do not consider that these are gimmicks than any company should tack on to a different management style. According to one experienced manager at the company, there are two important *musts* if either decentralization or management by objectives is to be of value:

1. The company must really mean to use them—otherwise don't bother to try to teach them.
2. The company must build them into the management system—otherwise no manager can really learn to use them.

So far as Honeywell Inc. is concerned, it has made a point of doing both.

---

1. The four firms are: Honeywell Inc.; General Mills, Inc.; Northwest Bancorporation; and Dayton's (a department store). The companies believe that the cooperatively sponsored course provides a good balance of the advantages of both in-house and "outside" courses. As in an in-house course, the companies can structure the content and teaching methods to suit their own needs. Like a course sponsored by an outside institution, the program provides the participants with the stimulation that accompanies studying with men from other firms with different approaches to common problems.

*Robert W. Fri*

# 3

# How to Manage the
# Government for Results:
# The Rise of MBO

These are bleak times for federal managers. Consider this:

• Confidence in the ability of government to produce useful results stands at a new low. Confidence waned long before Watergate; we learned in the late 1960s and early 1970s that the legions of new programs created in the last decade had failed to achieve the results we expected.

• The budget crunch is here to stay. Federal resources no longer grow faster than expenditures for existing programs. The fiscal dividend of the 1960s is gone—and shows no sign of returning.

• Like it or not, federal managers face a new and potentially unpleasant imperative. Caught between public skepticism and the budget crunch, they must weed out programs of low value, tighten up control of the rest, and produce results the public will understand and accept.

The trends of the times call for belt-tightening and place a premium on results. And federal managers must respond in many ways. One crucial response will be to improve government's ability to plan and control program operations—to set realistic objectives and ensure they are met. As witness to its importance, operational planning and control has already attained a rare status: It has Office of Management and Budget (OMB) support and a catchy name, management by objectives (MBO).

But it's not the OMB/MBO tag that confers importance to operational planning and control; rather, the times demand it. What OMB support and the MBO name mean is that all agencies will wheel about and start building MBO systems. And that presents a familiar danger—that MBO will become a fad, a management system to have but not to use. Some of us remember that the last time OMB pushed a management system with a fancy title was in the days of the Planning, Programming, Budgeting system (PPB).

It is hoped that we can do better this time. My purpose in this article is to increase our chances of doing MBO right. Having lived throug PPB, I want to draw some lessons from that experience and identify some

Reprinted by permission of the publisher, *Organizational Dynamics*, Vol. 2, No. 4, Summer 1974, pp. 19-33.

mistakes we need not make again. And, having participated in installing an MBO system in the Environmental Protection Agency (EPA), I want also to suggest some useful principles for the design and implementation of MBO elsewhere.

## Lessons from the Past

The stately progression of federal management from fiduciary accounting, through performance budgeting, to PPB is remarkable for its brilliant successes and for the catholicity of its failures. It is a history that leaves us with broad shoulders on which to stand and a rich choice of blunders not to make again. I have chosen from history's treasure six lessons that seem particularly important to recall during the development of MBO systems, either because they relate directly to MBO or because they are drawn from mistakes that have been repeated so often in the past as to be a positive menace to MBO or any other management approach.

First, *accept the President's Budget for what it is.* The President's Budget process stands accused of many sins. It is nonanalytic . . . it is the height of incremental budgeting, never admitting of real evaluation of base programs . . . it concentrates on inputs. And to some degree, it's all true.

The problem is that it is going to stay true, because there is only limited capacity and even more limited motivation to change the President's Budget process in any fundamental way. Putting together a $300 billion budget in less than three months will probably never be a comprehensive exercise in analysis. The budget is the President's chance to propose new initiatives and OMB's chance to prod legions of outstanding issues to resolution. As a result, there is a necessary preoccupation with increments, or at least with pieces. And the Congress rather likes the appropriation structure, since it's not a bad structure if your goal is to exercise oversight of agency expenditures. If fiduciary responsibility still counts for something, many appropriations will continue to deal in inputs.

This is not to say the President's Budget is perfect; it's not. But it is deeply rooted in needs and motivations that leave little room for making it wholly analytic, nonincremental, and output-oriented. The wise man will accept this fact. He should try to improve the budget, but not tilt at the windmill of turning the process into something it's not.

Second, *don't become preoccupied with accounting structures.* Some federal managers seem to have a nearly uncontrollable urge to integrate fully appropriation, program, and other accounting structures and to build devices to translate data easily and quickly among them. Particularly with the advent of PPB inordinate amounts of time and money went into techniques for moving data mechanically among accounting frameworks. A passion for neatness must inspire these efforts, because full accounting integration really isn't needed.

For example, what is really gained by linking detailed program structures to detailed budget activity structures in formulating the President's Budget? To the extent the budget is incremental, it's not really built up from these details. To the extent OMB and the Congress change the budget, there is not much neatness left. And I, at least, have never defended a budget on the grounds that it was built from compatible accounting structures.

I do not argue for sloppiness. The more compatible the structures, the handier it is. It's the preoccupation with neatness that softens men's minds and diverts their energies from the main chance, which is to use the structures to help plan and control operations.

Third, *systems don't set goals.* Many management approaches, especially PPB and MBO, begin with the simple idea of setting goals. They also often stop there, because system designers assume that sufficiently elaborate systems or clever analytic techniques will, by themselves, produce a set of agency goals. Yet, despite numerous attempts, I never figured out how to make a system—or, for that matter, an analysis staff—produce a set of agency or program goals I like. What does work for top agency management is creating their own set of goals.

The reason, I think, is simple. Organizations don't lead themselves; they require leadership. The *sine qua non* of top managers is to set the course. Moreover, as the political winds shift and as administrators and administrations come and go, few careerists want to guess at the basic goals of their top brass. I know I wouldn't.

It's not hard to set goals, the prevailing mystique about the difficulty of doing so in government notwithstanding. In fact, the real problem is that it's hard *not* to set goals. Legislation, Presidential statements, and a Secretary's chance remarks set them every day. The trick is to capture them, achieve a consensus on them, and make them operational guides for agency management.

Fourth, *the wish is not the fulfillment thereof.* Goals, structures, systems, and the whole baggage of management should aim at results, not plans. PPB, in particular, always seemed to lack the attention to the follow-through required to make things happen. But action is crucial, and indeed, it appears that OMB is setting out to redress the balance between planning and action through the institution of MBO.

Fifth, *build your own system.* The agonies of rapidy force-feeding Mr. McNamara's PPB system into the domestic agencies in 1965 have been widely reported. The underlying problem was simply that the original PPB program packages and five-year plans were developed for the Air Force, and revolved around weapons systems (program packages) and long-term investments (five-year plans). The original PPB perfectly re-flected this service's unique character, but outside the Air Force, this same uniqueness became a problem. Even in the Defense Department, PPB didn't always fit the other services. For the domestic programs, the fit was even worse. (As an aside, the Army's problem is to figure out how to relate millions of parts—people, weapons, supplies—to the readi-ness of combat units. This problem is conceptually different from the Air Force problem of grouping a few activities into programs around a limited number of large weapons systems. Most domestic programs are even less like the Air Force.)

Sixth, and finally, *keep it simple*. There is an inverse relation between the perceived complexity of a system and top management's willingness to use it. It takes time to learn a complex system, and time is just what top federal managers don't have. Less than 50 percent of Presidential ap-pointees stay on the job more than two years. Worse, the top managers stay together as a team for an even shorter time; only 23 percent of the Assistant Secretaries work for longer than two years with one Undersec-retary. To be useful to top federal managers, therefore, any system of management must be simple, easy to learn, and quickly responsive to a new manager's needs.

PPB and MBO, which depend heavily on top management's involve-ment in setting goals and reviewing performance, are particularly sus-ceptible to the disease of complexity. Complexity helped kill PPB with top management and presents a clear danger for MBO. In contrast, routine budgeting and accounting systems probably have survived in part precisely because top managers can safely ignore their complexities.

## Building the MBO System

Conceptually, MBO is simple enough: Managers set goals, allocate re-sources adequate to meet the goals, measure performance, and find and correct problems. It is, of course, easier said than done. I don't pretend to be able to lay out an all-purpose MBO system; to do so would be to ignore history's mandate that each agency develop its own system. But it is possible to spell out some principles that have general, if not uniform, applicability in fitting MBO to an agency's special needs.

Before getting into the details, however, it may help to look at a schematic of the system. As illustrated in Figure 26, an agency manage-ment system will generally have these familiar parts, the last three of which are usually thought of as parts of the MBO process.

• *Problem identification and analysis* is the continual process of sharpening management's understanding of the problem it's trying to solve and of the alternative ways of doing the job. Agency goals, program and

**Figure 26**

Main Elements of an MBO System.

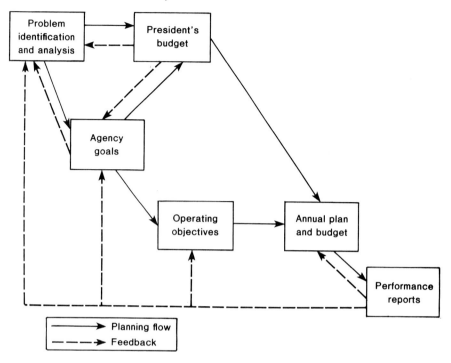

budget issues, and performance reports are fed into this process for re-view and analysis. From the process emerge many of, but not all, the insights that go into setting goals.

• *Agency goals* are based on management's current understanding of the problem before it, on statutes and Presidential directives, on agency performance, and, very heavily, on top management's judgment and desires.

• *The President's Budget* is both the cauldron in which agency goals are refined and the final determinant of what resources will be available each year to run the agency's programs.

• *Operating objectives* are statements of specific results that each agency program should attain. They must be precise enough (for ex-ample, issue 1,000 discharge permits) to tell a responsible manager just what is expected of him.

• *The annual operating plan* states the operating objectives to be met by each responsible manager during a one-year period and allocates the resources he needs to do the job.

• *Performance reports* measure how well the agency is doing in meet-ing its goals and objectives.

My experience suggests that people who build MBO systems run afoul of three particularly sticky points, and the three principles I want to discuss touch on each of these troublesome areas: setting goals and operating objectives; sequencing the tasks of preparing the President's Budget and the agency's annual operating plan; and getting useful performance reports. For convenience, I will refer occasionally to an EPA example in my discussion to illustrate what I want to say.

A final warning: MBO is not conceptually complex, nor need it be burdensome to use. But Lincoln said he would write shorter letters if he had the time, and, by the same token, keeping an MBO system simple is a fairly complicated design job. So the oversimplification required to keep the following comments to a manageable length should not be taken to mean that building an MBO system is an easy task.

### 1. Setting Goals and Operating Objectives

The mythology of federal management holds that it's nearly impossible to use goals systematically in an agency, because federal goals are broad and hard to measure. Some goals are fuzzy, to be sure. But a closer reading of the problem shows that goals can be used if the job is approached systematically and with top-management involvement.

The problem is not in a lack of goals and objectives. They exist in statutes and Presidential directives, in the minds of agency management, and in the hands of program managers. Some goals are very broad, some are no more than work-load measures. There are inconsistencies among them and often important gaps between them. But the raw stuff of goals and objectives is there.

Rather, the problem is that all this raw stuff is not organized into a coherent framework, an orderly hierarchy tied firmly to an agency's broad mission at one end and, at the other end, grounded on precise operating objectives that managers can use to prepare annual operating plans. Without such a framework, it's difficult to be sure agency goals make sense, and it's impossible to communicate even sensible goals to down-the-line managers. But it is possible to build a framework of goals and objectives, and I offer three guidelines for doing it.

• It is essential that top agency management get deeply involved in goal setting, simply because leadership must come from the top. Furthermore, the relationship among goals, from general to specific, is necessarily judgmental. Only the agency's leadership has the perspective and judgment to ensure that goals fit together.

• To get top management involved in goal setting, their participation must be made simple and direct. Top management usually have a fair grip on what's important to the agency; the need is to squeeze this valuable information from them. Yet there is nothing more frustrating to them than being detoured in getting to the important things by a system that forces managers through a hundred procedural steps along the way. Management's participation must be simple and direct, but their involvement cannot be entirely random. What is needed is some conceptual framework that permits management to think systematically and comprehensively about goals. Often, a simple grid is all that's required for organized thought. Shortly, I'll show an example of such a grid.

• Finally, there must be a small, capable staff that plays a key role in elaborating management's goals into the more detailed guidance that the MBO system needs to function.

An example from EPA's water pollution control program illustrates these guidelines. Of course, EPA is not exactly like any other agency. And, as with most illustrations, what follows sounds more orderly than it really was. Yet I have seen the same principles applied successfully, with a few necessary adjustments, in at least four other programs.

The goal-setting process in EPA began with management's trying to set the general goals of the water program. It was—as it often is—a judgmental exercise, with management's initial judgments refined later by the problem analysis process. In this case, management settled on three broad goals:

1. To meet shifting water quality standards by 1977, giving priority to areas of dense population with severe pollution problems and to a few other areas where protection of existing high quality is urgent.
2. To reduce pollutant loads each year, giving priority to selected industrial and municipal discharges—wherever located—that are responsible for the bulk of water pollution.
3. To issue the legally required regulations to implement the important features of the program by the statutory date, or so as not to delay program operations.

At this point, judgment gave way to analysis, for the initial goals had flushed out a serious policy issue: Should discharge permits be issued only after a complete abatement plan for a watershed had been developed, or should they be issued without much planning by simply requiring the use of the best abatement technology? The debate raged for several weeks, but it is sufficient to say that the issue was resolved when, after analyzing the consequences of each approach in some depth, management developed a policy slanted toward the technology option but requiring plans in areas of severe pollution where time and data permitted.

Armed with this decision, a small staff went to work to boil down management's overall goals to the more specific level of operating objectives. This called for a simple conceptual framework that permitted orderly and comprehensive analysis. The framework adopted was a grid constructed as follows:

- Across the top were listed management's three goals—*what* needs to be done.
- Down the side were listed the tools available to the agency to meet the goals—*how* the job can be done. In any given agency, the how-to may be best represented by program, by organization unit, or by function. It takes some skill to describe the how-to concisely, but it stands to reason that any agency that knows what it is doing can describe how it is doing it. In EPA's case, the how-to was functional: planning abatement needs and monitoring performance, issuing waste-discharge permits, and awarding grants for sewage treatment plant construction.

To fill out this grid, the staff had to figure out what each how-to function had to do to meet management's goals—for example, what must permit-issuance do to reduce pollutant loads? This is partly an analytic process; thus, the staff had to identify the water basins that met the priority criterion in the shifting quality goal. But it is partly a judgmental process, as well. The important things are to use the grid to force systematic thinking and to make sure all the cells of the grid are filled in.

After the usual staff iterations, the grid was completed, as is illustrated in Figure 27. The elements in this case are fairly explicit, and serve as operating objectives for an MBO system. A final, and easy, step was to divide the operating objectives into annual increments to form the basis for an annual operating plan. (If the first pass doesn't produce goals sufficiently explicit to serve as operating objectives, make a second pass. Thus, the goals in the cells of the first grid become goals across the top of a second grid, a new how-to list is created, and the second grid is completed. Each pass screens a set of goals against a how-to list to produce a more detailed set of goals, and, depending on the generality of the first set of goals, the process can be repeated until specific operating objectives are reached.)

This goal-setting method is a useful device for mapping an agency's existing goals and objectives. It doesn't guarantee that the existing objectives are right; doing that is more the job of the problem identification and analysis process. But both the MBO and the analysis processes need to start from a precise and coherent statement of existing goals and objectives. MBO needs the roadmap to tell operating managers what is expected of them. And the same statement is the foundation of the analysis process; unless the analysts know what exists, it's hard to determine what is right. But neither analyst nor operating manager needs or wants top management to give him detailed objectives covering every facet of every agency activity. Agency goals, and hence MBO, should concentrate on the important results to be achieved. And top manage-

## Figure 27
Grid for Analyzing Agency Goals

| | | | |
|---|---|---|---|
| **Overall Goal; Functions Performed** | Meet ambient water quality standards by 1977 giving priority to access of dense population with severe pollution problems and to a few other areas where protection of existing high water quality is urgent. | Reduce pollutant loads each year, giving priority to selected industrial and municipal dischargers—wherever located—that are responsible for the bulk of water pollution. | Issue legally required regulations needed to implement the important features of the program: (a) by the statutory date, or (b) so as not to delay program operations. |
| **Planning and Monitoring** | Complete by 12/31/74 detailed plans for 89 priority basins.<br><br>Complete by 12/31/74 monitoring surveys of 10 priority basins having serious non-point dischargers.<br><br>Complete revision of state water quality standards by 7/1/74.<br><br>Conduct monitoring needed to determine water quality status in 89 priority basins. | Complete by 12/31/74, 1,730 facility plans for essential sewage treatment plants.<br><br>Conduct monitoring needed to assess status of compliance of major dischargers and selected minor dischargers.<br><br>Complete by 12/31/74 inventories of all dischargers on 178 minor basins. | Each of the required regulations was identified, and a plan for producing each was developed. Because several organizations contributed to every regulation, each plan assigned objectives to responsible managers. However, to keep track of the end result, performance was reported against each plan, not by organization. |
| **Issuing Waste Discharge Permits** | Issue waste discharge permits to all dischargers in 89 priority basins by 12/31/74.<br><br>—First priority to 3,060 large dischargers.<br><br>—Second priority to 17,200 other dischargers. | Issue 16,150 industrial permits in minor basins, giving first priority to 1,200 major dischargers.<br><br>Issue 10,000 municipal permits in minor basins, giving first priority to 1,100 major dischargers. | Each of the required regulations was identified, and a plan for producing each was developed. Because several organizations contributed to every regulation, each plan assigned objectives to responsible managers. However, to keep track of the end result, performance was reported against each plan, not by organization. |

**Figure 27**–Continued

| | | |
|---|---|---|
| **Awarding Construction Grants** | Agree with states to revise treatment plant priority list to give high priority to plants in 89 priority basins. | Allot and obligate $5 billion in grant funds by 1/1/74. Initiate 2,500 construction projects. Complete 133 of the projects by 12/31/74. | Each of the required regulations was identified, and a plan for producing each was developed. Because several organizations contributed to every regulation, each plan assigned objectives to responsible managers. However, to keep track of the end result, performance was reported against each plan, not by organization. |

ment should rely on their subordinates to administer routine tasks on which the agency's success does not depend very much.

## 2. Preparing the President's Budget and the Annual Operating Plan

Once goals and operating objectives are in hand, two steps in the overall MBO process turn them into operational plans. (1) First, the agency needs to prepare the President's Budget and to propose new or revised programs better able to meet its goals in future years. (2) Second, an annual operating plan must be developed to give line managers resources and annual objectives for the current year. Sequencing these tasks is an important part of building an MBO system.

In the past, there has been a tendency to concentrate as many of these tasks as possible into the President's Budget process. That's a mistake, because the President's Budget process is nearly useless for developing an operating plan. Because it is inherently incremental, the process defeats the systematic look at the base program that an operating plan requires. Moreover, the budget is prepared months before the operating year begins, and OMB and Congress change it, sometimes drastically.

Once you accept the idea that the President's Budget cannot be reformed to carry this whole load, it's fairly easy to conceive of a workable planning cycle. The trick is to move the operational planning effort to the spring, leading to approval of the annual operating plan by mid-June. The resulting schedule, patterned after the EPA cycle, would look like the one in Figure 28.

The centerpiece of this schedule is the annual operating plan, which serves two functions. First, it is the means by which top management secures from operating managers a commitment to meet stated objectives. In EPA, it was a commitment reached in face-to-face discussion; this direct contact lends the stature and urgency that an agreement to produce results deserves.

The annual operating plan also serves as the financial plan for all the agency's resources. Since MBO objectives will probably not cover every agency activity, they do not cover all agency resources. Thus, in the operating plan, a commitment to selected objectives and a comprehensive financial plan must coexist.

The schedule in Figure 28 offers three important benefits. First, it puts most of the detailed work of digging into ongoing programs into the January-June period. During this time, there is an intensive period of planning the specific objectives to be achieved by every program during the operating year beginning in July. Some resource reallocation will happen, but, since it's not budget season, the bulk of the effort goes into securing commitments to operating objectives from managers. Assuming that real work goes into this process, the agency will emerge with a solid

**Figure 28**
The Annual Cycle for Managing by Objectives.

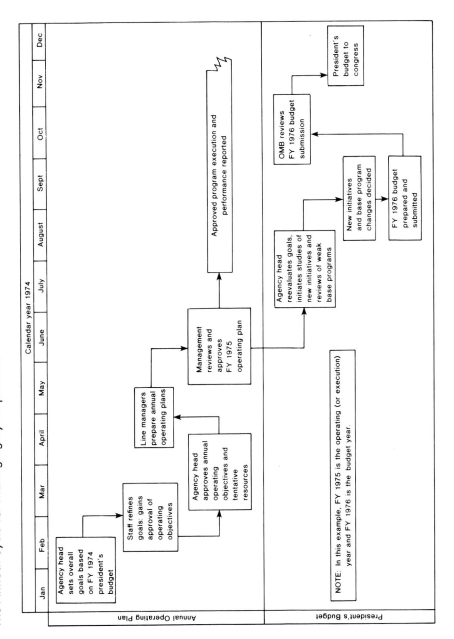

operating plan and an extraordinary understanding of the base program. Thus, the systematic review of the base—an automatic fallout of good operational planning—moves from the fall to the spring.

The second feature of this cycle is that it allows the agency to use the President's Budget process the way it should be used. Building on the intensive program review in the spring, the agency has at least three months before submitting its budget to redirect or tidy up weak programs in the base, and decide on the new initiatives (or increments) it wants to advocate in the President's Budget process and carry out the strategy or supporting studies needed to select and support the best of them.

Thus, by the time the budget is ready to go to OMB, the agency should be able to concentrate its efforts on the main chance—the increments and decrements in the President's Budget. And, with a solid operating plan in hand and a good fix on its base program, the agency is well equipped to thwart that greatest of all threats, an arbitrary cut in the base because "everyone knows you can always cut the base program by 5 percent."

Finally, although this cycle accepts the President's Budget as a largely incremental affair, it does not accept the notion of incremental budgeting elsewhere. In fact, this cycle builds in a thorough review of the base program in the spring. But it is mainly the increments that will get fought out in the President's Budget, and the agency's advocacy in that fall process needs to be geared to its incremental nature.

### Getting Useful Performance Reports

Performance reports close the loop back to agency objectives. They should give a clear picture of how things are going, flag problems, and help management take corrective action. They should, but they often don't.

One problem, of course, is that goals are not set systematically, so there is really nothing to report against. Another problem is the tendency to set up overblown reporting systems. A third is that progress toward an agency's more general goals can be measured only infrequently, because progress occurs slowly, but performance against annual operating objectives can and must be assessed quite often. This phenomenon defeats integrated systems that try to handle all reporting in the same way.

All these problems can be neatly side-stepped by first setting goals and then tailoring separate reports to the characteristics of each goal. For EPA goals, for example, it was determined that three kinds of reports would be needed.

1. Quantitative, monthly reports of results achieved against operating objectives (for example, the number of permits issued) in the annual operating plan.

2. Quarterly or semiannual reports on pollutant reductions, based on actual measurements in the field. This report is less frequent, because several operating objectives must be reached before a discharge is actually abated.
3. Annual reports on shifting quality, based on a sample of readings taken around the country. Such data are expensive to get, and are largely unreliable except in trend reporting; thus, there is no need to report them more often than annually.

In other words, there should be a closed-loop system for each type of goal. But there need not, and often cannot, be a pyramid of reports that cover all goals at once. This concept of tailoring avoids the swamp of the giant, integrated, pyramid-shaped reporting system—and happily, because rarely does such a pyramid have a point. The concept does require that management review several reports at different times and give some thought to the underlying problems of which bad reports are symptomatic—but then, that's what management is paid for.

## Implementing the System

Once the MBO system is designed, it has to be installed. Grafting a new management system on to a going agency takes some care and common sense. Recalling two lessons from the past, I should say that the keynotes of system implementation are keeping the system simple and tailoring it to the special needs of the agency. In my experience, system implementation tends to hang up at three points. First, integrating a system such as MBO into existing accounting structures is likely to get overly complicated. Second, there is the problem of assigning staff responsibilities for running the system. Finally, there is the risk of becoming too enamored of planning. Some pointers for avoiding these pitfalls are discussed below.

### Simplifying Structure Problems

MBO needs responsibility-accounting structures that permit resource allocations and performance targets to be set and monitored. Too few agencies have responsibility-oriented structures. That is bad news, for creating such a structure adds one more woe to the problem of integrating the existing accounting structures.

The good news is that the responsibility structure is simple. It is just a list of names, preferably of line managers, the specific workload goals in the operating plan for which they are responsible, and the resources they are allocated to do the job. For example, the administrator of EPA Region II has a total of $2 million for which he will produce X water discharge permits, Y construction grants, and so on.

It is important to note the implications of this concept. First, it is built around responsible line managers, not "programs"; if a program is managed by ten regional administrators, split it ten ways. Second, the concept presupposes that responsible managers actually control the resources they need to produce results. And third, it requires that cost accounting (*not* fiscal accounting) be done in terms of the responsibility structure.

The responsibility structure must, of course, fit with other, existing accounting structures. As was indicated earlier, full integration of all structures is *not* the way to achieve this fit; rather, a simple and selective approach is in order:

- There's not much need to relate the responsibility structure to appropriations during the President's Budget process. That process is incremental, and all that is needed is a good analyst to price out the increments and allocate them into appropriation and responsibility structures.

- The most difficult structural problem is to relate, in the annual operating plan, objectives, which may not cover all resources, to the comprehensive financial plan, which does. There are two issues here. First, the agency must decide whether to price out each objective. Often, it's not necessary, but the decision will depend on the character of each objective and the importance of knowing precisely how much it costs. Second, the agency has to determine when during the development of the operating plan to prepare the detailed financial plan. As a general rule it's best to concentrate on objectives first and financial plans later. To keep the entire process under some financial discipline from the start, it is usually possible to allocate funds at the outset only at the appropriation level. Then, toward the end of the process (when the commitment to annual objectives and broad resource allocations are pretty well fixed), each line manager should price out his plan by appropriation, budget activity, authorization, and whatever other financial structures may exist.

The law of averages being what it is, the sum of these price-outs will usually be within the financial constraints approved by OMB and Congress in whatever structures they are stated. If not, it is simpler to make the necessary changes in the operating plans near the end of the process (since the changes are almost always minor) than to carry the full panoply of financial data through from the start. (The law-of-averages system may sound risky, but it works. EPA had four appropriations, 30 budget activities, 50 separate authorizations, and ten reprogramming constraints—and managed to keep its head above water. The reason the scheme works is that appropriations are usually the most constrainting financial consideration, and absolute appropriation control is retained in the system.)

 • Financial accounting during the operating year must, of course, consider all financial constraints imposed on the agency. But financial data should be reported separately from operating results, not through a common system. With appropriate safeguards at the appropriation level, the law-of-averages system will keep spending within target, without the need for integrating financial and responsibility accounting.

 • Every other need for financial data (function, special analyses, cost by goal) is best satisfied by special studies.

In short, there is not much need to tie responsibility accounting directly to financial accounting. A close tie between appropriations and responsibility accounting is needed, but only for the operating plan. Cost and responsibility accounting should be coincident. Beyond that, it's best to let the systems run separately and to use special studies when translation from one structure to another is needed.

### Staffing the System

Who is going to do all the work of MBO? Should there be a special MBO staff? Some may recall the PPB staffs created in the 1960s that were of variable quality and tended to do battle with the budget office. Worse, line managers often ignored even their good work. In an MBO system, especially, it's a good idea to keep special staffs to a minimum. Small staffs are cheaper and they work better. And they are likely to do less fighting among themselves and with other organization units.

One very small special staff at the top is needed to support management in analyzing goals, developing performance measures, interpreting reports, and generally exercising quality control over the MBO system. The agency's central program and budget office should play its usual role of assembling the paperwork incident to budgets and annual operating plans and should keep things in line with financial constraints. But the bulk of the operational planning can, and should, be done by line managers; indeed, MBO won't work unless line managers develop their own operating plans.

There remain the special studies, such as strategy studies and base program reviews. The rule here is that if such studies are assigned solely to special staffs, top management had better be ready to lose the blood necessary to implement the study recommendations. Since management has only so much blood, special staff studies are best reserved for those critical issues that cannot successfully be attacked by others. For example, an entrenched program office that violently resists change may not be able to produce a sound study aimed at a substantial program redirection. If the redirection is clearly called for, an outside staff study is the only answer.

Short of this, however, it's best to assign the study to the responsible manager, or at least to ensure his full participation. Top management should make clear what issue is to be studied and why. It can, and often should, provide outside staff support to maintain quality control and supply special skills. But a study run by the office responsible for the issue is often done more quickly and accepted more gracefully than is one developed by a special staff.

## Avoiding Overplanning

It's easy to overplan, and it's bad to do it. Overplanning wastes time and diverts attention from the real work of agreeing on simple operating objectives and controlling performance to meet them. Unfortunately, there is no ironclad way to avoid overplanning, but a few common-sense rules on the subject will illustrate what I have in mind:

• *Don't worry too much about how planning gets done, but worry a lot about whether it works.* Far too much effort goes into writing manuals on how to plan. As a rule, however, the sophistication of the planning system bears absolutely no relation to the quality of the plan. The moral is clear: If you want good planning, hire a smart planner.

• *Insist that plans produce a commitment to specific results that are clearly assigned to someone for accomplishment.* The proof of planning is in the doing, and nothing will get done unless the plan spells out who must do what and when.

• *Plan sufficiently to produce specific targets, then quit.* Some planners seem to have a profound drive to elaborate on their plans, demonstrate their sophistication, and in general produce more paper than anyone needs. Don't do it; no one has time to read the stuff.

• *Don't waste time with planners who cannot deliver results.* A plan done by staff with no responsibility or ability to deliver the results is only an artifact. Deal with the line manager.

Common sense is a lot easier to talk about than have. But it can be used, and must be, if government is to be managed for results.

## A Closing Word

No wise man would deny the great advances in federal management of the past half-century. The integrity of fiduciary controls, the coherence of the unified budget, the power of the analytic tools of PPB—all these and more are landmarks in the effort to manage the incredible enterprise of government.

Now we talk of management by objectives, of goals and operational planning. Today's talk may be in the jargon of management theory, but it is not for the sake of management doctrine that these ideas have a new currency. The reasons go far deeper than mere doctrinal differences with the past.

The plain fact is that the public distrusts big government (and big business, big education, big labor, and big religion, for that matter), at least in part because government doesn't produce. Results, not promises, are the order of today. And if setting goals and carefully managing operations to meet these goals will produce results, that is reason enough to get on with the job.

I think we're on the right course. Americans are still pragmatic enough to believe that if government works it can't be all that bad—even if they no longer believe that government is good just because it works. Our job as manager is to decide what we can do, then do it. That having been said, one final note is in order to set MBO, or any other management system, in proper perspective. It is true that better management systems will help do the job of producing results, but no system ever produced any results by itself. People make results, and, in government more than in any other enterprise, the conscious act of managing is crucial to success.

## Selected Bibliography

For additional reading on the basic concept of management by objectives and the techniques for implementing this concept, see George S. Odiorne's *Management by Objectives: A System of Managerial Leadership* (Pitman Publishing Corp., New York, 1965); John W. Humble's *Improving Business Results* and *Management by Objectives in Action* (McGraw-Hill Publishing Co., Ltd., London, 1967 and 1970. Also see *Management by Objectives,* by David E. Olson (Pacific Books Publishers, Palo Alto, 1968); *Managing By—and with—Objectives,* by Walter S. Wikstrom (The Conference Board, Personnel Policy Study No. 212, New York, 1968); and *Appraising Managers as Managers,* by Harold Koontz (McGraw-Hill, New York, 1971).

Two of Peter F. Drucker's books, *The Practice of Management* (Harpers, New York, 1954) and *Managing for Results* (Harpers, New York, 1964), provide a general discussion of the opportunities of the effective business and of goal-setting strategies required to move an enterprise forward.

Extensive research on the subject has been done by Henry L. Tosi, John R. Rizzo, and Stephen J. Carroll. For a general discussion of the MBO process, see "Setting Goals in Management by Objectives" *(California Management Review,* Summer 1970). Also, see the following articles by Messrs. Tosi and Carroll: "Some Structural Factors Related to Goal Influence in the Management by Objectives Process" *(Business Topics,* Spring 1969), "Managerial Reactions to Management by Objectives" *(Academy of Management Journal,* December 1968), and "Some

Factors Affecting the Success of Management by Objectives" *(The Journal of Management Studies,* May 1970).

For readings on MBO in the federal government see Aaron Wildavsky's recent article, "The Annual Expenditure Incrementor—How Congress Can Regain Control of the Budget" (*Public Interest,* Fall 1973). Charles Schultze's book *The Politics and Economics of Public Spending* (The Brookings Institution, 1968) discusses the federal government's budgetary process. For a status report on MBO in government, see the *National Journal,* Vol. 5, No. 22, and Vol. 5, No. 33.

*John M. Ivancevich*
*J. Timothy McMahon*
*J. William Streidl*
*Andrew D. Szilagyi, Jr.*

# 4

# Goal Setting: The Tenneco Approach to Personnel Development and Management Effectiveness

Applying goal setting to an organization is intuitively appealing and seems seductively simple, but it is fraught with potential problems. The testimonials of goal-setting advocates are meaningless when an organization is attempting to implement, evaluate, and integrate such a program.

If we want to be able to develop managerial personnel to the limit of their potential, we have to ask ourselves a number of questions. Does each manager really have a clear understanding of his or her job responsibilities? Are superiors providing enough feedback on performance? Are managers given the opportunities and guidance to master their work, increase their skills and knowledge base, and receive promotions and move up to jobs with greater responsibility?

In this article we will examine the efforts of Tenneco Inc. to apply a goal-setting program for management development across relatively autonomous divisional and affiliated companies. By standing back and examining the sequence of activities implemented at Tenneco, we can acquire both a conceptual and an empirically based picture of the strengths and weaknesses of its effort. An analysis of the Tenneco experience provides insight into the use of a goal-setting system in a company in which top management is committed to such use. The initial results of the Tenneco program indicate that the goal-setting system has been successful in many areas, although a continual monitoring effort is needed to determine long-run performance changes.

## Traditional Goal-Setting Practices

When discussing an organization's goal-setting program, a person may have a number of different approaches in mind. Terms used to describe goal setting include management by objectives (MBO), management by results, work planning and review, and the charter of accountability concept. As George Odiorne emphasizes, goal-setting techniques involve:

Reprinted by permission of the publisher, *Organizational Dynamics,* Winter 1978, pp. 58-80.

> . . . a process whereby the superior and subordinate managers of an organization jointly identify common goals, define each individual's major areas of responsibility in terms of the results expected of him, and use these measures as guides for operating the unit and assessing the contribution of each of its members.

The different terminology used has led to some confusion concerning the basis of goal setting, where it is implemented, and how it works. The major implication, however, is that through discussions and active involvement in goal setting, a subordinate will be motivated to work harder and consequently improve his or her performance.

The philosophical rudiments of goal setting provide the basis for a process that includes a series of interrelated and interdependent steps taken by the superior and subordinate. These steps are illustrated in Figure 29. They include: (1) a *diagnosis* to assess the needs, job, personnel, and technology; (2) *preparation* via communicating what goal setting is, training in the process, establishing objectives, making action plans, and evolving criteria to assess whether the goals of the process are being accomplished; (3) *goal setting*, with special attention paid to goal clarity, superior-subordinate participation, and the establishment of relevant goals and goal priorities; (4) an *intermediate review* of the original goals, which is a form of feedback and provides an opportunity to modify the original goals; and (5) a *final review* or discussion and analysis of the results, which are used to initiate the next complete cycle of objective setting. The anticipated result of the planning, control, and organization goal-setting process is improved and motivated involvement that is based on accomplishments rather than personality or popularity. In addition, managers are encouraged to develop their skills and abilities within the framework of their jobs.

A number of important principles of action emerge from a close examination of this process:

*Principle I: Diagnosis.* The crucial first step in any goal-setting program should be a thorough diagnosis of the job, the participants, and the needs of the organization.

*Principle II: Commitment.* Goal setting requires the frequent and intensive involvement and participation of superiors and subordinates.

*Principle III: Meaningful Goals.* Goals should be established that, if attained, benefit organizational effectiveness *and* the personal growth and development of the participants.

*Principle IV: Feedback.* Goal setting relies heavily on feedback of results, which should be as closely connected to behavior and performance as possible.

*Principle V: Counseling.* The superior should be competent in counseling subordinates on the achieved results and the expected or agreed-to results for the next cycle.

**Figure 29**

Goal-Setting Model for Superior-Subordinate Objective Setting.

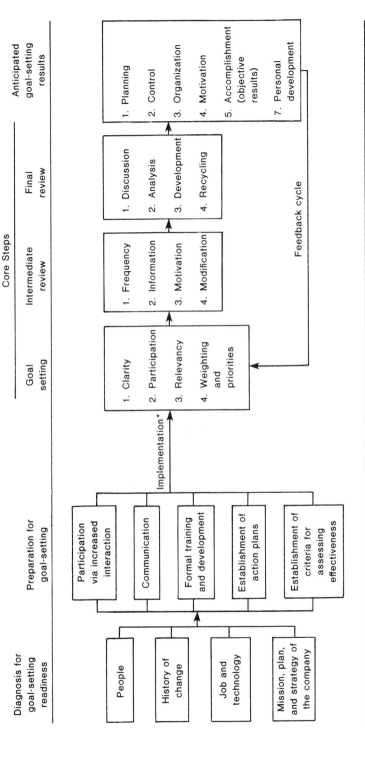

*After the preparation phase is completed it is necessary to develop a systematic plan for implementation.

These principles are based on a review of the empirically based goal-setting literature, which has been quite sketchy and limited considering the worldwide use of organizational goal setting. The vast majority of goal-setting literature that espouses its virtues is based primarily on testimonial claims of consultants, academicians, and convinced practicing managers. These advocates propose an attractive list of benefits that can accrue and, in certain instances, have accrued to organizations that implement and monitor goal-setting programs. Some of these benefits include:

- Improved short- and long-range planning.
- A procedure for monitoring work progress and results.
- Improved commitment to the organization because of increased motivation, loyalty, and participation of employees.
- Improved clarity of the manager's role.
- Improved communication between superiors and subordinates.

These and other benefits are certainly attractive to any manager. Unfortunately, some advocates assume that not only do these benefits flow easily from a goal-setting effort, but they do so in a relatively short time. These erroneous assumptions have not been evaluated in most reviews of goal-setting programs, and false claims have sometimes been made for the superiority of these programs. In addition, inflated expectations can emerge and have emerged that are impossible to fulfill in a short time.

A less vocal, but equally important, group of managers has experienced some of the negative consequences of goal-setting programs. Some of their complaints are:

- Goal-setting programs are used as a whip, particularly when they are closely tied to wage and salary programs.
- Many programs not only fail to receive continual top management commitment and support but do not reach the lower managerial levels.
- There is an overemphasis on production and productivity, or what are called "hard" performance indicators.
- Many superiors are not adequately trained in the goal-setting process or in the most effective manner of coaching and counseling subordinates.
- Goal-setting programs fail to provide adequate personal incentives to improve performance—the emphasis is only on the benefits to the organization and seemingly little concern for the development of the participating managers.

The advocates of goal setting in organizations project the impression that it is the panacea for motivation, leadership, change, development, and personal development. Because many organizations fail to recognize that goal setting is a comprehensive management process, they attempt to superimpose it on their existing structures, climates, and untrained personnel. This unfortunate imposition leads to some of the problems cited above, which probably account for the limited number of scientifically based success stories reported. Too, there is often a tendency to overemphasize hard performance factors in goal-setting programs. This type of focus fails to capture the developmental potential of goal setting. Another major block to creating a successful goal-setting system is the lack of top management involvement and support. The evidence is so clear cut that top management must be involved in each phase of the program that it is difficult to fathom why this issue is not a number-one priority.

## Concern for Development

Many goal-setting systems have been introduced with an emphasis on only the hard performance indicators for managerial jobs. The Tenneco emphasis on development that resulted from the task force efforts described below put a new definition on work development. Tenneco's goal-setting system recognized the importance of being able to measure the quality and quantity of work performed, but it also stressed the fact that measurements exist that will help meet manager development objectives at each level of the managerial/professional organization. Several management experts have recognized the need for making manager development the building block of all organization units. The catalyst is the manager-employee relationship and the degree of support for continuing development that comes from a relationship. In addition, there is the recognition that true development occurs over a period of time in an atmosphere that is related to the everyday work life of the employee and his ability to continue to improve, whether or not he is promoted (see Figure 30).

Tenneco, with headquarters in Houston, is a large diversified, multi-industry company operating in eight major industries. Among the Tenneco companies are J. I. Case, manufacturer and marketer of farm and construction equipment; Newport News Shipbuilding and Dry Dock Company; Walker Manufacturing Company and Monroe Auto Equipment Company, manufacturers of automotive equipment; Packaging Corporation of America, a vertically integrated supplier of paperboard, folding cartons, and corrugated containers; Tenneco Oil, producer, refiner, and marketer of petroleum and related products; Tennessee Gas Transmission Company, which administers Tenneco's natural gas pipeline activities; Tenneco Chemicals, marketer of a wide range of industrial chemical products; and Tenneco West, which produces markets agricultural products. Tenneco employs about 82,000 people, of which approximately 15,000 are managers and professionals.

**Figure 30**
Development Goal.

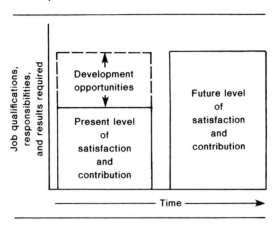

Tenneco's definition of development, as depicted in Figure 30, suggests that the basis for continued development is the ongoing dialog between manager and employee at every level of the organization. This dialog is expected to result in the development of hard performance indicators (defining what a good job is), while considering the manager's role, his or her unique qualifications, the formal organization structure, and the results expected from that employee. The result should be an emphasis on the individual employee's role in both providing his contribution (hard performance indicators) and obtaining personal satisfaction and self-fulfillment from that contribution. Concurrently, it should create a group of employees who are striving for perfection on their jobs and who will therefore become qualified to be considered for positions of greater responsibility.

Tenneco, like most organizations, utilizes hard performance indicators to determine whether results are being achieved. What is unique in the Tenneco approach is the attempt to tie in such achievement with the overall development objective, thereby pointing out how each employee contribution places the manager, employee, and organization as a whole in "win-win" positions.

## Emphasis on Top-Management Support at Tenneco

A task force that represented each divisional company in Tenneco was appointed by the office of the president. Each company had at least one representative (vice-president or director) on the task force. The task force established some important objectives for its work in instituting a goal-setting system. The task force decided that it would be necessary to (1) secure and maintain management commitment, starting with top levels of the company and moving through each succeeding level of management, to ensure that the new performance planning and evaluation (PP&E) system would be used and would become a "managerial way of life" rather than a personnel program; (2) ensure that a minimum of additional procedure and paperwork would be used in introducing and implementing the system; (3) ensure that the system was understood conceptually and that the managers who had to use it had the basic skills necessary for system implementation; and (4) attempt to communicate the system effectively so that participants—superior and subordinate—recognized the need for continual interface, dialog, and commitment to goals by both at each level of the organization to achieve the development objectives of the organization as a whole.

One form of top management support for the PP&E system is identified in the foreword to a booklet describing Tenneco's approach to goal setting with the following excerpted statement from Wilton E. Scott, chairman of the board and chief executive officer of Tenneco:

> It is my utmost concern that among our thousands of employees there may be highly capable people whose talents we do not recognize or to whom we do not give maximum opportunity. And if we fail to do that, in fact, if we fail to offer maximum opportunity to any one person in our organization, we are failing in one of our basic management responsibilities . . . accordingly, I expect this philosophy and method of management to receive enthusiastic support at all levels with in Tenneco.

Tenneco Inc. has an active office of the president. The above and similar statements of top management support were reinforced by the active participation of the office of the president in the formation of the task force and the introduction of the PP&E system through initial training efforts. Members of the office of the president did, in fact, participate in the same basic training workshops as other members of management. This type of involvement is often bypassed in less effective goal-setting efforts.

Simply stated, Tenneco's philosophy of goal setting suggests that a maximum opportunity for personal satisfaction and personal contribution to the organization can occur only when the job is well defined in terms of the outputs expected from it. These outputs can be defined only through an ongoing relationship between manager and employee at every level of the organization, and the discussion of such development opportunities provides a basis for continual development. Figure 30 illustrates the long-run goal of personal development that manifests itself in the form of improved satisfaction and increased organizational and individual contribution.

## Tenneco Preparation Phase

The top-management cadre was knowledgeable about problems encountered in other organizations with goal-setting systems. By studying the literature carefully, attending professional meetings, visiting with peers in other companies, and discussing goal setting with experts, the Tenneco team developed a set of scenarios of the crucial problems to avoid in implementing a goal-setting system within the company. This set included the following:

### Commitment

Failure to get top management's commitment and involvement is a quick way to lose the influence of a goal-setting system. Lack of support from the top causes goal setting to deteriorate into another futile bureaucratic exercise. It becomes something for middle managers who are expected to represent top management to fiddle with. The middle-level executive writes a set of objectives, looks it over, and files it deeply into a desk drawer to simmer for at least a year. These objectives are retrieved one year later and looked at before the next year's cycle begins. Thus goal setting is reduced to filling out a report, filing it away, and looking at it a year later in a casual fashion. Instead of an exercise, this sequence of events can more appropriately be called "a game."

### Evaluation

Many managerial processes and change interventions, such as goal setting, tend to have consultants carry out a diagnosis and evaluation of the system. This dual role of consultant and researcher is difficult to perform. The person or team performing the dual roles is likely to conclude that what ails the system can be treated by "their" package. Thus an organizational change expert finds that the problems can be remedied through goal setting; the transactional analysis specialist finds that TA is the answer; and the career planning advocate suggests that performance problems can be solved by developing career plans.

Tenneco decided to have an external group evaluate its goal-setting intervention. The roles of implementer and evaluator were separated on purpose. The internal task force decided to implement goal setting in the divisional companies. The preparatory steps for Tenneco's goal setting were conducted by representatives of the company and not by trainers from an institute or university. Although Tenneco was responsible for the preparation, evaluation was placed totally in the hands of John M. Ivancevich, J. Timothy McMahon, and Andrew D. Szilagyi, Jr., of the Department of Organizational Behavior and Management at the University of Houston.

### Status of Goal Setting

Many companies treat the goal-setting system as an appendage that is not too important. The status of the program is ambiguous and questionable. If more than marginally acceptable improvements in personal development are to accrue, goal setting must become one of management's top priorities. If not, it often begins to suffer from a lack of attention. When this happens, the program disintegrates rapidly and ends up on a back burner or as a "wooden" set of notebooks that adorns each manager's shelf and collects dust.

### Lack of Integration

Everyone always hopes that the goal-setting effort will be integrated with performance appraisal, managerial planning and controlling, and management development. Unless more than hoping is done the program becomes little more than useless. Integration with the normal managerial processes must be accomplished from the top down.

These four crucial issues were considered carefully by the task force. The task force produced specific strategies, policy suggestions, and action plans that addressed each issue. In working through their suggestions, the task force paid particular attention to failures reported by other companies that seemed to ignore the importance of commitment, evaluation, status, and integration.

## Training Phase

An early suggestion by the development task force was that the PP&E system be field tested through initial introductory training activities and implementation in two companies. Concurrently, one of the other companies, which had eight years' experience with a comparable goal-setting system, could continue to operate within that system. The knowledge gained by the pilot companies and the experienced goal-setting company would, in turn, be used to build a better overall system for Tenneco.

The company with eight years' goal-setting experience provided a director-level manager to serve on the overall corporate task force during initial PP&E system-design activities. At the same time, the task force member, along with Tenneco corporate staff members worked to develop an overall training package that could be used throughout all the Tenneco companies to introduce the system. Strengths and weaknesses found in the approach to introducing goal setting in the experienced company and that company's training materials provided additional input for both the task force and the sub-group that was assigned to develop the initial training package.

The pilot companies—one in a process industry, the other in manufacturing—were asked to carry out initial PP&E introductory activities before the total corporate training package was developed. The diversity and geographic spread of these companies provided an opportunity to field test some of the concepts built into the overall PP&E system, so that an introductory training package could be developed that was acceptable and effective across a wide range of industries.

The task force efforts and the specific training and introductory plans provided a conceptual basis of understanding and skill practice appropriate to each of the widely diverse companies within the Tenneco family of companies. Materials and "train the trainers" seminars for each divisional company were provided that set broad parameters for such training and had built-in flexibility to make the training and implementation suitable for each company. For example, in one large division of one of the companies, over 90 line managers were trained as PP&E trainers; in a smaller company with widely decentralized locations, one training and development specialist carried out the initial basic training.

The "train the trainers" sessions and the follow-up sessions in each divisional company resulted in the completion of basic goal-setting training for over 15,000 managerial and professional employees during 1976 in both the United States and overseas. This segment of of the training concentrated on the individual identification of major responsibilities and goals (performance planning). It did not attempt to provide detailed knowledge on performance evaluation, coaching, and counseling. Another PP&E training segment is being carried on now on a highly flexible and decentralized basis for the approximately 5,000 managers of other managers and professional employees. These managers of managers must be skilled in completing the PP&E cycle through performance evaluation, coaching, and counseling activities.

## Integrating PP&E with Normal Managerial Processes

The sheer size, diversity, and geographic spread of the Tenneco companies have provided some of the strengths of the Tenneco approach to date. At the same time, they could cause system weaknesses in terms of overall integration with its present and future management systems. As mentioned, the system has been installed throughout the various companies, utilizing basic training materials prepared at Tenneco's headquarters.

The corporate policy statement permits a considerable amount of divisional flexibility:

> The PP&E system represents a minimum standard to be achieved by all divisional companies and all Tenneco Inc. corporate staff groups. The minimum standard requires the continual use of formalized goal setting resulting from face-to-face meetings for the purpose of discussing, defining and recording responsibilities, expected results, priorities and target dates.

Tenneco has standard reporting systems (largely in the financial area), but there is considerable divisional autonomy in terms of other operating practices, procedures, policies, and systems. To date, each company continues to affect the integration of the PP&E system into its organization units in a manner appropriate for that unit. For example, within one of the larger manufacturing units, training methods, document flow procedures, audit and control activities, and so on are different for the international unit than they are for some of the domestic units. In fact, there are some variations between the major domestic units. This flexibility of approach ties back to making development the major objective. Currently, Tenneco corporate programs are being developed that will assist divisional managers to integrate their activities, but the approach will be through training and information rather than executive order.

## Tenneco System in Action

In recent years many executives have accepted the principle that the health and growth of their enterprise depend, in part, on the growth and development of employees. Tenneco's management believed that goal setting via a performance planning and evaluation system could be a vehicle for such growth and development. In its most basic sense, the PP&E system represents a program for improving work performance and management development for managerial and professional-level employees in all Tenneco corporate staff groups and divisional companies.

A number of objectives have been established for the PP&E system. The first is improved on-the-job effectiveness by each employee in his or her present position by requiring planned attention to goals and priorities. The second is self-development to assure each employee's future effectiveness and career growth. The final objective is to locate managerial personnel with the ability to handle greater responsibility. A pool of such personnel assures management continuity from within the organization. Taken together, the objectives of the PP&E system are intended to provide each employee with the maximum opportunity for personal development and advancement and to provide a tool for more effective management. In its most basic form, the PP&E system is as shown in Figure 31.

The PP&E system is composed of several sequential steps. Each has a specific purpose and is essential to the program.

### Performance Planning
In this first phase, the job and situation are diagnosed, and the employee states his or her job responsibilities and objectives for the year. The process includes:

**Figure 31**
Philosophy of the Basic PP&E System (Goal Setting).

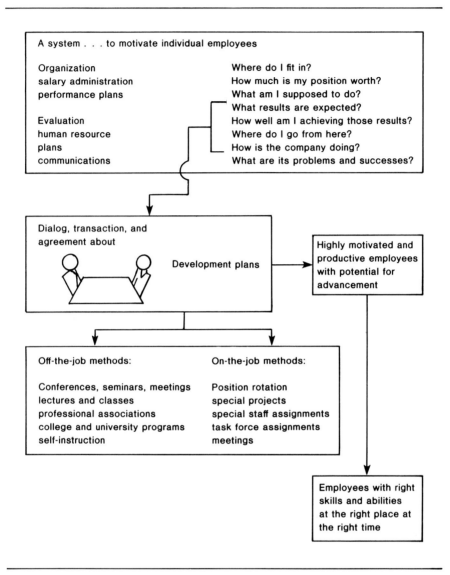

A system . . . to motivate individual employees

Organization
salary administration
performance plans

Where do I fit in?
How much is my position worth?
What am I supposed to do?
What results are expected?

Evaluation
human resource
plans
communications

How well am I achieving those results?
Where do I go from here?
How is the company doing?
What are its problems and successes?

Dialog, transaction, and
agreement about

Development plans

Highly motivated and
productive employees
with potential for
advancement

Off-the-job methods:

Conferences, seminars, meetings
lectures and classes
professional associations
college and university programs
self-instruction

On-the-job methods:

Position rotation
special projects
special staff assignments
task force assignments
meetings

Employees with right
skills and abilities
at the right place at
the right time

- Broadly defining the key responsibilities of the job.
- Expressing specific objectives to be achieved for each key responsibility.
- Assigning relative priorities to the desired results.

The first step is important because it allows the employee to discuss specific job aspects with his or her supervisor and to obtain agreement on goals. The agreed-upon plans are recorded on a form and reviewed periodically by the superior and subordinate to check progress, discuss ways to improve, and agree on changes in activities that may be necessary to adapt to changes in the business climate or other related conditions.

## Performance Evaluation

After one year, the results of the employee's actual performance are measured against stated objectives and priorities. The employee finds out exactly how well he or she is doing and any opportunities to contribute better results are fully identified. The evaluation phase has three basic parts.

- The supervisor completes a tentative evaluation of the subordinate's performance.
- The supervisor's superior reviews the tentative evaluation to assure consistency, equity, and quality.
- The supervisor discusses the evaluation with the subordinate, with a focus on developing the subordinate.

## Development

During the performance evaluation session, the subordinate is told how well he or she is doing, and specific plans for development are made, based on a discussion of:

- Strengths and weaknesses of past performance.
- Potential performance improvement opportunities.
- The subordinate's interest in development and aspirations for advancement.

After the performance evaluation session, the supervisor completes an assessment of the employee's potential for development. The report includes:

- Overall performance rating during the last period.
- Development needs and mutually satisfactory action plans.
- Progress and achievement from previous development plans.
- Interests and aspirations.
- Present promotability and potential for future achievement.
- Possible replacements.

This assessment is reviewed by the supervisor's superior and is maintained within each division and at corporate headquarters to serve as a source for locating employees with advancement potential.

Experience and research reveal that there should be a relationship between how well a job is performed and the financial rewards allocated. Many companies have found, however, that little employee development takes place in salary review sessions. Because of this, the PP&E system requires salary discussion interviews to be separate and distinct from progress reviews and development/evaluation sessions. The PP&E system is designed to plan for good performance, correct performance problems, achieve the goal plan, assist the employee in developing his or her optimal skills, and, most important, increase the job effectiveness and long-run career development of each managerial and professional employee. PP&E-related discussions take place many times during the review year, as plans are modified, different goals are achieved and new ones developed, and the supervisor assumes the role of a coach in assisting the employee to develop his or her skill utilization.

The proper procedure for determining what impact, if any, the PP&E system is having on the participants is to perform a continuous evaluation. One source of information is the participants themselves. What do they feel about the program? What do they like or dislike? How are they conducting goal-setting sessions? These are some of the questions that can be examined in the evaluation phase.

## Evaluation Phase

The scientific evaluation of the PP&E system focuses on five basic objectives:

1. Initially, to trace changes in attitudes throughout the PP&E system. After full implementation, to trace performance or on-the-job effectiveness.
2. To isolate problems participants are having with the PP&E system.
3. To determine how PP&E is being utilized on the job.
4. To gather scientific data so that modifications and changes in the PP&E system based on more than personal opinions or intuitive judgments can be initiated.
5. To compare Tenneco results with those in similar organizations that have implemented goal-oriented programs.

A survey methodology was used by external organizational researchers to achieve the evaluation objectives. The responses described attitudes about goal-setting activities, job characteristics, organization climate, and what it was like to set PP&E plans with a superior. It was assumed that positive and negative reactions to and attitudes about PP&E

had to be studied over a period of time to acquire a picture of what was happening within the units and divisions. Studying reactions and attitudes over a short period is not recommended; goal-setting initiated changes often take time to appear.

The timing for assessing reactions and attitudes is spelled out in Figure 32. The first time frame for taking measurements is referred to as the *baseline*. Baseline measures were taken during April-July, 1976. From late 1977 on, similar evaluations will be conducted at Tenneco, so that each of the five objectives can be accomplished with scientifically based data.

Because of the diversity of type of division and geographic location in the overall PP&E introductory effort, a wide range of approaches were considered and used to determine how well the system was meeting development needs. Personal visits and consultations with line and staff personnel responsible for system introduction and implementation have been carried out continually since the system was introduced.

Ideally, of course, it would have been appropriate to attempt to measure attitudes before any changes had been introduced to Tenneco or its individual companies by training and by establishing the task force. This approach was not used because the high interest in getting the PP&E system introduced and implemented generated its own momentum, and it was felt that the need for the system in terms of overall developmental objectives far outweighed any concern for getting pure baseline measurements.

This article reports only the attitude data; it does not cover development or performance indicators. These measures will eventually be combined with the attitude data to provide a comprehensive picture of the impact of the PP&E system. Goal-setting results from other organizations suggest that changes in attitudes typically precede improvements in performance. Thus the initial research spotlight centers on attitudes of Tenneco managers toward PP&E.

## Driver and Secondary Variables and Process Indicators

The Tenneco PP&E system appears to be stimulating, challenging, and pervasive enough to cause things to happen. It was assumed that after PP&E implementation, improvements would occur in such areas as job clarity, job tension, feedback, need satisfaction, and the linking of performance and rewards. The survey was designed to determine whether these attitudinal improvements were actually occurring.

**Figure 32**

Goal-Setting Process: Tenneco PP&E Evaluation Program.

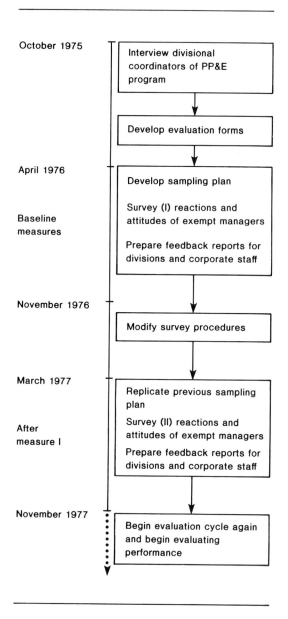

October 1975 — Interview divisional coordinators of PP&E program

Develop evaluation forms

April 1976

Baseline measures

Develop sampling plan

Survey (I) reactions and attitudes of exempt managers

Prepare feedback reports for divisions and corporate staff

November 1976 — Modify survey procedures

March 1977

After measure I

Replicate previous sampling plan

Survey (II) reactions and attitudes of exempt managers

Prepare feedback reports for divisions and corporate staff

November 1977 — Begin evaluation cycle again and begin evaluating performance

*Driver variables* is the term used to describe the central attitude changes, after PP&E is implemented, in such areas as goal feedback, participation, role clarity, job autonomy, and job tension. It was assumed that the driver variables would provide the impetus and starting point for performance and self-development improvements.

The *secondary variables* were assumed to be important, but were expected to take longer to show improvements. Included in this set were such variables as job satisfaction, organizational climate, and job characteristic variables such as autonomy, feedback, and uncertainty. Again, previous research on goal setting in other organizations has indicated that these factors would begin to show significant changes after a program such as PP&E was functioning smoothly.

*Process indicators* was used to refer to measures that assess what goes on between superior and subordinate in PP&E planning and performance evaluation sessions. Unfortunately, it is extremely difficult to determine exactly what does happen when a boss and a subordinate meet to discuss the subordinate's goals. A number of survey questions were aimed at learning more about these important processes.

A few sample questions from the *driver, secondary,* and *process* portions of the survey questionnaire are listed in Table 1. The responses to the attitude questions were used to create the baseline measures. A similar survey will be conducted annually to generate measures subsequent to baseline PP&E implementation. The monitoring of attitudes will enable Tenneco managers to investigate soft spots in PP&E implementation more thoroughly.

## Selected Results: Lots of Promise

The volume of data collected is too large to present in an article. However, a sample of the baseline results will provide some indication of the nature of PP&E at Tenneco. During the months of April-July 1976, over 4,500 out of a randomly selected sample of 5,300 surveyed at Tenneco responded to an attitude survey. These 5,300 were selected from a list of approximately 15,000 eligible managers. When the baseline data were collected, some managers were already using the PP&E system and others were not. A total of 2,131 repsondents indicated that at the baseline point they were using the PP&E system; 2,395 respondents said they were not. Thus they were divided into two groups: *user of PP&E* and *nonuser of PP&E*.

### User and nonuser: driver results

In analyzing each driver variable score, the user managers responded more favorably than the nonusers. All references to "more" and "less" in discussing results refer to statistically significant differences $\leq .05$. In other words, the probability of the differences being due to chance is 5 percent or less. The users report more goal feedback, more goal participation, more goal clarity, more role clarity, less job tension, and more job autonomy.

**Table 1**
Sample of Survey Questions

| Specific Portion of Questionnaire | Sample Questions |
|---|---|
| **Driver Variables**[a] | |
| Goal Feedback | I receive a considerable amount of feedback concerning my overall performance on the job. |
| Goal Participation | My superior usually asks for my opinions and thoughts when determining the results expected for my work. |
| Need Satisfaction | There is good opportunity for advancement. |
| Role Clarity | I feel certain about how much authority I have on my job. |
| Job Tension | I am unclear about just what the scope and responsibilities of my job are. |
| **Secondary Variables**[a] | |
| Pay Satisfaction | Considering the work required, the pay for my job is good. |
| Fringe Benefit Satisfaction | In general, I am satisfied with the personal protection (for example, hospitalization, surgical, and major medical) benefit plans I receive. |
| Organizational Climate | The organization places great emphasis on improving individual performance through training and development activities. |
| Job Characteristics | There are different types of work to do every day in my job. |
| **Process Issues** | |
| Time | How much time did you take to prepare your last set of PP&E plans? |
| Coverage | How many of your job duties were covered in your last PP&E session? |
| Involvement | To what extent were your PP&E plans determined by you? |

[a]The driver and secondary variable responses were made on a five-point Likert-type scale. An example would be a question to which the respondent marks one of the following: always, often, sometimes, rarely, never.

**User and nonuser: secondary results**

The positive improvements found in the driver variables were expected to be present to a lesser degree in the secondary variables. More time is generally needed to alter job satisfaction, organizational climate, and job characteristics. The users reported more pay satisfaction, promotion opportunities satisfaction, training orientation, work group cohesion, and job variety. Of the 18 secondary variables measured, the users reported more favorable attitudes on 16, more than anticipated for the baseline period. For one of the other variables, job difficulty, the mean scores were the same for users and nonusers. Only for satisfaction with co-workers was the nonuser score more positive, but the difference was not statistically significant.

**Process Results**

Only the user managers completed this section of the survey. A profile of the results indicate the following:

- About 20 percent of the PP&E session with the superior was spent on a discussion of results. (Given the age of this effort, 20 percent is acceptable. We expect this figure to rise later.)
- The majority of managers believed that they had more say than their superiors in establishing their individual PP&E plans.
- PP&E plans were arranged according to priorities.
- On the average, the PP&E participants met formally with superiors approximately two times to finalize their PP&E plans. The average meeting lasted about one hour.

The process results at Tenneco were compared with those obtained by user managers in other manufacturing companies using programs similar to PP&E. Answers from 800 managers responding to similar process questions were gathered from three non-Tenneco manufacturing organizations. The comparisons indicated that Tenneco managers were more satisfied with their goal-oriented program, but spent less time preparing for the planning sessions (one day versus several days) and focused slightly less on personal development during the sessions.

## Overall Picture at the Baseline: Positive

For Tenneco as a whole, the best way to describe the baseline results is "positive." The profile that emerges when the data are analyzed shows that users of PP&E display more positive attitudes about their jobs, company, and supervisor. These improvements emerged shortly after implementation of the PP&E program.

If the word "positive" is used to describe the Tenneco picture at the baseline, another word is needed, and that is "caution." The results focused on driver and secondary variables that were attitudinal and process indicators, which are subjective. The reactions, attitudes, and performance of PP&E participants must continue to be monitored. The missing links at the baseline are the performance measures. These are needed to complete the picture of Tenneco PP&E. If the positive results in attitude changes associated with PP&E are duplicated in the future with positive performance and personal development changes, the Tenneco approach may well serve as an important model for other organizations.

Although the performance indicators have not been tapped because it is too early to look for changes, the findings are positive. The 800 goal-setting participants in the three non-Tenneco manufacturing companies completed a number of driver, secondary, and process questions in earlier surveys. They were used as a comparison sample to judge the differences between PP&E and similar programs in other companies. The users in the comparison companies were at approximately the same point of implementation and experience in goal setting when the measurements were taken. The Tenneco findings are quite similar to the comparison findings. This is impressive, because each of the comparison companies reported significant quality, quantity, cost, and safety performance improvements approximately 15 to 18 months after full implementation of their goal-setting systems. There is every reason to assume that Tenneco performance changes will be just as positive.

## Some Weaknesses and Potential Problems

It would be exciting to be able to report that the Tenneco system has no weaknesses at its present stage of development. Unfortunately, this is not possible. First, because of the sheer size, diversity, and differences in processes used within each company it might be necessary to monitor or evaluate at different points in time. However, to encourage the evaluation of PP&E at all companies, it had to be done at a specific time by external parties. This has created some frustration among company executives, and may result in a decreased willingness to participate further in the evaluation. Managers whose divisions were not far along in the program felt anxious and threatened by the fact that they would not look as good on the reports evaluators submitted to corporate headquarters. Second, because of the flexibility purposely built into the programs within each company, some managers are not devoting the necessary time and energy to the PP&E system. Thus there is some unevenness across companies on how much they encourage managers to take the time to do a thorough job. The flexibility of the present arrangement may mitigate against correcting this defect.

In Tenneco's approach to goal setting, the flexibility is in the areas of policy, procedures, and training. Corporate policy is to establish minimum standards for the continual use of formalized goal setting. These standards provide a degree of continuity to the process of discussing, refining, and recording responsibilities, expected results, priorities, and target dates without being unduly restrictive. As a practical matter, Tenneco's policy gives divisional companies an opportunity to approach the goal-setting process in ways that will be the most helpful and applicable to them. For example, PP&E forms used by divisional companies differ in terms of general format and the categories of goals enumerated.

Flexibility is also reflected in the area of PP&E procedures. For example, the procedure requiring superior-level review (face to face) of a performance evaluation made by a supervisor before it is discussed with the affected employee is not always adhered to. In some cases the physical separation of the evaluating supervisor and his or her superior makes the face-to-face review impractical because of unavoidable time lags. Where this is a problem, divisional companies have developed their own procedures for handling hierarchical review.

Flexibility in training covers variations in the length of training programs used by divisional companies and in several cases modifications in the training materials developed at Tenneco headquarters to meet the specific needs of the different companies. In addition, some companies have used line people as trainers, others have used staff, and some have used a combination of the two.

Another important part of evaluation is that feedback from it can be provided to make important modifications. Because of the flexibility built into PP&E no specific feedback strategy is used across companies. Research indicates that systematic feedback is an important priority in establishing a program such as goal setting. Presently, each company is able to develop its own feedback plans. Some participants have commented that they have not received any feedback on the evaluation. Unless these complaints are remedied, cooperation between the PP&E participants and evaluators may become strained. It is a natural reaction after participating in a survey study to want some feedback on what was discovered.

There are no plans to allow each company eventually to tailor its own PP&E system. But because these companies have different customers, technologies, and problems, the PP&E efforts in each are expected to become more individualized. Initially, the objective was to get the companies involved in goal setting to use a common base—the PP&E system. However, it is becoming more obvious as the system becomes embedded that each company will have to make modifications.

## Implications

A number of implications for practicing managers can be derived from the Tenneco approach to goal setting and management development and the corresponding research effort to evaluate the effectiveness of the system. This experience with goal setting is unique for reasons other than its scope and the large numbers of participants. First, although performance goals are not ignored, the focus is on manager development. The usual goal-setting approach is just the opposite; development is totally ignored. Second, the effectiveness of the system is determined by external evaluators employing a detailed survey research methodology. Unfortunately, in many situations, the degree of goal-setting effectiveness is determined by managers' and/or consultants' (internal and external) testimonials. Third, the reports of the external evaluations provide the basis for an ongoing feedback system that focuses on specific variables and dynamics of the goal-setting system. In most instances managers faced with a sputtering goal-setting system must base their diagnosis and remedial action on intuition, hunches, or selected feedback from participants. The external evaluations have raised the level of the feedback, making it a valuable commodity for managers.

1. *Organizational goal-setting systems need participants to look closely at personal development goals and avoid the relegation of these goals to a second-class citizenship role in the program. Personal development goals may be the key to an improvement in the quality of work life.* It's no secret that most goal-setting systems focus on performance goals, with little if any attention paid to personal development. If goal setting is to be a proactive program that makes the concepts of sound human resource management operative and is intrinsically satisfying because the goals are meaningful, personal development goals have to be included. In fact, personal development goals may be more important than performance goals; they are surely not less important. Development goals are closely related to performance; they represent a medium for management improvement that will be reflected in performance. They serve as a major building block in a sound management resources program. And they can improve the quality of work life. Also, their value in terms of motivation and psychological involvement is important. Employees pay little attention to personal development goals because of the overemphasis on performance goals. Feelings of increased responsibility, growth, challenge, and achievement can all flow from the establishment of personal development goals.

2. *Top-management support needs to be conveyed by actual involvement in training, implementation, and integration efforts.* Information that points to the necessity of top-management support of and seriousness about goal setting is plentiful and there is no need to repeat it here. However, the intent of top management is reinforced by appointing a development task force, attending the actual goal-setting training, and engaging external evaluators. The probability that goal setting will be perceived as "just another program" is reduced by each of these actions. The seriousness of top management is conveyed when it participates actively, then subjects the program to objective evaluation, using evaluation results to solve problems and identify needed modifications. It also shows it means business when it involves people throughout the organization in the process. No one at Tenneco has complained that top management is not involved in the PP&E system. In fact, all members of the office of the president participated in goal-setting training, and all employees seemed to understand that the very top level of Tenneco was committed and active.

3. *A critical issue is how the goal-setting system is implemented. In many cases, the method of implementation can make the difference between positive and negative effects.* Tenneco diagnosed before it acted; it appointed key people from each divisional company as representatives; it established a development task force to work out the problems; and it trained participants and educated them before the program was initiated. Each of these steps was taken carefully so that complaints, discomfort, and misunderstandings would be minimized. In many companies there is a tendency to rush into goal setting without establishing the necessary foundation. The task force was the foundation that addressed the issues so commonly faced in an intervention such as goal setting. It served as an information processing unit and as the hub of PP&E activities.

4. *The use of external evaluators minimizes the probability of bias creeping into assessments because the psychological (ego) involvement of the internal evaluator and the economic motivation of the consultant are eliminated.* With all the time and money many organizations spend in implementing goal-setting systems it is surprising how seldom evaluations are made and with what lack of rigor in following scientific procedures. Perhaps the investment was too high to make any criticism palatable. Or the people involved may have gotten so wrapped up in the "means"—gaining acceptance, developing forms and manuals, and establishing training programs—that the "end"—an effective, well-integrated system—got lost. Another possibility is that managers saw implementing a goal-setting system as a one-shot deal rather than an on-going process that requires modification and an effort to sustain the system.

In any event, hiring qualified external evaluators on a contract basis has a number of advantages. Since these evaluators are not involved in the program design or implementation, they are not emotionally attached to its success and can be more objective. The scientific methodology they employ—data collection methods, data analysis, and standardized reporting formats—facilitate their objectivity. For example, the fact that participants can send unsigned questionnaires directly to the evaluators is likely to generate more honest responses than if they had to deliver them to the personnel manager, their immediate superior, or some executive committee.

Not only can the evaluation be more thorough and objective, but the management and responsibility for evaluation are removed from those directly involved. The result is that the evaluation is more likely to be completed on time. It is always advisable to separate implementation from evaluation for the reasons cited above, but it is also true from a pragmatic point of view that both processes will not be managed with the same vigor and rigor if they are handled by the same group.

External evaluators are also more likely to acquire and disseminate knowledge about goal setting in the form of research studies. There are exceptions, but internal evaluators usually limit distribution of their findings to managers within the organization (especially if the findings are unfavorable). External evaluators are typically more interested in adding to the body of knowledge. Their contribution to the knowledge base can stimulate further research, which should have positive payoffs for those interested in implementing and sustaining effective goal-setting systems.

5. *Previous research clearly projects the message that a system such as PP&E needs to be monitored over time. In fact, any major intervention needs to be traced longitudinally so that false or sleeper improvements can be identified.* An accurate assessment of the impact of a goal-setting program must include a strong interest in identifying cause-and-effect relationships. The only way to do this scientifically is to collect and analyze data at specific intervals over a period of time. Any other method leaves the validity of the findings open to question because of halo errors, extraneous influences, and other factors that cloud the cause-and-effect issue.

Continuing the evaluation effort over time also forms the basis for problem identification and feedback of information to managers for problem solving. Managers become more deeply involved in the goal-setting program; they see themselves as more than just employees carrying out requisite procedures. In addition, the longitudinal nature of the evaluation gives managers an opportunity to see the impact of modifications in the program; they can see to what degree changes in the system are reflected at the next data collection point.

Estimates by "experts" in the area of goal-setting systems indicate that the time required to make a smooth-functioning, effective system fully operational may be as long as five years. If this is the case, it stands to reason that one evaluation, six months after implementation, is insufficient.

## Conclusion

This report describes Tenneco's use of goal setting in nine divisional companies. Additional evaluations, testing, and modifications are to come. The preliminary finds, however, are encouraging and indicate that if goal setting is planned properly, implemented carefully, and evaluated, it has a potentially positive effect on employee attitudes. It is hoped that this article encourages organizations (1) to explore the options available to them for initiating and sustaining top-management involvement in goal setting carefully; (2) to consider emphasizing personal development goals at least as much as performance goals; and (3) to consider using external evaluators who can assess the strengths and weaknesses of an organization's goal-setting system objectively.

## Selected Bibliography

Management by objectives or goal setting has been the subject of books and articles for more than 20 years. The early perspective of management by objectives is captured in Peter Drucker's *The Practice of Management* (Harper and Bros., 1954) and George Odiorne's *Management by Objectives* (Pitman, 1965). More recently two very informative books that trace MBO in organizational settings are Stephen J. Carroll and Henry L. Tosi's *Management by Objectives: Applications and Research* (Macmillan, 1973) and Anthony P. Raia's *Management by Objectives* (Scott, Foresman, 1974).

There are numerous descriptive articles on MBO or goal setting in organizations. Some of the more informative are Harry Levinson's "Management by Whose Objectives?" *Harvard Business Review* (July/August 1970, pp. 125-134); John M. Ivancevich, James H. Donnelly, Jr., and James L. Gibson's "Evaluating MBO: The Challenge Ahead," *Management by Objectives* (Winter 1975, pp. 15-23); Wendell French and Robert Hollmann's "Management by Objectives: The Team Approach," *California Management Review* (Spring 1975, pp. 13-24); and Dale D. McConkey's "MBO—Twenty Years Later, Where Do we Stand," *Business Horizons* (August 1973, pp. 25-36).

An outstanding review article that examines research on goal setting is Gary Latham and Gary Yukl's "A Review on the Application of Goal Setting in Organizations," *Academy of Management Journal* (December 1975, pp. 824-843). Examples of scientific evaluations of goal setting in organizations appear in Gary Latham and James Baldes's "The Practical Significance of Locke's Theory of Goal Setting," *Journal of Applied Psychology* (February 1975, pp. 122-124) and John Ivancevich's "Changes in Performance in a Management by Objectives Program," *Administrative Science Quarterly* (December 1974, pp. 563-574).